LIBRARY
OF
ADVENTIST THEOLOGY

The Body of Christ

Series Editors:

George R. Knight
Woodrow W. Whidden II

Other books in the Library of Adventist Theology series:

BOOK 1: *The Cross of Christ* (George R. Knight)
BOOK 2: *Sin and Salvation* (George R. Knight)

Other books by Reinder Bruinsma include:

Faith—Step by Step
Key Words of the Christian Faith
Matters of Life and Death
It's Time
Our Awesome God

To order, call **1-800-765-6955**.

Visit us at
www.reviewandherald.com
for information on other Review and Herald® products.

THE
BODY
OF CHRIST

A Biblical Understanding
of the Church

REINDER BRUINSMA

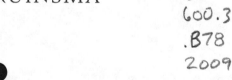

REVIEW AND HERALD® PUBLISHING ASSOCIATION
Since 1861 | www.reviewandherald.com

The Review and Herald® Publishing Association publishes biblically based materials for spiritual, physical, and mental growth and Christian discipleship.

The author assumes full responsibility for the accuracy of all facts and quotations as cited in this book.

Unless otherwise noted, Bible texts in this book are from the *Holy Bible, New International Version*. Copyright © 1973, 1978, 1984, International Bible Society. Used by permission of Zondervan Bible Publishers.

This book was
Edited by Richard W. Coffen
Copyedited by James Cavil
Designed by Trent Truman
Cover photo: © ernestking/istockphoto.com
Interior designed by Heather Rogers
Typeset: Bembo 11/13

PRINTED IN U.S.A.

13   12   11   10   09   5   4   3   2   1

Library of Congress Cataloging-in-Publication Data
Bruinsma, Reinder.
   The Body of Christ: an Adventist understanding of the church / Reinder Bruinsma.
      p. cm.
   Includes bibliographical references and index.
   1. Church. 2. Adventists—Doctrines. I. Title.
   BV600.3.B78 2009
   262'.067—dc22

                                        2009029332

ISBN 978-0-8280-2488-4

Dedicated to

My colleagues in ministry in the Netherlands

Contents

A Word to the Reader

A book on the "doctrine" of the church? Many, if not most, Adventists do not even think of the topic in doctrinal terms, even though number 11 in their statement of Fundamental Beliefs is dedicated to "The Church."

Such a doctrinal emphasis, many seem to believe, is more in line with a Roman Catholic theology or one aligned with the Orthodox or liturgical Protestant segments of Christianity. But the Bible has a great deal to say on the topic. Thus the significance of Reinder Bruinsma's *The Body of Christ: A Biblical Understanding of the Church*.

Bruinsma's discussion of this important subject is far ranging, to say the least, moving all the way from the Old and New Testament foundations of the doctrine of the church up through church government and on into such important issues as ordination and the future of the church. It is the most comprehensive treatment on this crucial fundamental belief in the history of the denomination.

As such, *The Body of Christ* fills an important gap in Adventist literature. It is the third volume in the Library of Adventist Theology, a series that over the next few years will explore in book-length treatments the central theological teachings of the Bible from an Adventist perspective. The series' first two volumes were *The Cross of Christ* (G. R. Knight, 2008) and *Sin and Salvation* (G. R. Knight, 2009). The fourth volume (by Woodrow Whidden, scheduled for release in 2011) will deal with the intricate and controversial topics of judgment and assurance. Future titles will focus on such issues as the Sabbath, the ministry of Christ in the heavenly sanctuary, principles of prophetic interpretation, conditional immortality and hell, great controversy theology, final events, and other topics of interest and importance to the church.

Meanwhile, we are indebted to Reinder Bruinsma for his very readable and informative treatment of a vital subject. We trust that *The Body of Christ* will be a blessing to both the Adventist movement in general and to each of its readers in particular.

George R. Knight and Woodrow W. Whidden II,
Series Editors

Chapter 1

Is the Church
About to Disappear?

The church is God's family; adopted by Him as children, its members live on the basis of the new covenant. The church is the body of Christ, a community of faith of which Christ Himself is the Head. The church is the bride for whom Christ died that He might sanctify and cleanse her. At His return in triumph, He will present her to Himself a glorious church, the faithful of all ages, the purchase of His blood, not having spot or wrinkle, but holy and without blemish.
—From *Fundamental Beliefs of Seventh-day Adventists*, no. 12.

If you have access to a library with a good section of Adventist books, take a careful look at the books on various branches of theology. You will find quite a few older and more recent titles on most subsections of theology, but hardly any major Adventist works on the doctrine of the church.[1] This, in itself, is food for thought.

The development of Seventh-day Adventist theology followed, in many ways, a similar course as that of general Christian theology through the centuries. The Christian church addressed in particular those areas in which the church faced controversy and/or had to deal with what it considered "heresy." It took many centuries before ecclesiology (the technical term for the branch of theology that studies the doctrine of the church) became a major theological concern in the church. In the Adventist Church, as in many other evangelical churches, the area of ecclesiology is still seriously neglected or, at least, underemphasized.

Today, however, we can no longer afford to downplay the importance of this area of systematic theology. Many people in today's world, especially in the West, are increasingly interested in spirituality but are highly suspicious of "the church." They are not so sure whether believers actually need organized religion with all the baggage it supposedly brings along. So the big question for many is: Do we still need the church?

For many, the fact that Christianity has split into thousands of fragments, all promoting their own variety of truth and defending particular rites and traditions, is an enormous stumbling stone. It seems a far cry from the unity Christ told His followers to pray for. If we need the church, where is the church? Do we find it in all these separate Christian traditions, or only in the one segment that has "the truth"? And, if it is only in one denomination or movement, which one?

Increasingly, people who have come to believe may ask for baptism but do not want to join any church organization. Is this biblically defensible? And should a church demand that its new members subscribe to a long list of doctrines as a prerequisite for baptism, or should it be willing to baptize anyone who simply expresses a sincere desire to follow Christ?

Other questions abound. What kind of church organization has the best credentials? Should local churches have total autonomy? Or is a hierarchical national, or even global, structure more in harmony with biblical principles? How do the roles of the "clergy" and of the "laity" relate? And what about the ordination of women to church offices and pastoral ministry? How can, or should, church discipline function in today's world? How do parachurch entities fit into a biblical concept of church? How must the concept of a "remnant" be defined? And so the list continues.

Thus, the study of ecclesiology is not only a fascinating theological exercise, but of enormous practical significance for the Christian church in general and, in particular, for the Seventh-day Adventist Church, its self-understanding, its ministry and mission.

Is the Church in Trouble?

Let's backtrack for a few moments and set the stage for our study. Many voices claim that the Christian church is gradually disappearing—at least in the Western part of the world. It is, many say, only a matter of time before the last worshipper (who will likely be a woman, because statistics tell us that women are more faithful church attendees than men) turns off the last light and leaves the last church for the last time. And indeed, the statistics are troubling, if not alarming, and academic studies as well as anecdotal evidence seem to point to an imminent demise of the church.

The picture in the United States may be a little less bleak than in Western Europe or Australia. In the U.S. most people still insist that they believe the Christian God exists. In many European countries the percentage of those who claim they still believe in the God of their parents and grandparents has often plummeted to around 50 percent. Many have said a definite goodbye to the denomination they belonged to, and as a result many denominations have seen a dramatic decrease in their membership figures. That has been especially true for the so-called mainline churches—the "traditional" churches that have a history of at least several centuries. This has been a steady diet of frustration for the past several decades to church members who have stayed, and especially for church leaders. The Adventist Church has not been immune to this trend, as for instance the membership statistics in the Scandinavian countries (which are among the most secular parts of the world) indicate. It is disheartening to compare, for instance, membership figures of 1980 with those of 2005, just 25 years later. For the countries of Denmark, Finland, Norway, and Sweden, combined membership has decreased from 18,702 in 1980 to 15,275 in 2005.[2] Other similar examples from the Western world could be quoted.

The decline in membership in the Christian church in general in several countries, and the inability of many denominations to recruit new members in any significant numbers (or even to keep enough of their own youth to maintain the numbers) has some far-reaching consequences. One of these is the drop in church attendance, which has been further accelerated by the fact that large numbers of people, even though they have retained their membership, no longer attend church on a regular basis. Fully trustworthy documentation about church attendance by the members of various churches in different countries is often hard to come by. But when one looks at available statistics from various sources it appears that some 40 percent of Americans still attend church on a regular basis. For Canada that figure has dropped to about 20 percent, while in most European countries it is even significantly lower than that and will often be found in the one-digit realm.

Decreased church attendance has financial consequences and has led to serious fiscal difficulties in local churches as well as denominations. Severe budget cuts have become a recurring phenomenon, and staffing levels have often been dramatically reduced. Many denominations have great problems in recruiting new priests or pastors. There is hardly any interest in pursuing a church career, even if there would be enough money in the denominational kitty to pay the salaries. In addition, it should be noted that in many countries church buildings are used far below their capacity, and because of high maintenance costs, large numbers of buildings have been demolished or given over to a new, often secular, use.

Institutional Christianity does not present a very encouraging picture.

In many parts of the Western world the church has become increasingly marginalized. Its voice in society no longer provides direction; its moral contribution to the national discourse is no longer a significant factor. And the many moral scandals in which clergy have been involved have done additional severe damage to the credibility of the church.

Does the Church Still Have a Message?

The decline of organized Christianity is a complex phenomenon. Low birth rates in many places in the West have had a negative impact on the potential for church growth. The low birth rate among the indigenous population has, at least in part, often been offset by successive waves of immigrants. But in many cases these people had a predominantly non-Christian background (as, for instance, the more than 3 million Muslims who migrated to Germany). These changes have forever changed the religious landscape of the West and are challenging the Judeo-Christian roots of Western society. Many other changes in the past few decades have also contributed to the enormous shifts in religious attitudes and in church allegiance of many people. Just to mention two important factors: increased mobility resulting in a slackening of traditional ties and social control, and the graying of large segments of the population.

But there is something else—something that has immensely affected the way people think, choose, and act. Western society has moved into a different era. The change has come gradually and stealthily, but is *has* come and is unmistakably continuing. Whether we like it or not, we are in the midst of it. After the Middle Ages the world moved into a new period of its existence: out of the premodern era into the era of modernity. After the medieval period with its nonscientific outlook, the Renaissance changed Westerners in a fundamental way: humankind, with its power of reason and its ever-increasing scientific skills and knowledge, became the center of the universe. This greatly impacted the religious outlook of people and had a great influence on theology and on how churches operate. It led, among other things, to an ever more secular view of life and an ever more secular approach to life's challenges.

More recently, however, in the post–World War II period, and more specifically, in the past few decades, the Western world has gradually been shifting from *modernity* into *postmodernity*. And this shift has, to a large degree, also shaped the development of recent Western Christianity. One cannot understand what has been happening to the Christian church in the Western world in recent years (including developments in current

Adventism) without having at least some awareness of the main facets of postmodern thought. On the one hand, the postmodern person has little use for organized religion. On the other hand, postmodern men and women tend to have a lot of interest in religiosity. But postmodern thinking emphasizes that all human beings should pick and choose what to believe in and should shape their own religion, while defining their own brand of truth. No longer, it is argued, can people believe in one absolute truth, which is expressed in a universally valid set of doctrines and forms the basis of one universally valid moral standard. No longer should we strive for uniformity in our worship or try to reach agreement and consensus as to what we should believe. Individual human beings, we are told, are supposed to be different and should be proud of their differences and rest content with their own personal truth. It is not difficult to see how this radically new approach to how people view themselves, the people around them, and the world has laid a powerful time bomb under the traditional ecclesiastical structures. The results have been no less than dramatic.

Millions of former church members have left their churches, because they no longer feel at home in a setting that continues to demand adherence to a set of doctrines they no longer consider relevant. The church no longer provides for the kind of spirituality they are looking for. Organized religion in its traditional forms no longer "works" for them.

Nevertheless, millions of other Christians have (at least for the time being) still retained a tie with their church. *But many look for change.* They want new ways to worship. They yearn for a church that appeals not only to their intellect but also to their emotions. They feel tired of church organs and traditional choirs and desire a different kind of music. They want to express their feelings in ways that are often labeled as "charismatic" and, therefore, in many circles unacceptable. They place less emphasis on doctrine and wish for more space for religious experience. They are no longer interested in many of the questions the church has traditionally worried about, but want to address new questions—those they consider relevant. They show but little interest in documents and plans that come "from above," from "higher" denominational administrative bodies. Their interest is in their local church, and they prefer initiatives that are lay-driven.

This postmodern influence on much of today's church life, unfortunately, often finds expression in what may be called a "consumer church." People want to pick and choose what they find attractive and what is convenient to them. The main question is no longer whether the church they go to is focused on biblical truth. Rather, the main considerations are, for example: Do I like the kind of worship, in particular the music? Do I like the pastor and the way he or she preaches? Does the church offer the kind of services that are good for my family? Can I park my car without any problem when I go to church? As a result, in our postmodern age we notice a lot of denominational switching and church "shopping." People shop for the congregation they like best and, unlike former generations, do not show great loyalty to the local church or the denomination in which they were once baptized or grew up.

But in all honesty, even the most severe critic of postmodernity will have to concede that not all church reactions are of a shallow consumerism type. Many local congregations, but also many denominations and church leaders, have tried to deal with the postmodern challenges in thoughtful and responsible ways. Many recognize that change does not necessarily conflict with fundamental convictions and that the Christian message should be packaged in such a way that it will have optimum appeal to the twenty–first-century person.

There is also a growing awareness in the church that this twenty–first-century individual often knows very little about the basics of the Christian faith and that the faith journey of such a person will different greatly from the faith journey of those who have been Christians for many years. And thus many new initiatives have been launched to attract nonbelievers. "Seeker-sensitive" services have been organized, and many congregations have realized that they will not survive unless they become "purpose-driven" and explore new ways of "being church." Many denominations have begun to utilize methods as the "alpha course" in their efforts to attract people they do not normally see in their churches and have started a church-planting movement in a concerted effort to establish new church assemblies in towns or neighborhoods where the church is not yet present or has lost its former presence. Those who are involved in such experiments often predict that the church of the future will undoubtedly look very different from what we are familiar with today. They emphasize the need for constant openness to where the Spirit may lead. More and more, one hears about the "emerging church"—a label that is, in the eyes of those experimenters who want to stay close to biblical principles, actually a less neutral term than it at first sight appears to be, and the emerging-church movement tends to move in directions in which not all will want to follow.[3]

The Church Is Not About to Disappear

The recognition that organized Christian religion is indeed facing enormous difficulties and also that many of the courageous efforts to turn the tide oftentimes bring only meager results should not lead us to conclude that Christianity is about to disappear from the face of the earth. That is not just a statement of faith but a conclusion fully supported by hard evidence. When we study recent developments in global Christianity, a few significant trends appear.

First, in the United States and Australia—and even in neo-pagan Europe—not all church bodies decrease in size. There are also growing churches (some even grow by leaps and bounds), and quite a few new churches are being planted. Many Christians have, sadly, lost their way, but there is a steady stream of new Christians who are somehow finding the Way. This is, in particular, true in the evangelical segment of Christianity. Whereas many churches have lowered the threshold and have relaxed membership requirements in their frantic efforts to win or retain members, it is, surprisingly enough, in the more conservative corners of Christianity that numerically most of the gains are made!

It may be that many mainline churches are losing members, but other denominations continue to enlarge. The growth of the Pentecostal movement has been nothing less than phenomenal. According to the world-renowned statistician David Barrett, the number of Pentecostals/charismatics rose to a staggering 523 million by around 2000 and may well reach more than 800 million by 2025.[4]

Among the fastest growing Christian movements is Seventh-day Adventism. While numbering but little more than 1 million a mere 50 years ago, there are today more than 16 million baptized Seventh-day Adventists in the world, and if current growth rates continue, the church may well have at least 50 million members by 2025.

Second, immigration of large numbers of Christians from the developing nations to the Western world has given a powerful impetus to the church in some areas where, for decades, it had been in continuous retreat. Sections of Amsterdam provide a powerful example. When the city planned a new extension in the 1970s, it was felt that no provisions needed to be made for church buildings, as church attendance in Amsterdam had dropped to almost zero. Today, however, this section of the Dutch capital is the most religious area in the entire country. Tens of thousands of immigrants worship in a vast array of Christian congregations with all kinds of European, Caribbean, and African traditions. The same pattern exists in many other cities in the Western world.

Third, the church is not so much disappearing as it is moving. It is moving south! Countries such as Brazil and Mexico are now among the main Christian nations in the world! Philip Jenkins, a renowned professor of history and religious studies at Pennsylvania State University, predicts that as the result of the rapid growth of the Christian church in Latin America, Africa, and Asia, by 2050 only one Christian in five will be non-Latin and White. "Soon," he adds, "a *white Christian* may sound like a curious oxymoron, as mildly surprising as a *Swedish Buddhist!*"[5] This will entail more than simply a geographical shift. It will also greatly influence the nature of the church, as the Christians in the south will tend to be considerably more conservative in many of their views than their sisters and brothers in the north.[6] Adventists who keep abreast of what is happening in their own church will know that this process is powerfully present in their own denomination. While the Adventist movement began as a white Anglo-American movement, today less than 10 percent of its members live in the West—and even there, large segments of their church are non-Caucasian!

Why This Book?

With so many momentous things happening in the Christian church— the Adventist Church included—why spend much time and effort on writing or reading a theological study of the church? Why focus on theological theory and not on the gigantic practical challenges the church faces? Will this book not seem like an echo of the oft-told story about the church council that was held in fifteenth-century Constantinople at the precise moment that this Christian city was about to be overrun by the Muslim Turks? The church leaders that had gathered for the council discussed the philosophical dilemma of how many angels can sit on the point of a needle and considered the question of the color of the eyes of the virgin Mary! Does our preoccupation with the theology of the church not show a similar insensitivity to the enormous practical issues the church must confront? And what is so complicated about the doctrine of the church anyway? Luther claimed that a girl of 7 knows what the church is. Why, then, did he pen thousands of words in order to explain what she understood?[7]

Most surely the church must address many practical challenges. Changes must be made. New methods must be developed. The church must rekindle—particularly in the secular West—its missionary drive. It must find ways to repackage the gospel message so that the contemporary listener will be interested and will stop to listen and be able to understand what is being said. There are all kinds of organizational and financial problems to be addressed. In addition, this postmodern age presents us with many new ethical and moral predicaments that the church must deal with. But in doing all this, it is easy to make mistakes. It is easy to start from the wrong premises, or to be unfaithful to the biblical witness that must remain the guiding principle. It is easy to introduce elements that reflect an unbiblical understanding of important issues or, on the other hand, to assume that certain things are thoroughly biblical while, in fact, they are no more than customs hallowed by a long tradition or by a gradual adjustments to culture.

All this provides ample reason to take time to study the doctrine of the church. It is important not only to emphasize that the church has a future, but that it also is just as important to have a clear idea as to *what kind of church we ought to have in the future.* Yes, a lot of change may be needed in the church. But how can we be sure that in adopting change we are not losing something that is fundamental and do not end up with something that may be an interesting social structure but is no longer a "church" in the biblical sense and in the way Christ intended? It may seem necessary to reorganize many of the ways in which the church operates. But are we sure that we know what organizational elements are no more than human ideas that may be changed at our human pleasure and what principles of organization are immutable because they are anchored in the Word of God? Postmodern people may not have much affinity with church discipline. Is that, however, enough reason to abandon all traditional forms of church discipline? And so the list continues.

Where Will This Book Take You?

This book wants to present a reasonably comprehensive picture of the various aspects of the doctrines of the church. It does so from both a general Christian perspective and also a specifically Adventist angle. The following chapters deal with all the major ecclesiological issues. The approach is fourfold.

Biblically and theologically—What does Scripture say? How can we build a theology of the church on the data provided by the God's Word? It is clear that the Bible does not present us with ready-made doctrines and theological positions. But the biblical data are the building blocks for the construction of the church's doctrines. It will be of interest to see how these building blocks have been used in various ways and what Adventist theologians consider the most balanced and defensible way.

Historically—How have various theologians and theological traditions developed their theologies of the church in the face of these biblical data? What does church history teach us? There are few situations today that have not, in some shape or another, already been faced by church leaders and church members in the past. Circumstances have changed, but often the same underlying principles are at stake. We do well to look at the response of history and to learn from the mistakes made and the successes attained.

Practically—How does theory translate into practice? How do we apply biblically sound principles when we face organizational matters? How should denominations deal with one another? What is the most desirable relationship between church and state? Countless practical issues should not just be solved in a pragmatic manner but worked out in the light of biblical principles.

Viewed through the lens of Adventism: its traditions, its needs, its challenges. Adventists believe that they are part of the church universal but at the same time claim a special role for their movement as being charged with proclaiming an end time "remnant" message. What are the implications for the Adventist self-understanding? for the way in which Adventists relate to other Christians? for the way in which they relate to their mission?

The People of God

Do we need the church? A great many people today claim that they can lead the life of faith without becoming a member of a church. The early chapters of this book will show this attitude to be wrong. We *do* need the church. Our life of faith would miss a vital ingredient if there were no faith community to which we may belong. Jesus Himself founded the church. Who, then, are we to say that the church is not needed? It is true: The institutional church in itself does not save us. Salvation does not come through an organization, but it comes through Jesus Christ. But we will see that the church is more than an organizational concept and more than a strategy for the efficient promotion of the gospel message. *The church is, first of all, the body of Christ—God's people.* "It is a people of God who are created by the Spirit to live as a missionary community. . . . It is God's personal presence in the world through the Spirit."[8]

The church is imperfect simply because the individuals who make up God's people are far from perfect. Nonetheless, whatever the statistics in the Western world tell us, the church has a glorious future, because the future of God's people is assured. It faces many challenges, but the good news is that the church does not dependent on human skills and wisdom for its survival. The words of Ellen White are as true as ever: "Enfeebled and defective as it may appear, the church is the one object upon which God bestows in a special sense His supreme regard. It is the theater of His grace, in which He delights to reveal His power to transform hearts."[9]

---

[1] With "doctrine of the church" we refer not to what the church believes or should believe about all kinds of theological subjects but about what the church believes about itself.

[2] See *118th Annual Statistical Report* (1980) and *143rd Annual Statistical Report* (2005), published by the Office of Archives and Statistics of the Seventh-day Adventist Church, in Silver Spring, Maryland. These statistics can be viewed on the Internet: http://www.adventiststatistics.org.

[3] For a short description, see "Ecclesiology" in William A. Dyrness and Veli-Matti Kärkkäinen, eds., *Global Dictionary of Theology* (Downers Grove, Ill.: InterVarsity Press, 2008), p. 259.

[4] David B. Barrett et al., eds., *World Christian Encyclopedia* (Oxford University Press, 2001), p. 1.

[5] Philip Jenkins, *The Next Christendom: The Coming of Global Christianity* (Oxford: Oxford University Press, 2002), p. 3.

[6] This is the theme of a new book by Philip Jenkins, *The New Faces of Christianity: Believing the Bible in the Global South* (Oxford: Oxford University Press, 2006).

[7] Edmund P. Clowney, *The Church* (Leicester, U.K.: InterVarsity Press, 1995), p. 71.

[8] Craig van Gelder, *The Essence of the Church* (Grand Rapids: Baker Books, 2000), p. 25.

[9] Ellen G. White, *The Acts of the Apostles* (Mountain View, Calif.: Pacific Press Pub. Assn., 1911), p. 12.

Chapter 2

Biblical Foundations:
The Old Testament Roots

J esus Christ founded the Christian church. Does this mean that we should begin our search for the biblical data concerning the nature and the role of the church in the New Testament? Or does the Old Testament also have something relevant to say about our topic?

If we were to begin our study of what the New Testament tells us about the church, it would not take long before we would discover countless pointers back to the Old Testament. John's Revelation, the last book of the Bible, presents us with an impressive panorama of last-day events and of the final outcome of the great conflict between good and evil. All who have rebelled against the Creator are collectively labeled Babylon, while the New Jerusalem, the heavenly city for the saints, becomes the symbol for the "bride, the wife of the Lamb" (Rev. 21:9)—the redeemed of all ages, or, in other words, the church triumphant. John the seer is at a loss to find words to describe this heavenly reality. But the magnificent composite of symbols leaves no doubt about the intimate connection between this New Testament vision of the redeemed and the Old Testament record of salvation history. He notes not only that the names of the apostles are written on the walls of the city but also that the names of the twelve tribes of Israel are also prominently displayed! Both the new and the old are there side by side.

This direct linking of the tribes of Israel of old and the leaders of the New Testament church is not a careless remark of a prophet who exercised his creative liberty. It rather is a striking, final, and exuberant reminder of the *continuity* in God's dealings with His people through the ages. Surely there is a distinct *discontinuity* between Old Testament Israel and the church, as we shall see in chapters 3 and 4, but we will do well first to underline the strong continuity between these two. It has been said: Starting at the New Testament is like picking up a novel and beginning halfway through. That is certainly true when we study what the Bible says about the church. So let's focus on the Old Testament first.

God Elects Individuals and Families

One of the things that stand out when we look at the Old Testament is that God *elects* individuals and groups of individuals for particular roles in His plan for humankind's redemption. However, the story of God's people does not begin with the call of Abraham as the father of Israel, as is often suggested. It begins with the creation of the world and the rebellion of the first two human beings, and thereby paints the background of a humanity in need of restoration.[1] Any attempt at understanding the nature of God's people—and thereby of the Christian church—must be based on a firm awareness of the fact that God created human beings for a purpose and on the assurance that He will not abandon His purpose, in spite of the tragedy that resulted when the first couple exercised their free will by choosing to disobey. And it is further based on the discovery of the first glimpse of the gospel message in Genesis 3, where it is predicted that the evil one will be allowed to continue to wreak havoc among God's creation but only to a limited extent. For, ultimately, he will not succeed, as at the appointed time Someone among Eve's offspring will "crush" Satan's head (verse 15). This is what the Bible is all about. The Bible reveals salvation history and relates how God fulfills His plans for the redemption of people.

From the very beginning, God wanted to work through people who were loyal to His instructions; who were prepared to work with Him to bring salvation to the world. Even before He made His covenant with Abraham and promised that he would be the progenitor of a special nation that would ultimately prove to be a blessing for the entire world (Gen. 12:1-3), God singled out particular families in the lineage of Adam, Seth, Noah, and Shem as the guardians of His truth. Among the people, who lived before the Flood, Noah "found favor" with God (Gen. 6:8, 13-18). Yet when God subsequently made His covenant with Noah (Gen. 9), promising that there would never again be a calamity that would destroy the entire surface of the world and establishing the rainbow as an eternal reminder of His mercy, He entered into this covenant with Noah and his sons, thus including all of the very few inhabitants of the earth at that moment. When we turn a few pages and come to the story of Abraham, we discover more clearly that one particular person and a special community were "elected."

God told Abraham to leave his homeland of Mesopotamia and, with his loved ones, to "go to the land I will show you" (Gen. 12:1). Then followed the unforgettable promise: "I will make you into a great nation and I will bless you; I will make your name great and you will be a blessing. . . . And all peoples on earth will be blessed through you" (Gen. 12: 2, 3). God established a covenant with Abraham and in so doing made certain concrete promises. A special ceremony sealed the covenant. Interestingly, God used a ritual that was customary in Abraham's days. (This is how God works—He chooses forms that people can recognize, packaging the unique content of His revelations to us human beings!) Abraham had to provide a 3-year-old heifer (young cow), a 3-year-old goat, a 3-year-old ram, a dove, and a young pigeon. The heifer, as well as the goat and the ram, were cut in half, and together with the dove and the pigeon were arranged in a particular pattern.

The lives of the animals symbolized the lives of those participating in the covenant. Those entering into the covenant were to walk between the pieces as a token of their perpetual faithfulness to the conditions solemnly agreed upon.[2] We find this very same ceremony still in use many centuries later during the days of Jeremiah (Jer. 34:18, 19). The ritual may seem rather bizarre to twenty-first-century readers, but for the as-yet-childless Abraham it was an impressive challenge to maintain faith in the promise that his offspring would be as numerous as the stars in the sky (Gen. 15:5).

Subsequently (see Gen. 17), the circumcision ritual was added as a most intimate reminder of Abraham's covenant with God. Again, this was not a unique ceremony that God devised for this occasion, but a rite that was practiced by other ancient peoples, and is, of course, practiced even today by many Jews, Muslims, and even some Christians. God deemed this ritual suitable to express the allegiance of His people and to underline that those whom God had singled out would belong to Him in a very special sense.

Although God is the Creator-God to whom all people owe absolute allegiance, He is in a very special sense the God of Abraham, Isaac, and Jacob. Moses was to tell the Israelites in Egypt that the God of Abraham, Isaac, and Jacob had sent him (Ex. 3:15). God made Himself known as God Almighty to Abraham, Isaac, and Jacob (Ex. 6:3). God's special bond with Abraham and his posterity continues to find an echo in the apostle Peter's speech in Solomon's porch on the eastern side of the Temple in Jerusalem, when he testified that "the God of Abraham, Isaac and Jacob" was the God who "glorified . . . Jesus" (Acts 3:13).

The Covenant Renewed

After Israel's deliverance from Egypt, God renewed the covenant with His people—the descendants of Abraham. Moses, who had led out in the exodus from Egyptian bondage, climbed Mount Sinai, where he experienced a special revelation from God. He received a clear commission: "This is what you are to say to the house of Jacob and what you are to tell the people of Israel: '. . . . If you obey me fully and keep my covenant, then out of all nations you will be my treasured possession' " (Ex. 19:5). Then these words, pregnant with meaning, are added: "You will be for me a kingdom of priests and a holy nation" (verse 6). We will return to these words shortly. The Ten Commandments (Ex. 20:1-17; Deut. 5:6-21) summarized in a new concise wording the principles that had always served as the covenant conditions and that would forever continue as such.

The *covenant* theme is a constantly recurring one throughout the entire Old Testament. God has chosen His own people—the people of Israel—and has covenanted with them. Unfortunately, we read again and again about the people's unfaithfulness to their oaths of loyalty and about the subsequent disintegration of the covenant relationship. We find, however, that Israel's leaders continued to be evaluated by their loyalty to the covenant. The ministry of the prophets had the primary object of giving back to the people the consciousness and a sound understanding of their election, such as existed in the beginning.[3] Prophets such as Hosea, Jeremiah, and Ezekiel made frequent reference to the covenant. Jeremiah, in one of the most famous passages of the Old Testament, emphasized how God "will make a new covenant with the house of Israel, and with the house of Judah." The prophet looked forward to the time when the divine conditions of the covenant relationship would be engraved not just on tables of stone but in the hearts of the people. *That* is the *newness* of the covenant. The terms were the same, and were as gracious as ever. But the response would, at long last, truly be one of the heart and not of outward compliance at best (Jer. 31:31-34).

Election and covenant are among the central realities of the Old Testament. The Hebrew word for election (*bachar*) usually expresses the idea of free, unmotivated choice. In His infinite wisdom God makes His free choice as to whom He wants to use for a special purpose, as the apostle Paul explains in his profound theological essay about God's sovereign election (Rom. 9-11). The crucial place held by the theme of election is expressed by a wide variety of images to underline the close union

25

between God and His special people.[4] And it should be pointed out that these very same images are later used to characterize the Christian church. This is certainly no coincidence, but points to the continuity between the people of God in Old Testament and New Testament times.

The marriage union is probably the most prominent image, and is used by a number of the prophets (see, for example, throughout the book of Hosea; also Jer. 2:1-7; 3:11-22; Eze. 16 and 32; and Isa. 50:1; 54:5-10; 62:4, 5). It underlines the element of faithfulness, as well as the fertility the union was expected to bring. The vineyard theme is a variant of the marriage theme (for example, Hosea 2:12). Another image is that of the father-son relationship (for example, Ex. 4:22). Numerous times God is referred to as the Father of His people. Finally, the image of the shepherd and the flock strikingly emphasizes the absolute dependence of the people on their God (see, for example, Ps. 23).

Election is not for a particular elevated status, but for a task. This basic truth applies both to elected individuals and to the chosen community. God wants to bless all nations, and He chooses to do this through His people. They are elected for service and are His servants—a term frequently used for individuals (Moses was referred to as a servant of God more than 40 times) but also for the people as a whole. Deuteronomy 32:36 provides an example in which the terms are used interchangeably: "The Lord will judge his people and have compassion on his servants!"

Israel's mission to the nations is often insufficiently recognized. God's intention was that through the posterity of Abraham all nations would be blessed—just as the church later received a mission mandate to preach the gospel to all peoples and in all cultures. Israel failed to a large extent in the fulfillment of that task, but there are many indications in the Old Testament that this missionary awareness did, at least to some extent, survive. Moses became a missionary to the Egyptians. Daniel, likewise, lived and worked as a missionary among the Babylonian elite. Naaman, the Syrian, was "evangelized" by the prophet Elisha. Jonah preached his message of repentance to the metropolis of Nineveh. At the dedication of the Jerusalem Temple, King Solomon prayed that non-Israelites would come to worship in the house of worship that he had been allowed to build, "so that all the peoples of the earth may know your name and fear you" (2 Chron. 6:33). Isaiah emphasized this same goal: "My house will be called a house of prayer for all nations" (Isa. 56:7). The prophets Isaiah and Micah presented their audience with the ultimate vision that "in the last days" all this would at long last become reality, when "many peoples will come and say, 'Come, let us go up to the mountain of the Lord, to the house of the God of Jacob. He will teach us his ways, so that we may walk in his paths" (Isa. 2:2, 3; Micah 4:1, 2). In retrospect the continuity between the era of the ancient people of Israel and that of the church is abundantly clear.

This election for *mission* happens within the framework of God's covenant. It is important to understand that this covenant was not imposed on God's people as a burden—in the form of a dispensation of works, as opposed to the later dispensation of grace—as is still vigorously but completely erroneously argued by many Evangelical Christians. Yes, the covenant is a bond, and it presupposes obedience and faithfulness. But it is nothing less than a gift of grace, full of rich and undeserved promises.

Jon Dybdahl, Old Testament scholar and missiologist, points out that among the many synonyms that exist for the somewhat old-fashioned sounding word "covenant" (such as "contract," "bond," "alliance," "agreement," "treaty") the best is probably *relationship*, because the covenant is a defined relationship between God and His people.[5] It is initiated by God and sustained by Him. He does all He can to maintain the relationship with the kind of patience that is far beyond what human beings have a right to expect.

God's Holy People

The people of Israel were referred to as His "holy people" (Deut. 28:9) and as a "holy nation" (Ex. 19:6). God's people were set aside for a specific purpose. Israel did not deserve the label of holiness; it had no credible claim to moral purity. God had consecrated Israel to Himself. When Peter later referred to the members of the church as "a chosen people, a royal priesthood, a holy nation, a people belonging to God" (1 Peter 2:9), he simply quoted a phrase that had already been applied to the people of God in Old Testament times. God told Moses that he could confidently tell the people: "Although the whole earth is mine, you will be for me a kingdom of priests and a holy nation" (Ex. 19:5, 6). Deuteronomy uses similar wording. Israel is the people of God's inheritance (Deut. 4:20). Israel should know that they were "chosen . . . out of all peoples on the face of the earth to be his people, his treasured possession" (Deut. 7:6). Israel will remain God's people, and in spite of their recurring unfaithfulness, they will be called "His people" and "sons of the living God" (Hosea 1:10; 2:23).

Israel is also called an "assembly" (or "congregation") that had been called out (Acts 7:38). This term is repeatedly used throughout the Old Testament (see, for example, Ex. 16:3; Num. 14:5; 1 Sam. 17:47; Job 30:28; Ps. 22:22). The Septuagint, the ancient and prestigious Greek translation of the Old Testament that originated in the third century B.C. (and was in use during the time of Christ), uses the word *ekklesia* (church) to translate the Hebrew word for assembly (*qahal*) more than 100 times. The New Testament authors seized on this very term *ekklesia* when they spoke about the church. Once again we find a remarkable bridge between then and now! In the next chapter we shall return to the term *ekklesia*.

Why Israel?

We cannot emphasize it enough: The people of Israel did not owe their immense privileges to the fact they had any special virtue to commend themselves. The book of Deuteronomy reminded the Israelites at the time of their "conquest" of Canaan that they were not even very numerous. In fact, they were "the fewest" of all people (Deut. 7:7). But why should that in retrospect surprise us? Christ told His followers that important things tend to start rather small. He compared the kingdom of heaven with a minute mustard seed, which is small at first but eventually may grow into a huge tree (Matt. 13:31, 32).

What began with Abraham in Genesis 12 was, humanly speaking, indeed a very modest beginning. But that was God's deliberate choice: to fulfill His plan by starting small, with one man in one particular place.[6] Many great enterprises have begun small. Take the U.S. Air Force as a rather recent example. Established as part of the U.S. army in 1907, it consisted of three men—an officer and two enlisted men. At one point in time, when the world was at war, it grew to more than 100,000 officers and more than 1 million enlisted individuals!

The story of the election of Abraham and through him of the people of Israel also teaches us that great things may have a small beginning, that God often takes His time, and that He demands that people have faith in what He sets out to do. Of course, when we try to grasp with our limited understanding why God brought Abraham into the land of Canaan and why He chose that particular spot in the ancient world to locate His people, we can see some advantages. The land where Israel was to settle is a relatively small area surrounded by sea and desert. Even today visitors to the modern state of Israel tend to be amazed at how small the country actually is. But it is located where three continents intersect—Europe, Asia, and Africa—in the very center of the ancient world, between the famous cultures of Egypt and Mesopotamia. It could not have been located more strategically.

Why, however, try to look over God's shoulder and question the whys and wherefores of His election of Israel? God chose His people. He gave them an important mission. He decided that Palestine would be the best home base for His people. He cared for His people by entering into a covenant relationship with them. The way in which He treats His people is, however, not based on geography or on some temporary physical arrangements. It is His eternal love for humanity that made Him choose a people then and makes Him choose a people in the here and now.

Israel was instructed how to structure its worship of the covenant God. The sanctuary—at first in the form of a rather small portable tent and later in the shape of some other rather modest sanctuaries and, of course, eventually in the more prestigious Jerusalem Temple in its various architectural phases—served as the rallying point par excellence. This was where God's presence was experienced in the most direct possible manner. This was where the ark of the covenant resided, and where, from the days of Moses until the Babylonian conquest of Jerusalem, the eternal principles of conduct toward God and fellow humans were physically kept, engraved on tablets of stone. An elaborate system of sacrifices and feasts ensured that the Israelites and others who became acquainted with them would be constantly reminded of the covenant. They would serve as a perpetual symbol of the ultimate remedy for the sin problem. They were tools in the accomplishment of Israel's mission but ceased to function as such when the true Lamb was slain (Mark 15:38). Nevertheless, the tabernacle and the Temple, along with the priesthood and its sacrificial system and feasts, would always remain powerful sources of inspiration for the church and, in particular, for the ways in which the church would develop its worship.

After the Assyrian and Babylonian invasions in the eighth and sixth centuries B.C., Israel became dispersed throughout the entire Middle East. For a considerable period of time there was no Temple in which to worship, and, of course, many people with Israelite roots never returned to the land of their fathers. At some time during the so-called intertestamental period, after the last of the Old Testament prophets had moved off the scene, a new institution developed: the *synagogue*. Its origin remains a matter of much speculation. There is no mention of any synagogue in the books of Ezra and Nehemiah, which shed so much light on the period of the return of groups of exiles to the land of Palestine and on the rebuilding of Jerusalem and its Temple in the fifth century B.C. There is plenty of first-century evidence (both in the Bible and in other sources, such as those of the historian Josephus), however, that by then there were many synagogues not only in Palestine but also in Egypt, Asia Minor, and elsewhere. The earliest Christians, at least for some time, would still visit the Temple, and both Christ and the apostles had no qualms about regularly attending synagogue services. Clearly the synagogue—with its emphasis on prayer, Scripture reading, and teaching from the Torah—served as an important bridge between worship by the Old Testament people of God and the church.

A Remnant

One other concept needs to be mentioned: the *remnant*. No other Christians have as much interest in "the remnant" as do Adventists. They see the special significance of this aspect of the people of God not only in the Old Testament but also in a famous passage in the Revelation, which holds great importance for their self-understanding. Revelation 12:17 refers to the "rest" or "remaining"—a term that reminds us of the remnant concept—of the end-time people of God (see also Rev. 2:24 and 3:2).

This idea of a limited number of people who remain faithful, even when a large majority does not, and have a special mission is a recurring theme in the Old Testament. Through the ages, after wars and calamities, there usually was a remnant group among God's people that stayed true to the covenant and continued to represent God's chosen people. In the days of Elijah, when apostasy was so rampant that the prophet believed there were no true believers left anywhere, God told him that He knew who were His and that there was still a remnant of 7,000 men and women who had not turned away from Him in favor of the Baal (1 Kings 19:14-18). Isaiah and other prophets foretold that even after the deportations by the Assyrians and Babylonians a faithful remnant would remain and would eventually return to Jerusalem (Isa. 10:20-22; 11:11, 12; Jer. 23:3; 31:7; Micah 2:12; Zeph. 3:13).[7]

We should note that the remnant concept has two facets: one catastrophic—only a remnant will survive, and the other full of promise—a remnant will escape and enter salvation.[8] The idea of a "remnant," which appears so frequently in the writings of prophets, shows how God can be at the same time (1) the righteous Judge, who has no other credible option than to bring punishment upon His disobedient people, and (2) the faithful Savior, who wants nothing more dearly than to bless His elected people.

Closely connected with the remnant concept is that of the gathering of God's people, in particular after the Babylonian exile. This term *gathering* is used with the meaning of helping, delivering, healing, redeeming. The central passage where this is expressed is Deuteronomy 30:1-6. In chapters 28-30 of Deuteronomy the "blessings" of obedience to the covenant as well as the "curses" resulting from disobedience are outlined. Willful disobedience to the covenant conditions by the people of God will lead to its dispersion among the nations. But when Israel repents, the Lord will "restore the fortunes" of His people and will "gather" them from everywhere. Then, He will "circumcise the hearts" of His people, so that they may love Him with all their heart and with all their soul, and live!

[1] Gerhard Lohfink, *Heeft God de kerk nodig?* (Gent, Belgium: Carmelitana, 2001), pp. 15ff.

[2] *The Seventh-day Adventist Bible Commentary* (Washington, D.C.: Review and Herald Pub. Assn., 1953-1957), vol. 1, p. 313.

[3] Edmond Jacobs, *Theology of the Old Testament* (London: Hodder and Stoughton, 1967), p. 204.

[4] *Ibid.*, see pp. 202ff.

[5] Jon Dybdahl, *Old Testament Grace* (Boise, Idaho: Pacific Press Pub. Assn., 1990), p. 70.

[6] Lohfink, pp. 50ff.

[7] Ranko Stefanovic, *Revelation of Jesus Christ* (Berrien Springs, Mich.: Andrews University Press, 2002), p. 392.

[8] Jacobs, p. 323.

Chapter 3

Biblical Foundations: The Earliest Beginnings of the Christian Church

Histtory bristles with examples of large corporations that have started in a shed or garage. A bit of Googling on the Internet leads to numerous remarkable stories of small beginnings that brought unexpected success. Two young men, Bill Gates and Paul Allen, started the world-famous Microsoft Company in a garage. Back then Gates and Allen were just two "geeks" who were more interested in writing software than they were studying in school. In fact, Gates dropped out of Harvard, worked on his home business, and produced MS-DOS. The rest is history. Some admire and love Microsoft and all it stands for, whereas some hate it, but the fact is that it currently dominates the software industry.

Many major institutions were never intended to become anything but a small, local initiative. Someone started something, and then others latched on to it, and it simply became bigger and kept on growing and eventually mushroomed into something larger than the originators could ever have imagined. Had they known what they would unleash, they might have thought twice. Superficially it would appear that this has also been true of the history of the church. That it began very small is undeniable. But from the very start the church was planned as a global enterprise that would reach to "every nation, tribe, language and people" (Rev. 14:6) and would remain until the end of time.

A Very Modest Beginning

The four Gospels provide us with stories about Jesus and with a record of some of the things He said. Of course, they contain only a very tiny selection of what Jesus actually did and said. Several decades after Jesus had been resurrected and ascended into heaven, the four Gospel writers each made their inspired choice as to what to include from what they remembered or had been told. That they all referred to the "calling" of the disciples is hardly surprising. Later in the first century, as the church was growing and several of these earliest disciples had become leaders, there must have been a strong interest in the stories of how these men first came to be attached to Jesus.

The three so-called Synoptic Gospels (Matthew, Mark, and Luke) give us a list of the men who are usually referred to as "the twelve disciples." Some of these names appear frequently in the New Testament, whereas others do not figure so prominently in the earliest annals of the church. This is the list: (1) Simon Peter, also referred to by his Aramaic name, Cephas; (2) James, the son of a certain Zebedee, a professional fisherman; (3) John, another son of Zebedee and thus a brother of James; (4) Andrew, a brother of Simon Peter and a former disciple of John the Baptist; (5) Philip; (6) Bartholomew, who, since the early Middle Ages, has usually been identified with Nathanael (see John 1:45-51); (7) Matthew, the tax collector; (8) Thomas; (9) James, the son of Alphaeus; (10) Thaddaeus, also referred to as Jude, the probable author of the letter with that name in the New Testament; if he was a brother of James, "the brother of the Lord," this would make Thaddeus or Jude also a half brother of Jesus;[1] (11) Simon the Zealot or the Cananaean; and (12) Judas Iscariot, who was later replaced by Matthias (Mark 3:13-19; Matt. 10:1-4; Luke 6:12-16; see also John 6:67, 70, 71, where reference is made to "the Twelve").

The twelve disciples occupied a unique position. They were destined to be the apostles, the leaders of the early church. Luke 6:13 explicitly tells us that Jesus "chose twelve of them, which he also designated apostles." There were, however, many others who became disciples of Jesus Christ. According to the Gospel of Luke (10:1-24) Jesus sent out 72 (or 70, as some Bible manuscripts indicate) on a short-term mission trip. Later traditions furnish complete lists of names, but, however interesting this may be, it is nothing but worthless speculation. We should not be surprised to find that most of the disciples the Bible refers to were men. That is to be expected in a world of male dominance, but let us not conclude that discipleship is a male prerogative! Many women followed Jesus (see, for example, Matt. 27:55, 56; Mark 15:40-47; Acts 1:12-14), and the events surrounding Jesus' crucifixion, burial, and resurrection certainly proved them to be true disciples.

Called by Jesus

Many teachers in the ancient world had disciples who came to learn from their masters and would often live in close association with them.

33

Usually the aspirant disciples were the ones who chose a teacher. But in the case of Jesus' disciples, that order was reversed. Jesus chose His disciples, rather than vice versa. But that is not the only difference.

The call to Christian discipleship is not just a call from someone who has hit upon a good *idea* and now invites other people also to learn about that idea and help to promote it. When Jesus calls people to be His disciples, it has primarily to do with attachment to His *person*. Of course, the attachment of any follower to any teacher is usually characterized by a personal bond. This is how we usually define discipleship. For that reason the Latin word *discipulus*—with its composite meaning of learner, adherent, and imitator—has become a key word in the Christian vocabulary. It became the translation for the Greek word *mathetes* (literally, a learner; used more than 250 times in the New Testament) and was used for the members of that band of close followers of Jesus. Being called *by Jesus* has a more dramatic impact on people, and has more far-reaching—temporal and eternal—consequences than any other kind of call from any teacher can possibly have.

Several times the Gospel stories about the calling of the twelve mention the word "immediately" when reporting about the response. Mark, in particular, has a great predilection for the word *euthus* ("immediately"), which he uses more than 40 times. It may, however, most of all be Mark's way of providing a measure of suspense to his narrative. Maybe we should not overly stress the immediacy of the response to the call, as if Christ suddenly appears as an unknown but utterly impressive kind of guru, to whom people react within seconds with an unconditional willingness to follow.

The calling of the twelve may not have been as sudden as many tend to suppose. The account in Luke 5 tells us that the calling of Simon, James, and John took place in the context of a public sermon by Jesus. The actual call was further preceded by the miraculous catch of fish, after Jesus had challenged Simon Peter to go fishing where the water was deeper, while during the previous night all fishing had remained totally unsuccessful. In John 1 we see a clear connection between John the Baptist's ministry and the early ministry of Jesus, and there the calling of the first disciples is placed in that particular context.

This, however, takes nothing away from the dramatic and drastic nature of Christ's call. The fishermen decide to abandon their boats and nets. The sons of Zebedee leave their father and his employees. Matthew hands in his notice to the fiscal authorities. We are not informed about all the details. At least several of the disciples were married and had families (see 1 Cor. 9:5), and we are left in the dark as to what their acceptance of the call to follow Christ meant for their family life. What the stories, however, succeed in bringing across is the radical nature of following Jesus Christ.

In his famous book *The Cost of Discipleship* Dietrich Bonhoeffer describes this in the following magisterial words: "The disciple simply burns his boats and goes ahead. He is called out, and has to forsake his old life in order that he may 'exist' in the strictest sense of the word. The old life is left behind, and completely surrendered. The disciple is dragged out of his relative security into a life of absolute insecurity (that is, in truth, into the absolute security and safety of the fellowship of Jesus), from a life which is observable and calculable (it is, in fact, quite incalculable) into a life where everything is unobservable and fortuitous, out of the realm of the finite (which is in truth the infinite) into the realm of infinite possibilities (which is the one liberating reality)."[2]

Jesus Did Not Call Perfect People

Peter was afraid he could not be with Jesus: "I am too much of a sinner to be around You," he says (see Luke 5:8). It is, in particular, a vivid reminder of our own fundamental unworthiness to be associates with the Lord, that Jesus called Matthew, a member of the much-hated guild of tax-collectors. The twelve were far from perfect people, who by nature were qualified to be leaders and role models for others. They "were distinguished by their ordinariness, not by their talent, power, or position."[3]

But while discipleship does not begin with any degree of sinlessness that human beings might bring along, it does presuppose honesty. This is the main emphasis in the short account of the calling of Nathanael (John 1:46-49). Nathanael was not very impressed when Philip told him he had found the Messiah, Jesus, the son of Joseph from Nazareth. Nathanael's gut reaction was very straightforward: "From Nazareth! How in the world can anything good come from there?" This was no reason for Jesus to put Nathanael on temporary probation, as we might do with people we find rather too outspoken. Jesus appreciated openness and honesty.

Honesty is a key requirement for true discipleship. One cannot possibly be an authentic disciple if one is not completely honest with oneself. Likewise, discipleship cannot succeed if the disciples lack integrity among themselves. They will not be able to follow their Lord with one mind and one soul, if they cannot be transparent to one another. And, of course, one cannot be a true disciple of the Lord unless one is totally honest with Him, knowing that He knows us even better than we can ever know ourselves. He knows exactly under which fig tree we are sitting (John 1:48).

Disciples Must Be Willing to Learn and Serve

Several new Bible translations in a variety of languages no longer use the word "disciple" but consistently suggest the word "learner" as the closest rendering of the Greek term that most traditional translations render as "disciple." This is not to say that discipleship is first of all an intellectual process. It is primarily learning about a new way of being, about learning to live the new life that Christ has on offer. It entails learning about our real self and about life as God intended it to be lived. It is about learning to lead the life of faith. There is, however, definitely an intellectual component. After all, we are to love the Lord also with all our mind (Mark 12:30). What's more, followers of Christ are people who think, or to put it more precisely, people who think Christianly. Os Guinness pointedly reminds us that "thinking Christianly" is not just thinking *by* Christians. It differs from merely thinking about Christian topics or having a Christian line on every issue. It requires the miracle of a "new mind" to think under the lordship of Christ and thus to think about everything in a consistently Christian way. Yet, that is what real disciples must learn.[4]

True discipleship also implies a disposition to serve. The Galilean fishermen were asked to abandon their fishing trade and become fishers of men (Mark 1:17). They would not lead a quiet life of mere prayer and meditation (although that is most assuredly also part of the learning process for anyone who is willing to accept the call to discipleship), but would be active in the kingdom of their Lord. It is no accident that the story of how Andrew and Philip found fellow disciples has been recorded. Discipleship is not a privilege to keep for oneself. Ultimately, that is why the church was established: to start the process of disciples-making-disciples (Matt. 28:18). This implies evangelism and the ministry of teaching. But more than anything else, it requires a life of discipleship that will inspire others also to become disciples.

Why *These* Twelve?

By human standards the apostles were not the most likely candidates for church leadership. Yet they were suitable clay in the hands of the Master Potter to mold them into the kind of people He could use. When we compare what is said about their origin with the record of their deeds in the book of Acts and in some of the New Testament Epistles, we are truly amazed by what being subjected to divine teaching and example can bring about. They were a very mixed group. Ellen White emphasized that they "differed widely in habits and disposition. There were the publican,

Levi Matthew, and the fiery zealot Simon, the uncompromising hater of the authority of Rome; the generous, impulsive Peter, and the mean-spirited Judas; Thomas, truehearted, yet timid and fearful, Philip, slow of heart, and inclined to doubt, and the ambitious, outspoken sons of Zebedee, with their brethren. These were brought together, with their different faults, all with inherited and cultivated tendencies to evil; but in and through Christ they were to dwell in the family of God, learning to become one in faith, in doctrine, in spirit. They would have their tests, their grievances, their differences of opinion; but while Christ was abiding in the heart, there could be no dissension. His love would lead to love for one another; the lessons of the Master would lead to the harmonizing of all differences, bringing the disciples into unity, till they would be of one mind and one judgment."[5] And, very aptly, the same author says: "The first step was now taken in the organization of the church that after Christ's departure was to be His representative on earth."[6]

Built on the Rock

As was stated at the beginning of this chapter, the church did not "happen" by accident. God wanted to have a church, a community of His people, just as He wanted a people in Old Testament times. If there still remains any doubt, it should be removed by the unequivocal statement Christ made, that is recorded in Matthew 16:13-20. This passage tells us about a conversation between Jesus and Simon Peter, while they were somewhere in the region of Caesarea Philippi. When the Lord asked His disciples what opinions people had about Him, He was told that the answers to His question varied greatly. Some identified Him with John the Baptist, but others believed He was a reappearance of Elijah or Jeremiah or one of the other ancient prophets. Then Jesus rephrased His question in a very personal way. Granted, He says, that there are different opinions, but what interests Me most is what *you*, as My closest associates, think! Peter replied first: "You are the Christ, the Son of the living God." That is the background for the famous statement that follows: "On this rock I will build my church" (Matt. 16:13-20).

The fact that Jesus declares He will found His church on "this rock" has given rise to vehement theological disagreements (and worse). Roman Catholics suggest that the apostle Peter is the rock, and they use this text as the foundational statement about the special authority of Peter and his (papal) successors. Protestants—Adventists among them—point to the play on words: "You are *petros,* and on this *petra* I will build my church." They defend the view that *petros* and *petra* are related but different words. *Petra* is used to denote a large solid rock, and *petros* refers to a small stone. This is a very credible explanation, for which solid arguments can be found, even though some scholars disagree. The Catholic doctrine of the special authority of Peter and his successors rests on flimsy evidence indeed. When all New Testament evidence is put together, there does not seem to be any other option than to conclude that the Catholic teachings about the role of Peter and the popes, as his successors, is based on traditional arguments rather than firm scriptural evidence.

The church is not founded on a vague theory or lofty ideal. It is based on the fundamental confession that Jesus *is* the Christ. That makes the church into the *Christian* church. *The Protestant explanation agrees with all the biblical testimony, which emphasizes that Christ Himself is the foundation of the church* (see 1 Cor. 3:11; Eph. 2:20; 1 Peter 2:4-7; Acts 4:11). "The Rock of faith is the living presence of Christ in the church."[7]

Shortly after this discussion about who Jesus in fact was, during the final days of His earthly ministry, when the Last Supper (Matt. 26:26-29 and parallel passages) was celebrated, Christ instituted the new covenant with His disciples as the representatives of the church that He wanted built. They would serve as the leaders of the new people of God. The passages about the Last Supper are not just important because of their bearing on that significant event and the meaning of the Communion Service which developed from it, but also for the wider concept of a worldwide community that would practice this solemn rite henceforth until Christ's second coming.

This community, the church, would not just be an association of people who enjoy their social activities or meet regularly for spiritual edification. We will discuss later in more detail that the church was established because there was a mission to be accomplished, just as ancient Israel had a mission. The mission is, in fact, the raison d'être for the church. The Great Commission to preach the gospel in all the world (Matt. 28:19, 20 and parallel passages in the other Gospels) leaves us in no doubt about the missionary task of the Christian church.

Ekklesia

Jesus said: "On this rock [the confession that I am the Christ] I will build my *ekklesia*." The New Testament writers frequently use the word *ekklesia*, which is commonly translated into English as "church." We already saw in the previous chapter that the word predates the New Testament and was used in the ancient world as well as in the Septuagint, the Greek translation of the Old Testament. It is a contraction of two words: *ek* (out) and *kalein* (to call). Literally, therefore, the word *ekklesia* refers to those who have been called out. A related word—*kletos*—means "the one who has been called," and the plural form of this word is more or less synonymous with *ekklesia*. The word for "church" in many modern languages has its root in this Greek word: *Kirche* (German), *kirke* (Scottish), *kyrka* (Swedish), *kerk* (Dutch), *ecclesia* (Italian), etc.

This word *ekklesia* appears in the New Testament more than 100 times. But it occurs only three times in the Gospels, more specifically in two passages in Matthew (16:18; 18:17). The word is mostly used in the book of Acts and in some of the Epistles after the Holy Spirit had been poured out at Pentecost, when the *ekklesia* began to take shape. Once again, it is important to remember that the idea of "being called" is closely connected with the concept of the church. The church comes into being not by any human initiative, but in response to a divine call.[8]

For most people today the word "church" can have a number of very different meanings. When they speak of "a church," they often mean a particular building, as, for instance, when they describe the Notre Dame cathedral in Paris or the St. Peter's in Rome as famous churches that are worth visiting. Often, also, the word "church" is used to refer to a denomination. We speak of the Presbyterian Church, the Baptist Church, or the Seventh-day Adventist Church. The word "church" may also be applied in a more general way, as the collective term for religion—its worship and its institutions—as, for instance, when we discuss the relationship between church and state.

However, the biblical focus of *ekklesia* is specifically that of people. An analysis of the various uses of the word in the New Testament is most instructive. Twice it is used with reference to the Old Testament congregation and three times for a secular assembly. The word is used six times in a general, nonspecific sense and 13 times for the universal church (for example, Eph. 1:22; 3:10, 21; 1 Cor. 10:32). But 90 times it clearly refers to one or more local congregations in specific localities (for example, Rom. 16:1; Rev. 2:3; 1 Cor. 1:18; 14:19) or to a house church or a small group of believers (for example, Rom. 16:5; 1 Cor. 16:19).[9] Never is it used for buildings or in the other ways that we use the word "church." The key thought that is embedded in this important word is not linked to any of the material aspects of an organization or institution. The church is the people who have been called out of the world and now belong to the Lord. *The church is the people of God.*

The Church in the Book of Acts

We can glean more information about the origin of the church from the book of Acts, written around A.D. 60 by Luke, a physician and traveling companion of the apostle Paul, to whose activities some two thirds of the book is dedicated. Immediately after the departure of the Lord, there was a community of believers in Jerusalem. The disciples—who were now called "apostles"—were the key figures (with Matthias replacing Judas to fill the vacant position among the twelve [Acts 1:12-26]). Other leaders were soon added, as the Jerusalem church grew. The fragmentary information in Acts 2:42-47 suggests a kind of communal life. It is also noteworthy that the synagogue and the Temple still played an important role for the early believers.

The early Christian community saw immediate significant growth. Even members of the Jewish clergy joined the Christ believers (Acts 6:7). Acts 2 gives the explanation for the increase in membership. The outpouring of the Spirit during the Feast of Pentecost provided the supernatural infusion of power that catapulted the small Christian community onto the first-century religious stage. Visitors from many different regions heard the good news of Christ in their own language and took their new insights with them after they returned home. Opposition led to a wide dispersion of believers in Judea and Samaria (Acts 8:1). Acts 8 reports the activities of Philip in Samaria and his contacts with a dignitary who was on his way back to Nubia. Acts 9 informs us about the church in Damascus. And so the story continues. Note that, from the beginning, the church was *ethnically very diverse!*

The remainder of the book of Acts deals, as was already mentioned, mainly with the missionary exploits of the apostles, and, more specifically, of Paul—the apostle to the Gentiles. If your Bible contains a set of maps, most likely you will find one that shows where Paul traveled on his four missionary journeys, establishing churches wherever he preached. Bible sources tell us less about the missionary exploits of the other apostles. We meet the apostle John, toward the end of his life, as a prisoner on the tiny Greek island of Patmos, and early Christian traditions indicate that he regained his freedom and subsequently, at a very old age, worked in the city of Ephesus. Tourists to that city, which is now part of modern Turkey, are shown the place where he supposedly was buried. Other ancient and very credible traditions tell us that Thomas preached the gospel message as far as present-day India. Similar traditions about extended mission journeys exist for several of the other twelve.

The book of Acts also reports about early organizational developments. The apostles who had, as disciples, been with Christ played a key role. They were soon assisted by seven other leaders, often referred to as "deacons," even though the author of Acts does not use that term to designate them (Acts 6:1-7). Later in the book of Acts and in the Epistles we see the first traces of local organizational development, when elders (or "overseers") and deacons (1 Tim. 3:8-13) make their appearance. The word "elder" is first applied to a local church leader in Acts 11:30. A comparison of Acts 20:17 with Acts 20:28 (see also 1 Tim. 3:2-7 and Titus 1:5-9) leads to the conclusion that the terms *presbyteros* ("presbyter") and *episkopos* ("overseer" or "bishop") are used as synonyms. The qualifications and offices of an elder and a "bishop" are the same. (For other passages that mention "elders," see 1 Peter 1:1; 5:1-3; James 5:14, 15; Acts 14:23; 15:1, 2, 4, 6. In chapter 7 we will have to say more on this topic.)

The book of Acts suggests a significant degree of solidarity (see Acts 2:45 and Acts 5) among the earliest believers in Jerusalem. Subsequently we learn about financial assistance for the church in Jerusalem from other local churches (Rom. 15:31). Acts 15 is a pivotal chapter. It describes an international church council at which an issue that had arisen and had impacted all congregations was discussed. It is significant that a meeting such as this could be held at such an early date and that its authority seems to have been generally accepted among the churches that had thus far been founded.

The Theology of the Church in the New Testament

The Bible provides us with the building blocks for our theology. This is the reason we have started this book about the doctrine of the church with a survey of the biblical data. This is the way in which any project in systematic theology ought to proceed. But there are also other approaches to the discipline of the theology. Some theologians specialize in historical theology and investigate how particular theological ideas have developed and sometimes changed over time. Another important approach to theology is that of biblical theology. This appears, at first sight, to be a rather puzzling label, for is not all theology supposed to be biblical? Certainly, but biblical theology has a special aim. It tries to determine what special focus can be found in particular books or portions of the Bible.

The books of the New Testament do not furnish a ready-made, complete systematic theological picture of the church. But some of the various books offer some significant insights that are not, or not as clearly, found in other sections. It should, of course, be noted that the sequence in our Bibles of the 27 writings that were incorporated in the New Testament does not represent the order in which they were written. These documents originated throughout a period of about 50 years, with Paul's First Letter to the Thessalonians probably being the oldest and the "Johannine" writings most likely being among the last to be written. Some development of thought and difference in perspective is to be expected.

The New Testament writings do not only reflect the teachings of Jesus and the apostles—notably of the apostle Paul—but also inform us about issues that, apparently, were relevant in the faith communities to which the Gospels were first addressed. That Matthew emphasizes Christ's mission to His own people is directly related to the fact that this Gospel originated in a Judeo-Christian context. John, who wrote a few decades later and whose ministry was to a large extent in an environment where Christians "from the Gentiles" formed a majority, wrote a Gospel that breathes a different atmosphere. John 3:16 knows of no ethnic or cultural limitations: God so loved the *world*!

The content of the Gospels therefore reflects the *Sitz im Leben* (the term German theologians have coined to refer to the setting in real life) in particular local churches or among particular membership segments. After all, what was recorded was just a tiny selection of what actually happened and what was said. It informs us about what was remembered and what was clearly considered by the early communities as having extra significance and relevance.

The Gospel of Mark was probably the first Gospel to be written. It was clearly addressed to an audience of Gentile ethnicity and may well have originated in the context of the church in Rome (as some external historical evidence suggests).[10] It emphasizes that greatness consists in service to others rather than in exercise of power and authority (Mark 10:41-44). The church must pattern itself after the Son of Man (verse 45).[11] Luke's Gospel very much exhibits the same kind of traits.

A few more words should perhaps be devoted to Matthew's Gospel. This exhibits a more developed ecclesiology than is found in Mark, as we can, for instance, discern in the various discourses of Jesus. From a late-first–century Judeo-Christian perspective, the Sermon on the Mount reminds its readers that the church is a community of disciples that fulfills the Mosaic law as interpreted by the Messiah (Matt. 5-7). This Gospel also focuses on the church's missionary task. Although Jesus limited His own mission largely to the lost sheep of the house of Israel (Matt. 10:5, 6; 15:24), the risen Lord, more strongly than in the other Gospels, commissions the church to make disciples of all nations (Matt. 28:18-20).

Why did Matthew include the parable of the weeds (Matt. 13:24-43) and that of the great net (verses 47-50) in his Gospel? Was it because it seemed relevant in view of some problematic situations in congregation(s) that first received this Gospel? Was Matthew confronted with a church that had weeds as well as wheat? Is that also why he includes instructions for dealing with those who had gone astray (Matt. 18) and why express warnings are included about "false prophets" (Matt. 7:15-23)?[12] Peter C. Phan, a native of Vietnam and currently teaching at the Catholic University of America, aptly summarizes Matthew's perspective: The church is a community instructed in all righteousness, missionary in nature, empowered to discipline its members as it waits for the Son of man, who will separate the bad from the good. Phan also clearly points out that there is continuity as well as discontinuity between Israel and the church.[13]

The Gospel of John was probably the last of the Gospels to be written and differs greatly from the other three. This Gospel seems to be especially interested in the status and role of Christ. Two images dominate John's theology of the church: the sheepfold (John 10:1-18) and the vine (John 15:1-10). Both emphasize the need of an intimate connection between Christ and His followers. An important point is made by referring to Christ's statement that He has other sheep who do not belong to this fold (presumably the community that first received John's Gospel [John 10:16]). The community of believers is guided by the Holy Spirit, whom the Father sends in Jesus' name (John 14:26). The old forms of worship in Temple and synagogue no longer satisfy, and the church is now challenged to worship in "spirit and truth" (John 4:21-24) as the members wait for the imminent return of their Lord.[14]

The other books of the New Testament also make their contribution—directly or indirectly—to the rich theological treatment of the theme of the church. Paul's Epistles have much to say about the Christian *ekklesia*, both in its local and supralocal forms. One key metaphor for Paul is that of the church as the *body* of Christ, as we shall discuss in the next chapter. But numerous other metaphors also illustrate the multifaceted nature and function of the church. Paul's letters are, as we shall discuss later, also a mine of information about the early developments of the various Christian ministries in the church during its earliest decades.

The letter to the Hebrews does not claim Pauline authorship. The traditional view that Paul was the author is contested, even among Adventist scholars. This question does not impact, however, its inspired nature and the deep meaning of the book of Hebrews, which, according to most specialists, dates from about A.D. 70. Although often referred to as a letter, it, in fact, rather seems to resemble a sermon. More than any other New Testament book it systematically stresses the continuity between God's people in Old Testament times and the Christian church. But also, more than any other part of the New Testament it argues categorically for the superiority of Christianity, with Christ's priesthood as far superior to what preceded in the old sanctuary service (Heb. 7-10). The story of Israel and the story of the church are distinct chapters of one and the same story, the author of Hebrews tells his readers. But in Christ something new has dramatically entered history as the fulfillment of what went before.[15]

The book of Revelation is probably one of the latest parts of the New Testament to be written. Majority opinion dates the Apocalypse around A.D. 95.[16] Of course, this last book of the Bible can be read and interpreted in many different ways. But those who fail to pay attention to what is said or implied about the church miss an extremely important dimension. Chapters 2 and 3 provide us with a lot of insight into church life, with all its challenges, in Asia Minor during the late first century, while at the same time presenting us with a sevenfold mirror for the church of all ages. Christ knows what is happening in His churches (Rev. 2:2, 9, 13; 3:1, 8, 15). The entire book is about a church that faces untold hardships; it is about times of martyrdom (see, for example, Rev. 6:9-11) and the unfortunate occurrence and reoccurrences of the most serious kinds of apostasy (for example, Rev. 17 and 18). But it is also the story of a church that, in the end, will be utterly triumphant, and the glorious story of a last-day remnant (Rev. 12:14) that will survive all divine judgments and, with the saints from all ages, will constitute the great multitude (Rev. 7:9-17) who will inherit the kingdom (Rev. 21 and 22). The destiny of the church is to be the bride of the Lamb.[17]

The first chapter sets the tone. It presents Christ as walking among the seven lampstands, which symbolize the Christian churches (Rev. 1:20). What more comforting message can there be than this marvelous picture of Christ "walking" amid His churches? The first characteristic of Christ that was revealed to John in his vision is that He is present among the congregations of His people. Everything else that may be said about the church must be seen in that glorious light.[18] In the days of Moses God promised His people: "I will walk among you and be your God, and you will be my people" (Lev. 26:12). And even now "He has not left His people to fend for themselves or to endure the tortuous course of history without Him."[19] The New Testament ends on the highest possible note: The Lord of heaven will for ever and ever be with His people!

---

[1] See "Jude, Epistle of," in: *Seventh-day Adventist Bible Dictionary* (Washington, D.C.: Review and Herald Pub. Assn., 1960, 1979), pp. 630, 631.

[2] *The Cost of Discipleship*, rev. ed. (New York: Macmillan Co, 1959), pp. 62, 63.

[3] Benjamin C. Maxson, *The Missing Connection: Where Life Meets Lordship* (Silver Spring, Md.: Stewardship Department, General Conference of SDAs, 2005), p. 39.

[4] Os Guinness, *Fit Bodies, Fat Minds* (Grand Rapids: Baker Books, 1994), pp. 135, 136.

[5] Ellen G. White, *The Desire of Ages,* (Mountain View, Calif.: Pacific Press Pub. Assn., 1898), p. 296.

[6] *Ibid.*, p. 291.

[7] *Ibid.*, p. 414.

[8] John S. Hammett, *Biblical Foundations for Baptist Churches—A Contemporary Ecclesiology* (Grand Rapids: Kregel Publications, 2007), pp. 26-31.

[9] *Ibid.*, p. 31.

[10] Donal Guthrie, *New Testament Introduction*, vol. 1, *The Gospels and Acts* (Chicago: InterVarsity Press, 1965), pp. 53-59.

[11] Peter C. Phan, *The Gift of the Church: A Textbook on Ecclesiology* (Collegeville, Minn.: Liturgical Press, 2000), p. 4.

[12] *Ibid.*, p. 5.

[13] *Ibid.*, p. 6.

[14] *Ibid.*, pp. 7-9.

[15] Donald A. Hagner, *Encountering the Book of Hebrews* (Grand Rapids: Baker Academic, 2002), p. 183.

[16] Among those who accept that the same John was the author of the Gospel of John and of the Apocalypse, some argue that the Gospel was actually written later than the book of Revelation.

[17] Phan, p. 19.

[18] G. B. Baird, *The Revelation of Saint John*, in Henry Chadwick, ed., *Black's New Testament Commentary Series* (Peabody, Mass.: Hendrickson Publishers), p. 25.

[19] Jacques B. Doukhan, *Secrets of Revelation: The Apocalypse Through Hebrew Eyes* (Hagerstown, Md.: Review and Herald Pub. Assn., 2002), p. 25.

Chapter 4

Biblical Foundations:
Themes and Metaphors

In this chapter we will take a further look at the biblical data regarding the church, but we will do so from a different perspective. First we will briefly look at the issue of how the church is related to another prominent New Testament concept: the kingdom of God. Are these two concepts synonymous? And if not, how do they fit together? Then we will address another matter: the relationship between the church and Israel. We referred already several times to a distinct continuity between the two but also pointed at the radical discontinuity. However, more needs to be said about this important issue. Then later in the chapter we will focus on a number of important metaphors used by the biblical authors to catch various significant aspects of the nature and role of the church.

The Church and the Kingdom

The kingdom of God is one of the prominent themes in the Gospels. The kingdom is closely connected with the church, but the two concepts are not to be confused, as was often done by many theologians through the ages, from Augustine to the sixteenth-century Reformers.

Various views have been held about the kingdom. Among nineteenth-century liberals, with the German Adolf von Harnack (1851-1930) as the best known example, the kingdom was interpreted in this-worldly terms, as completely belonging to the here and now and not as something that would come at the end of time. Others, as, for instance, the famous Swiss physician-theologian Albert Schweitzer (1875-1965), proposed the completely opposite position and saw the kingdom as totally future. (Schweitzer believed that Christ, however, was deluded, for His predictions of a soon–coming kingdom failed miserably!) It would be a rewarding exercise to explore the history of the interpretation of the kingdom concept a bit further, but this is not the place to do so.

Although the exact term *kingdom of God* is not found in the Old Testament, the idea is present. God is often pictured as the one and almighty King, ruling His people (see, for example, Isa. 9; 11). The kingdom clearly is a central theme in the Gospels (see, for example, Mark 1:14, 15 and Matt. 4:23). Matthew often speaks about the kingdom of heaven. This term betrays the Jewish-Christian milieu of this Gospel. The Jews tried to avoid using the word "God" and often substituted the word "heaven." The terms *kingdom of God* and *kingdom of heaven* are, however, fully synonymous.

When all Gospel material is brought together, various emphases are visible, but the conclusion is clear. The kingdom has already come and is a present reality. This is stressed in Luke 4:21, where the prediction relating to God's kingdom is quoted from Isaiah 35:5, 6 and where it is stated that this prediction has now become present reality. (See also Matthew 12:28; Luke 17:20ff.; and many other passages that emphasize the present reality of the kingdom.) Yet at the same time it must be remembered that the kingdom is present only in a preliminary form and that its full and ultimate realization in eternal glory is future and will come about when all things shall have been made new. The Lord taught His disciples to pray for the future coming of that kingdom (Matt. 6:10) and made it clear that His people would only after the day of judgment "enter the kingdom" (Matt. 7:21-23; 25:41, 46; Mark 10:17-31; Luke 13:22-30).

Several passages point to the mysterious nature of the kingdom. Notice, for instance, the metaphors of the mustard seed and the yeast (Matt. 13:31-35), descriptive of the nature of the heavenly kingdom. From a small, insignificant beginning it will develop into something that is substantial and that will have a penetrating influence in whatever it comes in contact with.

Mysterious it is indeed. For how can something be both present yet still future? How can it be *already* and *not yet* at the same time? This is the kind of paradox the human mind cannot fathom. Humanly speaking, a phenomenon must be past, present, or future. The divine reality, however, does not fit so nicely into human categories. We are often confronted with paradoxes (apparent contradictions), in which two or more aspects, which in our human experience seem to exclude each other, somehow are simultaneously true in God's supreme reality.

The church already lives on the basis of the ethics of the kingdom, as expressed in the teachings of Christ on the Mount of Blessing and thereby is a great blessing to the world. The church is the seed, the sign, and the instrument of the kingdom. It is a dynamic force in humankind's journey toward the eternal kingdom that we await.[1] The kingdom of God may be best defined as the redemptive rule of God. The church lives in the tension between the *already* and *not yet* as the community that has its feet firmly planted in this present world but at the same time prepares, as best as it can, for the world to come.

However, there is no tendency in the New Testament to identify the visible church with the kingdom of God. "The church that makes such an identification will soon begin to invite God to endorse its very own human policies and practices, will equate the people of God with those nice people who share its particular beliefs and participate in its services, and will reckon the advance of the kingdom in terms of its numerical growth!"[2]

The church is the human community that lives under God's rule. One might say that the kingdom creates the church and the church, in turn, witnesses to the kingdom. It does so, not by its efficient management of the missionary enterprise—through human strategies and resources. Important though these may be, it would be superficial or even wrong to say that the church must build the kingdom in the world. Concepts such as "building," "extending," "promoting," and "establishing" stand in stark contrast to the biblical language used to define the relationship of the church to the kingdom of God. Words such as "receiving," "entering," "seeking," and "inheriting" emphasize the redemptive gift character of the kingdom of which the church bears witness.[3]

The Church and Israel

Few issues are as controversial in contemporary Protestantism as the relationship between Israel and the church. We already saw that the topic is touched upon in many places in the Gospels and in other New Testament books, but a number of the apostle Paul's writings deal with the topic in greatest depth.

Contemporary Christendom holds widely divergent standpoints. Throughout the centuries many Christians have had utterly negative views of Judaism and have often promoted, or at least tolerated, anti-Semitic sentiments. It has, with at least some justification, been claimed that the Christian church, with its explicitly anti-Jewish theologies and ever-recurring anti-Jewish sentiments, has been responsible for many of the outbursts of anti-Semitism around the world. Most of that is fortunately in the past, and a majority of contemporary Christians has a much more positive view of the Jews and their religious traditions, recognizing that there is much in the past to be ashamed of. Today many evangelicals have, however, gone to the other extreme and often appear to be totally uncritical in their attitudes toward the Jewish state and its policies. They continue to see an important role for Israel as a people and as a nation in the plan of God. They view the rebirth of the state of Israel in 1948 as a striking fulfillment of Bible prophecy. They believe that the prophecies that predicted Israel's restoration are nonconditional and must therefore all be literally fulfilled.

One very influential approach is that of dispensationalism, pioneered by John N. Darby (1800-1882). This theory expects the present era of the church soon to be succeeded by the era of a restored Israel. Although it may be argued that the term *dispensation* is a biblical word[4] and that the word had been used by theologians prior to Darby, the modern dispensationalists have given it a totally new content, which "involves some basic principles of interpretation that depart radically from the historic Christian faith and are often diametrically opposed to what the church has always believed."[5] A *dispensation* is defined as a period during which humanity is tested in respect to obedience to some specific revelation of God's will. The issues at stake with regard to this test differ from one dispensation to the next. God works, according to the dispensationalists, in different ways in different periods of history, and He sets different requirements as history unfolds. The so-called secret rapture is also part of the conglomerate of dispensationalist ideas.

The number of dispensations that are distinguished by dispensationalist Bible interpreters varies, although the list provided by the notes in the very popular *Scofield Reference Bible* (first published in 1909 and widely distributed in the United States ever since) has found broad acceptance among dispensationalists. The most important periods, from our current perspective, are the last three: the period of Mosaic law (between Moses and Christ), the age of the church in which we now live, and the coming literal millennial reign of Christ on earth. For those who believe in this scheme, a literal understanding of the Bible is a key principle. Thus, when the word "Israel" is mentioned, it should always be taken as literal and never as symbolic. Israel is the nation of Israel, and the church is the church! A key passage that dispensationalists fondly quote is Zechariah 12:8–10, in which the prophet predicted a time that all would go well for Israel. Israel would fully accept Jesus Christ. "They will look on me, the one they have pierced" (verse 10, NIV).

The dispensationalist view has an enormous impact on how one views the church. It greatly restricts the role of the church to only a temporary intermezzo. For those who hold this theory, the coming of the kingdom is the restoration of Israel and not the consummation of the church.[6] Professor Clarence Bass is right when he concludes: "An emphasis upon the national restoration of Israel is, at the same time, a de-emphasis upon the triumph of the cross, by which believers are made members of the body of Christ, the church."[7]

Others, Seventh-day Adventists among them, point to the *conditional* nature of Bible prophecy. They believe, as Ellen White also indicated, that "the promises and threatenings of God are alike conditional."[8] They do not consider the re-establishment of the state of Israel as a significant part of God's plan of salvation, since the founders of the state of Israel and its present leaders are not operating on the basis of the divine conditions. The *Seventh-day Adventist Bible Commentary*[9] provides an excellent overview of this important issue.

One traditional Christian view, which is still widely held, is that the church has replaced Israel in God's plan. This is usually referred to as the substitution theory or replacement theology. In this context the church is often referred to as "spiritual Israel." Although that term is not found in the New Testament, it is believed by many that the concept is amply supported by the New Testament text. This used to be the majority opinion among Adventist theologians and possibly still is.

More recently, however, a considerable amount of discussion has arisen about this topic. Some Adventist scholars (for example, Jacques Doukhan and Richard Elofer, both of Jewish pedigree, but also others) argue that the supporters of the substitution theory overstate their case and that there is sufficient biblical evidence to defend some continuing role for the Jews in the salvific (salvation-historical) purposes of God.

Studying the topic with an open mind, we cannot avoid being impressed by signals of continuity—the continuing significance of Israel in God's plan. We notice the statements that underline how Jesus came as a Jew to the Jewish people, to the "lost sheep of Israel" (for example, Matt. 15:24; 10:5, 6). Jesus and His disciples—and later the early Christians—continued to worship in the Temple and the synagogue. It is also significant that many Jewish leaders eventually joined the Christian movement (Acts 6:7). We read in the last Bible chapters that the New Jerusalem is linked to the names of the 12 tribes of ancient Israel as well as with the names of the 12 apostles. The apostle Paul, though in particular targeting his work toward the non-Jews (Gentiles), continued to be pleased that he was a Jew. He belabored the point: "I am an Israelite myself, a descendant of Abraham, from the tribe of Benjamin" (Rom. 11:1).

But we should not only focus on the continuity between Israel and the church but also recognize the discontinuity. We need to pay attention to passages that emphasize the broader perspective, beyond the Jewish people and to the universal nature of the gospel message. Peter's vision of the clean and unclean animals (Acts 10) functions as an important passage in this respect. At the very beginning of his Gospel, Luke makes the point that Jesus was rejected by His own people in Nazareth (Luke 4:16-30). Matthew 24 and parallel chapters point to the fate of Jerusalem, which would be destroyed as the unmistakable signal that the era of the Jewish people as the special people of God would end. Matthew 23:37, 38 is unequivocal about the rejection of Israel: "O Jerusalem, Jerusalem, you who kill the prophets and stone those sent to you, how often I have longed to gather your children together, as a hen gathers her chicks under her wings, but you were not willing. Look, your house is left to you desolate."

What becomes abundantly clear in the New Testament is that, whatever our origin—whether we are Jew or non-Jew—we receive salvation only through Jesus. If you have any doubt, read and contemplate Ephesians 2:11-22. Salvation is rooted in a spiritual relationship and not in ethnicity (Gal. 3:26-28). And even though there may be some problems with the concept of the total substitution of Israel by the church, it cannot be denied that the exclusive or special status of Israel as a chosen nation has been abrogated. This term, once applied to Israel, is now applied to the church (compare 1 Peter 2:9 with Ex. 19:5).

And yet it might be advisable not to take too dogmatic a stance on this topic, as if we know every detail of God's plan of salvation. Romans 9-11 certainly leaves us with the impression that God's end-time people ("all Israel"), symbolized in Romans 11 by an olive tree, will not be complete until some (or many?) of the natural branches that have been broken away will once again "be grafted into [the original] olive tree!" (Rom. 11:24).

It may well be that, as Jacques Doukhan suggests, "the strong apologetic concern of some Seventh-day Adventist theologians and evangelists against the dispensationalist theory has led them to overemphasize the idea of God's rejection of Israel and even a curse upon the Jews."[10] Through the ages, he argues, the Jews have continued to play an important role in witnessing to crucial biblical concepts, as, for example, the divine law and the Sabbath. Does God have an increasingly important role for them as the end of time approaches? Whatever questions remain unanswered, the mission of bringing the message of the Christ, the Messiah, to the people who have provided the Christian church with its Scriptures and roots needs to remain a high priority for Adventist Christians. Several statements made by Ellen White about the Jews seem somewhat puzzling,[11] but other statements are crystal clear, as this one is: "Many of the Jewish people will by faith receive Christ as their Redeemer."[12]

The Body of Christ

The Bible informs us about many other aspects of the church through a variety of metaphors. Paul S. Minear (1906-2007), an eminent American New Testament scholar, in his well-known book *Images of the Church in the New Testament*[13], lists 96 different metaphors for the church that are used in the Bible. Some are only alluded to or mentioned once or just a few times. But some of them are used with great frequency and deserve close exploration. Some are well known, such as the *family*, a *pillar*, a *fortress*, a *flock*, and an *army*. The "brother" and "sister" language that has become common in many Christian movements has, of course, its basis in the family metaphor (for example, Heb. 2:11). The army metaphor (see, for example, 2 Cor. 10:3-5) is closely connected with the more extended imagery of the spiritual life as a battle against demonic powers, which must be fought with appropriate spiritual weaponry (Eph. 6:10-18). The Salvation Army has latched on to this imagery as a significant part of its identity. Other voices, however, suggest that this metaphor may be less suitable in today's climate of thought, as the church has often not shown its most loving and lovable face in times when it was most militant.

But let us first be clear about what a metaphor is and what it is not. One technical definition that I came across is: *A metaphor is an implied comparison between two unlike things that actually have something important in common.* An often-used example illustrates what is meant. It is quite common to refer to the Internet as a superhighway. When we employ this image, we use a *metaphor*. The concept of a highway as a stretch of pavement between two population centers is quite far removed from that of the Internet, which is based on an invisible worldwide network of computers that can be accessed almost instantly and provides enormous amounts of information. But underneath this vast difference we detect some common attributes: connectivity, speed, a medium for the masses! The metaphor is a unique teaching tool that helps us "see" some vital aspect of the object or topic under discussion.

The various biblical metaphors that describe aspects of the church provide crucial insights. But we must, from the outset, also recognize their limitations. They do not provide an analytic description whereby every element of the image can also be applied to the church. They are rather catchwords that focus on one particular aspect or just a few characteristics of a given phenomenon. The various metaphors should not be played off against one another. They each emphasize one or more particular aspects. *Together* they help us grasp, to some extent, the complete picture. Metaphors should not become the launching pad for unlimited allegories or, worse, unbridled fantasies. But they are powerful and enlightening pictures.

One of the most common of these metaphors is that of the church as a *body*, or more specifically, as the body of Christ. In Romans and 1 Corinthians the terminology points specifically to the local church, as the body of Christ in that particular place. Read, for instance, 1 Corinthians 12:27, which summarizes the concept: "Now you [church members in Corinth] are the body of Christ and each one of you is part of it." Earlier in that chapter this was more fully developed (verses 12-26). The body is a unit, though it is made up of many different parts. Some parts appear to play a more prominent role than other parts, depending on the spiritual gift or gifts they have been endowed with, but each of these parts has its own unique function, and none can be lost without causing damage to the wellness of the body as a whole. No part should complain about its role, for God has arranged the parts of the body, "just as he wanted them to be" (verse 18). The emphasis clearly is on unity, which is not primarily an organizational unity (though that aspect is present as well), but first of all a spiritual unity. It is, however, most explicitly a unity in diversity. While this is easy to understand, it is far less easy to put into practice, and the church knows from its long and often tragic experience that it takes a supernatural infusion of God's Spirit to bridge the natural divisions that so often tend to plague us. The body is united because it is united in the Spirit and in the fundamental truths of the Christian faith: "One Lord, one faith, one baptism; one God and Father of all, who is over all and through all and in all" (Eph. 4:5, 6). The entire passage (verses 1-16) breathes the need for, and beauty of, mutual support in love and care. "The one body means absolute solidarity in suffering and glory."[14]

But in Ephesians and Colossians the reference is to the universal church, and another aspect is added, that of the role of the head of the body. The believers constitute the body with all its limbs and organs, but Christ is "the head of the body, the church" (Col. 1:18). "In Him all things hold together" (verse 17). The teaching that Christ is the head of the church highlights the idea of His provision for the nourishment of the church, which is needed for continuous growth. First-century medical writers believed that the head was both the ruling part of the body and the source that provided nourishment and sustenance,[15] and Paul clearly adopted this notion. The problem is that the believer often loses his connection with "the Head, from whom the whole body, supported and held together by its ligaments and sinews, grows as God causes it to grow" (Col. 2:19). But the idea that the head is the ruling part must also not be forgotten. "Recognizing that Christ's authority in the church is supreme prevents us from exaggerating the importance of any church official or organizational structure. The church needs organization, of course, but no organization should obscure Christ's authority."[16]

Catholic theologians have often extended the image of the church as the body of Christ beyond sound biblical limitations and have not stopped at comparing the church with a body but have gone further by actually identifying the church as the Eucharistic body of the risen Lord. In so doing they make the church into a kind of reincarnation of Christ. This is incorrect. The church cannot exist separately from Christ, but Christ remains distinct from the church. Christ is perfect, whereas the church, as long as it is here on earth, remains imperfect.

The Bride of Christ

The metaphor of the church as Christ's bride focuses on another aspect of the church: purity, loyalty, intimacy, and love—that is, on the closest possible relationship. Perhaps the body metaphor is pressed to its most extreme point in the New Testament representation of the church as having united with Christ in marriage.[17] Christ Himself used the imagery a number of times. In His parables Jesus presented, for instance, His second advent as the coming of the Bridegroom (Matt. 25:6) and also spoke of the future wedding feast (Matt. 22:10-14)!

We need to remember that in the history of the church the bridal image has sometimes been loaded with ideas that went far beyond their intended application. For example, medieval women, at times, introduced strong sexual sentiments into their relation with the Bridegroom, and this has been true until today for some who have entered a convent to become "a bride" of their Lord. But the metaphor of the church as the bride of Christ is a powerful image. The Old Testament prophetic picture of Israel as God's spouse comes, of course, immediately to mind (for example, Isa. 54:5-7). Also, idolatry is often described as an adulterous relationship, in which the people have replaced the Bride with prostitutes. The early chapters of the book of Hosea provide the most striking illustration.

The metaphor strongly affirms the closest possible unity between Christ as the head and the church as His bride. "As his bride, the church must remain pure and faithful to her one husband, Jesus Christ." But, once again, "there is no support for the view that the apostle [Paul] regarded the church as a literal incarnation or extension of Christ."[18]

God's Temple

The Old Testament sanctuary was the place where God "lived," that is, where He manifested His presence in a very special manner. The antitype of this impressive symbolism is both God's presence in the heavenly sanctuary and the divine presence in the New Jerusalem, the ultimate habitat of God's people (Heb. 12:22; Rev. 21:3). While we still remain on this earth, the church is, in a sense, the holy temple of the Lord. God's people "and members of God's household" are "built on the foundation of the apostles and the prophets, with Christ Jesus himself as the chief cornerstone. In him the whole building is joined together and rises to become a holy temple in the Lord," or, in other but similar words, it becomes "a dwelling in which God lives by his Spirit" (Eph. 2:19-22). The believers are the "living stones" of this "spiritual house" (1 Peter 2:5).

"The Spirit is the mortar that holds the stones together. The church is not to be held together by social bonds such as being of the same race or class or income, but by the spiritual bond of a common possession of the Holy Spirit. . . . The New Testament is clear that the church must not become a club of one type of people but a community that transcends all those things that divide people in society. . . . God fitly joins together the stones in his holy temple with the mortar of fellowship. To switch the metaphors, the Holy Spirit is the lubricant that eases the friction" that so easily pollutes the temple.[19]

Because the church is God's temple, it must of necessity be a worshipping community in which all believers are involved in the church's ministry! And the temple is also a place of relationships. The Spirit strengthens our relationship with Christ, the Cornerstone, and joins us with the other stones that form God's spiritual house.[20]

In a derived sense the local congregation also is God's temple, as is clear from 1 Corinthians 3:16, 17, where the Corinthian church is addressed as God's sacred temple. In addition, the individual believer is described as a temple of God. Paul warns the believers against sexual sin and reminds them that the body of each one of them is "a temple of the Holy

Spirit" that is not to be defiled by any immorality but is an instrument to honor God (1 Cor. 6:19, 20).

What better imagery could there be than to describe the corporate church and every member of the church as a sanctified place where God wants to be present?

The temple metaphor has an interesting extension. During His earthly ministry Jesus said that the Jerusalem temple was to be destroyed but would be resurrected after three days (Mark 14:58). Jesus spoke of his own work as replacing the Jerusalem temple in the plan of God. The literal temple—the traditional center of the worship of God—was to be replaced by a new temple that Jesus was building—a temple built not of stones but "of the gathered members of the new Israel, which He is incorporating into Himself."[21]

The People of God

The metaphor of the church as the people of God also underscores the continuity in God's plan: He always had and always will have a group of people that belong to Him in a special sense. (See, for example, 1 Peter 2:9, which echoes Exodus 19:5, 6; Deuteronomy 4:20; 7:6; Hosea 1:10; 2:23.) They are God's elect, commissioned with the task of acquainting the world around them with the one and only God and with His plan of salvation for humanity. God says of His church: "I will be their God, and they will be my people" (2 Cor. 6:16).

The people of God are also called "saints" (Rom. 1:7), people "called to be holy" (1 Cor. 1:2). Some 60 times God's people are called "saints" or "the holy ones." This does not mean they are superpious or nearly perfect. But He has set them apart from other peoples to serve as His witnesses. They have been "redeemed," that is, purchased by the Redeemer, who paid for their redemption with His blood (Ex. 15:13, 16; Acts 20:28). This language reminds us of the Old Testament practice of "redeeming" what had been lost from the family possessions (see, for example, Ruth 3; 4; Jer. 32).

The Priesthood of All Believers

The New Testament further describes the church as the priesthood of all believers. The churches of the Reformation rediscovered this truth and emphasized the superiority of this biblical view over the sacerdotal system of the medieval church, which defended a sharp distinction between a priestly hierarchy and the "ordinary" believers, who depended on the former as their mediators for access to God.

The new people of God do not have a priesthood in their midst, as did

Israel in Old Testament times. The Letter to the Hebrews points out that the old sanctuary services have been replaced by a new and "better" ministration, with Jesus Christ as the perfect high priest (Heb. 9:23-26). He is the one and only mediator (1 Tim. 2:5). All members of the church—men and women—are priests (Rev. 1:6; 5:10; 20:6). Baptism is the ordination to the priesthood, in which all believers share (1 Peter 2:9, 10). Just as it was with ancient Israel, so there was nothing in the believers in the early church, nor in us, that qualifies for special consideration.[22] "The church is what it is because of what Jesus is, not because of who its members are."[23] That is why Paul writes to the Corinthian church: "Not many of you were wise by human standards; not many were influential; not many were of noble birth. But God chose the foolish things of the world" "so that none may boast before him. It is because of him that you are in Christ Jesus" (1 Cor. 1:26-30).

The New Testament refuses to make any qualitative distinction between clergy and laity. The church appoints people who have special responsibilities, as we shall later discuss in this book at some length, but the difference between those functionaries and the other church members is not that those who hold a church office relate to God in a more direct way. All members have, through their prayers, direct access to God. All depend in the same way on the intercession of the great High Priest. All share in the same way in the mission of the priesthood, to "mediate" the message of redemption (in the sense of communicating and being a channel) to the world. The Christian church has often neglected this aspect that all members are ministers, but fortunately in more recent times this has received greater emphasis than before.

---

[1] P. C. Phan, *The Gift of the Church,* p. 109.

[2] John Bright, *The Kingdom of God* (New York: Abingdon Press, 1953), p. 236.

[3] C. van Gelder, *The Essence of the Church,* p. 87.

[4] It is a translation of the Greek word *oikonomia,* and is rendered as "dispensation" in the King James Version of Ephesians 3:2-4.

[5] Clarence Bass, *Backgrounds to Dispensationalism* (Grand Rapids: Wm. B. Eerdmans Pub. Co., 1960), p. 17.

[6] *Ibid.,* p. 31.

[7] *Ibid.,* p. 33.

[8] Ellen G. White, *Selected Messages* (Washington, D.C.: Review and Herald Pub. Assn., 1958), p. 67.

[9] Vol. 4, pp. 25-38.

[10] Jacques B. Doukhan, *The Mystery of Israel* (Hagerstown, Md.: Review and Herald Pub. Assn., 2004), p. 8.

[11] Doukhan analyzes these statements in the last chapter of *The Mystery of Israel* (see pp. 117-143).

[12] Ellen G. White, *Evangelism* (Washington, D.C.: Review and Herald Pub. Assn., 1946), p. 579.

[13] London: Lutterworth Press, 1961.

[14] *Ibid.,* p. 192.

[15] J. S. Hammet, *Biblical Foundations,* p. 42.

[16] Richard Rice, *The Reign of God* (Berrien Springs, Mich.: Andrews University Press, 1997), p. 214.

[17] Alan Richardson, *An Introduction to the Theology of the New Testament* (London: SCM Press Ltd., 1969), p. 257.

[18] Raoul Dederen, "The Church," in Raoul Dederen, ed., *Handbook of Seventh-day Adventist Theology* (Hagerstown, Md.: Review and Herald Pub. Assn., 2000), p. 548.

[19] Hammett, p. 8.

[20] *Ibid.,* p. 49.

[21] Richardson, p. 261.

[22] *Ibid.,* p. 257.

[23] *Ibid.,* p. 215.

Chapter 5

The "Marks" of the Church

The oldest Christian confessional document is the *Symbolum Apostolicum*, usually in English referred to as the Apostles' Creed. At one time people believed that this ancient text originated with the apostles, but nowadays scholars agree that we can say only (with any degree of certainty) that it is a short and early summary of the teachings of the apostles, which contains vital truths of the Christian faith, in accordance with the New Testament. Most likely it originated as a baptismal confession. The precise text probably fluctuated, and its present written form cannot be traced to any point prior to the end of the fifth century. However, in essence it is much older than that.[1] It contains six short paragraphs outlining the crucial Christian convictions regarding God the Father, Jesus the Son, the Holy Spirit, the church, forgiveness of sins, and eternal life.

The Apostles' Creed expresses four fundamental convictions about the Christian church. It underlines (1) its unity, (2) its universality, (3) its holiness, and (4) its apostolicity. It reads, in part: *[I believe] in the holy catholic church, the communion of saints*. We find one additional word in the *Nicene Creed* (which was adopted at the famous Council of Nicea in 325), as enlarged in 381 during the Council of Constantinople: "[I believe] in one holy catholic and *apostolic* church."[2] These four characteristics—oneness, holiness, catholicity (universality), and apostolicity—became the four classical "marks" (Latin: *notae*) of the church. They were, in the minds of the leaders of the church in the early centuries, the key criteria that one must use to determine whether a theologian or a group of Christians was part of the true church or was rather to be regarded as heretics, who had no right to the claim of being the church or of belonging to the church.

These four marks originated in the context of the church's struggle to define itself against a variety of challenges, in particular Arianism, Montanism, Novatianism, and Donatism. For a long time these four *notae* were held in high esteem, but, as we shall later see, from the sixteenth century onward the churches of the Reformation believed that more needed to be said and that some other marks also needed to be present in the church. According to the Reformers, the possibility exists that the church outwardly might conform to the four *notae*, without having a vital relationship with Christ.[3]

The formula found in the Apostles' Creed and in the Nicene Creed is, of course, not a direct quote from the Bible. The words "holy," "oneness," and "apostle" are known biblical terms, whereas "catholic" does not occur in the Scriptures. Yet, although the formula is a later construction, it is important to deal at some length with these four marks, considering the prominent role they have played in the history of the church and in almost any serious work on ecclesiology. Whether or not a word actually occurs in the Bible does not determine if a concept harmonizes with the Bible or not. The word "Trinity," for instance, is also not found in the Bible, yet the concept, so conservative Christians—including Adventists—believe, is fully biblical and is foundational to the Christian faith. The crucial question to be discussed is: What have people through the ages *meant* when they referred to the church as "one," as "holy," as "catholic," and as "apostolic"? Have they interpreted these concepts in a biblical way? And what meaning is given to these words today, and can they still have significance for us?

Are these words useful for *Adventist* Christians as they formulate their view of the church? Or are they so ambiguous that it might be better to look for other terms? That they can be filled with various meanings, as is often suggested, is certainly true, but that in itself, I would argue, should not keep us from using them. For this could also be said of many other theological terms, and if we were to avoid any term that can be ambiguous, we would be forced to create an entirely new theological vocabulary. And that would hardly help us in making clear to others what we believe.

One preliminary question needs to be addressed briefly before we look at the four marks in some detail. Do these marks belong to the church in general, or do they apply in particular to the local church? Roman Catholics usually tend to think of their own worldwide church as *the* church to which these *notae* directly apply. Protestants are inclined to think of the church in more general terms and tend to view the characteristics as ideals that should mark the worldwide Christian church, and although this objective is lofty, many would say that unfortunately it is far from reality but nonetheless remains the goal to be reached.

There may well be a third way of approaching this matter.

Denominations are structures in which the visible church exists. Some are closer to the ideal of the Apostles' Creed than others. Might one say that denominations can claim to be truly part of the church universal only as long as they are serious about maintaining these marks of the Christian church? Could we also say that the Seventh-day Adventist Church will have and keep the right to view itself as being God's church (albeit not exclusively so, as if they were God's only children on this earth) only to the extent that it is committed to realizing true unity, true holiness, true catholicity, and true apostolicity in its community? And would it not be true to say that this applies to the denomination as a whole as well as to any local congregation? Local churches are, in fact, *the* church in the place and among the people where they exist. If the world church must be one, holy, catholic, and apostolic, that must also be true for the local churches in Hannover, Rio de Janeiro, and New York, and the village churches in tropical Africa. This consideration ensures that the discussion about these marks does not remain on an elevated level of academic theology but will actually touch the lives of the individual church members in whatever small or large church they worship.

It is important to devote some space to a discussion about the characteristics that identify the "true" church over and against heretical movements that pretend that they also (or only) represent the church. It is a very practical question. Where does one draw the line between what might be considered as bona fide Christian churches and what is definitely outside that realm? Can such churches as, for instance, the Unitarian Church (that denies the doctrine of the Trinity) and the Mormon Church (that has other holy writings in addition to the Bible), in which fundamental aspects of apostolic doctrine are denied, be considered as part of the invisible church? And are churches in which basic beliefs are in flux, or parachurch entities in which there is no administration of baptism or celebration of the Lord's Supper, be considered church in the full sense of the word?[4] A clear understanding of the marks of the church may help us to answer to such questions.

One

Christ prayed that all His children should be one (John 17). The image of the vine and the branches (John 15:1-17) refers to Christ's desire that all His followers should be one. Several other metaphors referred to in chapter 3 (the one body with its many organs, the one family with its many members, and the one temple with its many building blocks) also imply the

existence of a fundamental unity that must supersede the tragic fragmentation of the Christian church. There may be thousands of denominations,
sects, and modalities, but this does not deny the basic truth that there is
only one good news (Gal. 1:7), one Lord, and only one baptism, one faith,
and one hope (Eph. 4:5; 1 Cor. 12:12, 13).

The divisions in Christianity are often referred to as a stumbling
block for unbelievers. And they are. Sinful human beings have time and
again chosen to go their own way rather than the way of Christ. Many
believe that this situation will last as long as we are on the earth and that
true unity will remain an eschatological dream. Even though this tragic
assessment is largely true—for biblical prophecy certainly points that
way—it also remains a lamentable reality that the Christian church becomes a less-credible witness of the reconciliation of people in Christ
Jesus to the extent that the unity of Christ believers is impaired or only
realized very imperfectly.[5]

Of course, there can be a great difference between unity in Christ and
organizational unity. This realization will determine our attitude toward
ecumenical projects. Not all "unity" is automatically the kind of unity the
New Testament refers to. Many still follow Church Father Cyprian in his
unacceptable notion that the union of the church is to be realized through
a close union with the bishop of Rome. Many church leaders and theologians today understand the desire for unity first of all in terms of organic
union and find it hard to conceive that there are Christian believers who
refuse to get involved in ecumenical projects. To them this is disobedience
to Christ's command that we all be one. We will return to this issue in
chapter 10, for it is a relevant issue also for the Seventh-day Adventist
Church. Let it just be stated at this point in our discussion that division and
theological disagreement do not necessarily have to manifest themselves in
competition and hostility. Denominations can exist and bear their witness
in a spirit of humility, well aware of their own imperfections, rather than
in a spirit of vindictiveness and triumphalistic superiority.[6]

Unity is not only the polar opposite of fragmentation, however. It is
also often understood in contrast to diversity. The concept of diversity can
be quite shallow and may actually cover deep divisions about very essential elements of the Christian faith and Christian ethics. To suggest that
Christian denominations may coexist in a spirit of reconciled diversity[7] is,
therefore, not all that helpful. It may be better to state that unity among
believers does not imply a strict uniformity in language, rites, cultural
forms, and the application of principles. The oneness Christ told His fol-

lowers to pray for (John 17) is a spiritual oneness and reflects on a human plane the oneness between the members of the Godhead. It is a "tie that binds," but not in ecclesiastical handcuffs.[8] This unity is not primarily theological agreement (even though this is an important goal). It is far more than a spirit of camaraderie—it is a spiritual communion that is rooted in divine gift love: agape.

Yet let us, in pointing to the spiritual nature of this unity, not forget that it has also very concrete this-worldly ramifications. The concept of unity in Christ has, for instance, a direct implication for the way a denomination such as the Adventist Church functions across regional and national borders and across ethnic and gender lines—and not in the least for the way in which a local congregation wants to be "church." It has very immediate implications for the way in which resources are allocated, conflicts are resolved, and governance issues are addressed.

Striving for true spiritual unity in the church is not optional. Paul exhorts the believers in Ephesus to "make every effort to keep the unity of the Spirit" (Eph. 4:3). The Greek wording implies that this is a matter of great priority and that a total dedication to true spiritual unity is required.

Holy

What do people mean when they confess belief in a *holy* church? Do they believe in holiness as the ultimate, but as yet unreachable, goal of the church? Or do they believe that the church in some sense is holy even now, in spite of the fact that its members may yet be very unholy? In today's postmodern climate the institutional church is under deep suspicion and tends to be defined in terms of hypocrisy rather than in terms of holiness. To many who use the word "holy" in its most common—moral—sense, the church's reputation is extremely poor. Organized Christianity ("the church") has shown too many dark sides and has been too much tainted by internal politics, corruption, and blatant obsessions with power, and too many of its functionaries have shown terrible lapses of moral judgment to make the idea of a "holy" church even remotely credible.

One of the first theological retorts in dealing with this uneasy subject is to define "holy" in a less-confrontational way. It is correctly argued that the root meaning of "holiness" is being set aside, no longer being available for profane purposes but reserved for service to God. The Bible calls all kinds of things "holy"—the Holy City, God's holy mountain, holy vessels, holy sacrifices, and, of course, a holy day, the Sabbath. Likewise, persons who had been set aside to minister in the sanctuary were "holy," and Israel is "God's holy people." Holiness, therefore, is primarily a matter not of moral distinction but rather of assignment to a particular purpose. And therefore the holiness of the church has first of all to do with the mission of the church. God's people constitute a holy nation that has been assigned to "declare the praises of him who called you out of darkness into his wonderful light" (1 Peter 2:9).

It is important to keep this biblical usage of "holy" in mind. Nonetheless, it does not offer the complete picture. For it cannot be denied that holiness definitely also has a moral dimension and that it stands in contrast with sinfulness and separation from God. The apostle Peter wrote: "Just as he who called you is holy, so be holy in all you do; for it is written: 'Be holy, because I am holy' " (1 Peter 1:15). Of course, in view of the radical distinction between God in His seamless perfection and humanity with all its inherent restrictions, we must immediately conclude that men and women in the here and now can never hope to be perfect in the same unlimited qualitative sense as God is perfect. But being a holy people who have been called to a holy task, we read in Deuteronomy 28:9, is conditional upon the way His people live: "The Lord will establish you as his holy people, as he promised you on oath, if you keep the commands of the Lord your God and walk in his ways." A relationship with God presupposes an eagerness to lead a life that tries to incorporate the kingdom's values. It is God's will, Paul says, that we should be sanctified. And, in one and the same breath, he contrasts this holiness with immoral, sinful behavior that is to be avoided (1 Thess. 4:3). Living as children of the light is not just realizing that one is set aside for a specific purpose, missionary or otherwise, but is "to put on the new self, created to be like God in true righteousness and holiness" (Eph. 4:24). Christians cannot be content with the knowledge that God wants them as citizens of His "holy nation," and will manifest in their daily lives the fruits of an evercloser relationship with their Lord (Gal. 5:22; John 15:1-8).

Believers are often referred to as the holy ones, the saints. They strive for the fruits of holiness, but they can never claim to have reached perfection. The empirical truth is that no human being can in truth make that claim (Rom. 3:23). "If we claim to be without sin, we deceive ourselves and the truth is not in us" (1 John 1:8). In actual fact many church members (see, for example, 1 Corinthians 1 and 2 and Revelation 2 and 3) were—and are—far from perfect. But the glorious truth is that imperfect people can be saints as long as they trust in Christ for their ultimate perfection. They are justified and sanctified in the Lord Jesus by the power of the Holy Spirit (1 Cor. 6:11).

So in spite of all the shortcomings of the corporate church and of its individual members, we can confidently confess that we believe in a holy church. The church is holy because it is a spiritual entity, because God created it through the Spirit.[9] It is holy because it is the body of Christ.

Yet the sinfulness of the church in all its dimensions is a painful fact. One cannot solve this dilemma by maintaining that the church in its essence is perfect while admittedly the members are sinners. Nowhere in the New Testament do we find a basis for the idea of the church as an abstract phenomenon that exists separate from its members. Nowhere in the New Testament, also, do we find the adjective "holy" in conjunction with the word "church." The church is in a very real sense a community of the saints, the believers who have made a commitment to Christ. But the church is also a school for sinners. The church embodies the people of God who are still on their pilgrimage. As a corporate body the church must continue to struggle with all those corporate sins that so easily "entangle" (Heb. 12:1).

The Reformers affirmed that the church is *semper reformanda*, that is, it must always undergo a process of reformation. In one of the documents of the Second Vatican Council a similar wording was used. The church, it said, is *semper purificanda*, that is, it must always be purified. Martin Luther is known for his dictum that man is *simul iustus et peccator*—at the same time he is fully justified while he remains a sinner. Similarly, as long as the church is in the world, we must live with the paradox that the church is at once a "holy" communion of the saints and a place of refuge for repentant sinners. This begs the question how we can make sure that in our view of the church the elements of holiness and sinfulness are kept in balance. An overemphasis on holiness, understood as absolute moral perfection, will almost certainly lead to fanaticism and sectarianism. An imbalance in the other direction will easily lead to worldliness and superficiality. Examples of both abound in the history of the church. We will in a later chapter return to the related question of church discipline. What role can church discipline play in our pursuit of a holy church?

Catholic

Many Protestants in the pew puzzle over why official documents of the denomination they belong to assert the belief in the "catholicity" of the church. What does the word "catholic" mean? And since the Roman

Church so fiercely claims to be *the* Catholic Church and expresses its doubts, or even at times denies, that other branches of Christianity can be "church" in the full sense of the word, would it not be better for Protestants not to confuse the issue by avoiding the term altogether? To some this seems the preferred option. But many Protestant theologians and church leaders do not agree. We should not let the Roman Catholic Church get away with the suggestion that they can simply appropriate the term and restrict its meaning to what *they* want it to mean. It is, they say, important that Protestant Christians in their various denominations do not lose sight of the catholicity of the church and do not succumb to the temptation to view only the organization to which they belong as the full body of Christ. And, I would add, it is important also for Seventh-day Adventist Christians to balance their emphasis on the unique role of their movement with the realization that the church of Christ stretches far beyond their own denominational borders and beyond 1844 across the past centuries.

It must, first of all, be remembered that the word "catholic" was already in use in the early church centuries before the church in the West became the Roman Catholic Church. At the very beginning of the second century Ignatius of Antioch wrote to the church in Smyrna: "Where Jesus may be, there is the universal [*katholike*] church." And Polycarp, leader of the church in Smyrna and who was martyred around A.D. 155, wrote to "all brothers and sisters of the holy and universal [*katholikes*] church sojourning in every place."[10] The Greek word *katholikos* is derived from *kat'holos*, according to the whole. Its basic meaning in the Greek of that period is "full," "whole," or "general."[11] To speak of the *Roman* Catholic Church is, in fact, a contradiction in terms, something like wooden iron. The universality that the word signifies cannot be linked to the particularity of one single denomination, whether it has a billion members or 20 million. The early Church Fathers used the term in particular to emphasize the universal nature of the church. They argued that however important and indispensable the local church may be, the church of Christ is more than the local congregation.[12]

The church of Christ is "catholic" in a number of different but interrelated ways. First of all, it is catholic in a geographical sense. The church must be present in all parts of the world. It can and should have respect for other world religions, but it cannot accept that there remain people groups where Christ is not known and where the preaching of the gospel is restricted. Its mission field is the entire world. The gospel is to be preached to all nations (that is, all people groups) and in all languages

(Matt. 28:19, 20) "to the ends of the earth" (Acts 1:8). The "eternal gospel" must be preached to the entire world and break through every barrier of geography, language, and culture (Rev. 14:6). And, as a result, God's people will ultimately consist of men and women from "every nation, tribe, people, and language" (Rev. 7:9; 21:24). Those who are committed to the preaching of the good news, with those special biblical emphases that make their witness "present truth," must never lose sight of this "catholic" dimension of the church. They can never feel satisfied to see their witness restricted to particular geographical areas in the world. If they have something of real importance to proclaim, it must be proclaimed everywhere. The church by its very nature reaches out to the whole world with the whole truth.[13]

In addition, there is a time element to be considered. The history of the church began at Pentecost, and ever since the church has existed and born witness of its Lord. The churches of the Reformation did not invent the church, and the rise of Adventism does not mark the real beginning of Christianity. There are admittedly many dark pages in the annals of church history. There have been periods when dark clouds hung over the church and almost completely obscured its witness. The prophetic word that there would be times of apostasy has certainly been fulfilled. But there have always been disciples of Christ, individually and in communities, who have kept the gospel flame burning.

Ellen White emphasized this time and again: "From the beginning, faithful souls have constituted the church on earth. In every age the Lord has had His watchmen, who have borne a faithful testimony to the generation in which they lived. These sentinels gave the message of warning; and when they were called to lay off their armor, others took up the work." And "through centuries of persecution, conflict, and darkness, God has sustained His church."[14]

The church today must ever remember this historical dimension and understand how it fits into God's long-term plans for humankind. The lessons of history must be learned. The annals of the church of the past serve as solemn warnings about terrible failures and abuses of power and privilege. But they also contain magnificent inspiration that will nourish and stimulate believers today. The church today must be relevant to the people of today, but in this process of fulfilling its mission it has the enormous privilege of borrowing from the rich resources in theology, religious art, religious writing, liturgy, and hymnody of the church of all ages. Such use will have to be critical and selective, but a judicious and grateful incorporation and adaption of the treasures of the Christian past is very much part of what true catholicity means.

In its proclamation, the church must be true to the entire gospel message and not neglect certain truths while narrowly focusing on just a few aspects of the truth. The church would do well to keep the words in mind of Cyril of Jerusalem, the leader of the Jerusalem church in the middle of the fourth century: "The church is thus called 'catholic' because it is spread throughout the entire inhabited world, from one end to the other, . . . and without leaving out any doctrine which people need to know. . . . It is also called 'catholic' because it brings to obedience every sort of person, whether rulers of their subjects, the educated and the unlearned. It also makes available a universal [*katholikos*] remedy and cure to every kind of sin."[15]

Our belief that the one holy church is "catholic" also has connotations in the sphere of ethnicity and culture. In this respect the terms "oneness" and "catholicity" become almost synonymous. We earlier emphasized that unity in Christ does not presuppose full uniformity. By confessing the catholicity of the church, we insist that the church transcends the boundaries of culture and can be a vibrant reality within a wide diversity of cultures. The walls that brought separation between Christians with a Jewish background and Christians with a Gentile milieu, "Greeks" and "barbarians," slaves and freedmen, and men and women were broken down in Christ (Gal. 3:28; Eph. 2:14-16). This must similarly be true of all other walls that may exist in the church of our time.

Craig van Gelder, a professor of mission at the Luther Seminary in St. Paul, Minnesota, aptly comments: "Like the Bible, the church through the Spirit is inherently translatable into every specific cultural context. . . . The church's capacity to be contextualized, to be made relevant to any and every cultural setting, is a logical extension of the confession that the church is catholic."[16]

It is fully biblical that the one universal church may manifest itself in different forms in America, Europe, Africa, and China. There is no inherent problem when a specific congregation ministers to a specific ethnic audience, or when a congregation wants to organize church services that are intended to appeal in particular to young people or to older folks. However, these and similar phenomena must be embedded in a strong conviction that beyond all pluriformity in form and approach, we believe in the oneness and rich catholicity of the church and thereby condemn all hidden or not-so-hidden provincialism, sectarianism, and racism.[17]

These are important things also for Adventists to keep in mind. The Adventist Church is not an American church, even though much of its organizational and financial strength is located in the United States; it is not a developing countries church, even though the vast majority of Adventists now live in the developing world; it is a church that must always strive to move beyond such categories as a special part of God's universal church that welcomes all and reaches out to all.

Apostolic

The fourth mark of the church is its apostolicity. This term indicates that the Christian church is directly related to the ministry of the original apostles. A number of denominations hold that the top leadership in the church must be appointed via apostolic succession (that is, that the main leadership jobs are passed on from the first apostles in a direct line of succession). Most Protestants—including Adventists—deny the need for this unbroken connection between the first leaders and today's leadership, since they believe there is no biblical proof that this was God's intention. We already saw in chapter 3 that the statement in Matthew 16, which has often been interpreted as pointing in that direction, does not provide the hard evidence the supporters of papal governance and of apostolic succession look for. And empirical evidence that an unbroken line between church leaders of today and the apostles of the first century guarantees purity in doctrine is sadly missing.

A rejection of the concept of apostolic succession does, however, in no way involve a denial of the importance of the apostolic witness. The church of today must be faithful to the apostolic doctrines, which were based on the inspired recollection and experiences of those who had been with Jesus. Their role in the church was unique. When, after Judas' suicide, the remaining 11 apostles discussed his replacement, they agreed that they should be looking for "one of the men who have been with us the whole time the Lord Jesus went in and out among us" (Acts 1:21). Hans Küng, a Roman Catholic theologian whose critical attitude with respect to the doctrine of papal infallibility brought him in sharp conflict with his church, used these words to point to the unique role of the apostles: "As direct witnesses and messengers of the risen Lord, the apostles can have no successors. . . . Apostleship in the sense of the original and fundamental ministry of the first witnesses and messengers died out with the last of the apostles."[18]

The church is apostolic because it is built on the unique and unrepeatable foundational work of the apostles. Led by the Spirit, they accepted their commission from "Jesus, the *apostle* and high priest" (Heb. 3:1). Their writings have the same authority as the Old Testament Scriptures (2 Peter 3:2). "Apostolic," therefore, means adhering to the teachings of the apostles. The apostles had been with Jesus and were the trustworthy witnesses of what He had said and done. The church is built on the foundation of the prophets and the apostles, with Jesus as the chief cornerstone (Eph. 2:20). What authenticates the church is not a continuous, uninterrupted line of individuals from the original apostles until today, but "a continuous line of faithfulness to the testimony of the apostles."[19] Like the early believers, Christians today should "devote themselves to the apostles' teaching" (Acts 2:42).

Jürgen Moltmann rightly summarizes: "The apostolic succession is, in fact and in truth, the evangelical succession, the continuing and unadulterated proclamation of the gospel of the risen Christ."[20] The apostolicity of the church is therefore found in a special sense in its unreserved acceptance of its mission. The word "apostle" comes from the Greek verb *apostello*, meaning "to send." As the apostles' total focus was on their mission to proclaim the risen Christ to the entire world, likewise the church must remain truly apostolic in the pursuit of its task to preach the gospel to all people.

Other "Marks"?

Are these four classical *notae* then the only distinguishing marks of the church? The church Reformers of the sixteenth century felt that some additional characteristics needed to be added. For them such elements as the pure preaching of the Word, the administration of the sacraments in a biblical way, and in particular for John Calvin, a faithful application of church discipline were also essential marks. In some traditions and particular denominations within these traditions, other characteristics of the church receive special emphasis. In the charismatic tradition, the gifts of the Spirit, often with an emphasis on the gift of tongues, are seen as characteristics par excellence. Adventists lay stress on the keeping of the divine commandments and faithfulness to the "testimony of Jesus" (Rev. 12:17) as marks that are of special significance in the time of the end. One might, with some justification, argue that all these aspects are included in the apostolicity of the church, as they are included in the apostolic heritage found in the New Testament writings. Each of these will demand our attention in subsequent chapters.

[1] Philip Schaff, *The Creeds of Christendom* (New York: Harper and Brothers, Pubs., 1905), vol. 1, pp. 14-23.

[2] *Ibid.*, pp. 24-29.

[3] H. Berkhof, *Christian Faith: An Introduction to the Study of the Faith* (Grand Rapids: William B. Eerdmans Pub. Co., 1979), p. 409.

[4] P. Clowney, *The Church,* pp. 99f.

[5] Thomas P. Rausch, *Towards a Truly Catholic Church* (Collegeville, Minn.: Liturgical Press, 2005), p. 136.

[6] S. Hammett, *Biblical Foundations,* p. 54.

[7] Anton Houtepen, *People of God: A Plea for the Church* (London: SCM Press, Ltd., 1984), p. 170.

[8] Clowney, p. 78.

[9] Van Gelder, *The Essence of the Church*, pp. 116-126.

[10] Edgar J. Goodspeed, trans., *The Apostolic Fathers* (London: Independent Press, Ltd., 1960), pp. 230, 247.

[11] Rausch, p. 138.

[12] Hans Küng, *Credo: The Apostles' Creed Explained for Today* (London: SCM Press, Ltd., 1993), p. 137.

[13] R. Dederen, "The Church," in *Handbook of Seventh-day Adventist Theology,* p. 563.

[14] G. White, *The Acts of the Apostles,* p. 11.

[15] Alistair McGrath, *Christian Theology: An Introduction* (Oxford, U.K.: Blackwell Pubs., 2001), p. 501.

[16] Van Gelder, p. 119.

[17] Hammett, p. 119.

[18] Hans Küng, *The Church* (New York: Sheed and Ward, 1968), p. 355.

[19] Dederen, p. 563.

[20] Jürgen Moltmann, *The Church in the Power of the Spirit* (London: SCM Press, Ltd., 1977), p. 359.

Chapter 6

The Spirit in the Church

The mystery of the Trinity receives a miraculous extension in the church. God the Father always wanted to have His own people and to establish a loving relationship with them. He sent His Son, Jesus Christ, to reconcile His people to Him when they had gone astray. Christ, the Son and the second person of the Godhead, was the founder and the cornerstone for the spiritual building we call "church." And the church got off to a tremendous start and has remained alive through the centuries because of the life-giving presence of the third person of the Godhead, the Holy Spirit. To His role in the church we now turn.

Placing our discussion of the Spirit's role in the context of the Trinity is intentional and important, for it underlines what we mean when we confess that we believe in a triune God and that this triune God is totally involved with His church—in the past, in the present during which we live, and in the glorious future. While the Bible attributes specific functions to the Holy Spirit in connection with the church, we realize that it is never possible to fully separate the actions of one member of the Godhead from those of the other two. Therefore, when we point to activities of the Spirit, we are well aware that somehow God as Trinity is involved. It is thus not without profound meaning that those who enter the church are baptized in the name of the triune God—Father, Son, and Holy Spirit (Matt. 28:19). In Eastern Orthodox Christianity the church is seen as an icon of the Trinity, reproducing on earth the mystery of unity in diversity. As in the Trinity the three are one, so in the church a multitude of persons is united in one body, yet members preserve their personal diversity unimpaired.[1]

Belief in the Trinity, theology professor David G. Bloesch comments, has far-reaching implications for our spiritual life and thus for how we experience the church. It means that the God we worship as a community "is not a solitary detached being, but a living, personal God who can enter into meaningful relationships."[2] It is "through the Spirit" that our triune God leads, inspires, and sanctifies His church.

What Does the Spirit Do?

That the Spirit would play a prominent role in the church comes as no surprise. The coming of the Spirit fulfills multiple promises made by the Old Testament prophets. Peter, in his speech to the crowds in Jerusalem on Pentecost, said that the "outpouring" of the Spirit, with its peculiar visual and audible manifestations, was "what was spoken of by the prophet Joel" when he foretold that "afterward" God would "pour out" His Spirit "on all people" (Acts 2:16-21; Joel 2:28). The prophet Ezekiel also had prophesied that the time would come when God would give His people a special experience. God would, he said, give His people a new heart. Through the prophet God promised: "I will put my Spirit in you" (Eze. 36:26, 27).

Jesus had emphasized that He would not leave His people "as orphans" (John 14:18), that is, without divine guidance when He would return to His Father. He said to His disciples: "I will ask the Father, and he will give you another Counselor to be with you forever—the Spirit of truth" (verse 16). The word "another" is significant. It translates the Greek word *allos*, which means "one of the same kind" (referring to more than one but with all manifesting the same character), in contrast with another word for "other"—*heteros*—which denotes another of a different kind. (See, for example, Matthew 11:3, the text that reports a question asked by John the Baptist about Jesus, whether He was the one who was promised or if another [*heteros*] should yet be expected.) By the use of the word *allos* Christ wanted to underline that the Spirit who would "come" to assist the church as the *Parakletos* (see below) was as divine as He was.[3] He was another of the same kind. The last thing Christ did before His ascension was to remind His followers one last time that they would not be left without supernatural resources. They should not even attempt to start anything, but wait in Jerusalem for "the gift" that the Father had promised. "You will receive power when the Holy Spirit comes on you; and you will be my witnesses . . . to the ends of the earth" (Acts 1:4, 8).

Jesus called the Spirit the *Counselor*, or, as other versions read, the *Comforter*. In theological literature the word *Paraclete* is often used as an English transcription of the Greek *Parakletos*. Just as the word *ekklesia* (church) is rooted in the word *kalein* (call), so is the word *parakletos*. Literally the word means "the one who is called alongside." A *paraclete* is thus a person who is called alongside to help. The word could have a legal connotation, just as our word "counselor" still has, as is suggested in John 16:8–11.[4] But this meaning does not seem to be the prominent one as we compare the various passages in the Gospel of John that describe the role of the Spirit. The few other places in the New Testament where cognate words are used indicate that, in particular, the elements of prophetic guidance and exhortation must not be lost sight of.[5]

Let us take a closer look at the various aspects of the work of the Holy Spirit on behalf of the church and its members.

The Spirit gives us assurance of our adoption into God's family. He is with us when we make our entrance into the family of God. Jesus says to us, just as emphatically as He told Nicodemus, "No one can enter the kingdom of God unless he is born of water and the Spirit" (John 3:5). If we do not have the Spirit in us as we make our pilgrimage of faith, we do not "belong to Christ" (Rom. 8:9). The apostle Paul adds, "Those who are led by the Spirit of God are sons of God" (verse 14). And, "the Spirit himself testified with our spirit that we are God's children" (verse 16).

The Spirit is the Spirit of truth. The Holy Spirit was the divine agent in the writing of the Scriptures (1 Tim. 3:16). "Men spoke from God as they were carried along by the Holy Spirit" (2 Peter 1:21). The same Spirit ensured that people through the ages might hear and understand the message of God as they read or heard the Word. And He does so today. He is the Spirit of truth, who "will guide you into all truth" (John 16:13). He is not the Spirit of purely intellectual truth. The truth is always embedded in love. We grieve the Holy Spirit, "with whom [we are] sealed for the day of redemption," if our pursuit of the truth takes place in a context of bitterness and is not aimed at building up ourselves and others (Eph. 4:30). Paul admonishes us never to "put out the Spirit's fire" (1 Thess. 5:19). The Spirit of truth guides us, individually and collectively, in our choices between what is right and wrong (Rom. 9:1). He convicts us of our guilt, often through a faithful preaching of the Word (John 16:8).

The Holy Spirit directs the proclamation of the gospel. Without a powerful presence of the Spirit, evangelism remains utterly ineffective (Acts 1:8; Luke 24:49). Paul wrote to the Corinthians that he met with success when he came to evangelize them only as long as he was aware of his own weakness and inability to convince. His message was not "with wise and persuasive words, but with a demonstration of the Spirit's power" (1 Cor. 2:4). He knew from his own evangelistic experience that it is the Spirit who convinces. When human arguments fail and we do not know what to say to reach our audience, the Holy Spirit inspires us with what we should say (Luke 12:11, 12).

Finally, *the Spirit directs the worship of the church*. We will return to this later in the chapter, but in this short summary of what the Spirit does, this important aspect must not be left out. Real worship is impossible without the involvement of the Spirit. God seeks worshippers who will worship "in spirit and in truth" (John 4:24). It is only through the Spirit that we can address God as "Father." We "received the Spirit of sonship. And by Him we cry: 'Abba, Father' " (Rom. 8:15). In a similar vein we are told: "No one can say, 'Jesus is Lord,' except by the Holy Spirit" (1 Cor. 12:3). Without the powerful assistance of the Spirit, who always stands ready to assist Christ's church, our prayers would remain dry and empty (Eph. 6:18, 19). The Spirit "helps us in our weakness. We do not know what we ought to pray for, but the Spirit himself intercedes for us with groans that words cannot express" (Rom. 8:26).

A Spirit-filled Church

It is a common observation that the church of today urgently needs a strong infusion of the Holy Spirit. The church, many say, would be much stronger and much more meaningful if it would rely to a far greater degree on the power of the Holy Spirit. David Watson, a British pastor and author who since the mid-1960s has worked hard to revive dying churches, made the following provocative statement: "Take Him [the Holy Spirit] away, and you have no church: an institution, an organization, a building, a structure, perhaps; but no church of the living God. Yet, Dr. Carl Bates [a well-known Baptist preacher] once commented: 'If God were to take the Holy Spirit out of our midst today, about 95 percent of what we do in our churches would go on, and we would not know the difference.' "[6]

I hope the first part of this chapter has sufficiently emphasized the truth of the statement that there is indeed no true church without the Holy Spirit. Whether most local churches and denominations have ignored the resources of the Spirit to the tragic extent that is suggested by Dr. Bates is difficult either to gainsay or to confirm. For how does one exactly measure the extent to which individual Christians and Christian bodies open themselves up to the Holy Spirit?

Too often the degree in which the power of the Spirit is present is evaluated on the basis of what can be seen and heard. However, the kind of outward manifestations that are often associated with the presence of the Spirit are, at most, only part of the story. The Spirit is compared with the blowing of the wind. One can certainly see the results when the wind escalates into a powerful storm, but in the first century when Jesus used this metaphor, it was also true that one could "not tell where it comes from or where it is going" (John 3:8). Our meteorological knowledge has increased, but the point is clear. The Spirit is not under our control, just as even today we cannot increase the power of the wind by simply flipping a few switches. Richard Rice reminds us correctly that there seems, especially among conservative Christians, a "widespread failure to recognize the social or corporate dimension of the Spirit's work." He believes that this is due to a one-sided "preoccupation with individual religious experience" that is so characteristic of a major part of western Christianity.[7] The presence of the Spirit "affects human beings in their togetherness," Rice continues. "The primary manifestation of the power of the Spirit in this world is the presence of genuine Christian community."[8]

The fact remains, however, that most of us individually and that many churches and denominations (the Adventist Church included) have not reached the ideal of being filled with the Spirit. This is a serious reality that needs our urgent and constant attention. If we confess that we regard Christ as our ultimate role model, we need to note that He was "filled" with the Spirit when He started his ministry. John the Baptist saw it with his very eyes: "I saw the Spirit come down from heaven as a dove and *remain* on Him" (John 1:32). The Gospel story provides abundant testimony that the Spirit indeed stayed with Jesus and that a new era had begun.

The Spirit, who had inspired the prophets of the Old Testament, seemed to have been rather absent or distant during the intertestamental period, after the last of the Old Testament prophets had done his work and before the Messiah appeared. The literature of that period—the apocryphal and pseudepigraphal writings—often signal a consciousness of the loss of the Spirit and of the end of the prophetic period.[9] But now the Messiah had come and the Spirit was present, even on a far more elevated plane than in ancient Israel. When reading from the Word in the synagogue at Nazareth, Jesus chose precisely the passage from the prophet Isaiah (chapter 61) that speaks of the Spirit of the Lord as being "on me, because he has anointed me," and He made sure to comment, "Today this Scripture is fulfilled in your hearing" (Luke 4:18-21).

Christ ministered in the same Spirit who was to give the church its enormous first boost at the day of Pentecost, just 50 days after the Resurrection morning. Pentecost was not just a one-time event. When the people, having listened to the apostolic message that everyone could miraculously hear in their own language, asked: "Brothers, what shall we do?" Peter told them to repent and be baptized. Immediately he added: "You will receive the gift of the Holy Spirit." And this was not something that was available only on that memorable day. "The promise," Peter said, "is for you and your children and for all who are far off—for all whom the Lord our God will call" (Acts 2:37-39). This text should radically eliminate any idea that the Holy Spirit limits His powerful presence to particular time periods or special groups.

The Holy Spirit is not the possession of a denomination or a special group in the church.[10] That truth soon became clear as the church grew during the apostolic period. The record of the acts of the Spirit is found in the section of the Bible that we, rather inadequately, refer to as the Acts of the *Apostles.*[11] The apostles were able to face the spiritual elite because they were "filled with the Holy Spirit" (Acts 4:8). The members of the community of Christ believers in Jerusalem likewise "were all filled with the Holy Spirit and spoke the word of God boldly" (verse 31). Stephen, one of the seven who were chosen to assist the apostles, was "a man full of faith and of the Holy Spirit" (Acts 6:5). The Spirit, who had done such miraculous things at Pentecost, continued to do so. When Philip had sealed his Bible study with the Ethiopian dignitary with a baptismal service, "the Spirit of the Lord suddenly took Philip away" (Acts 8:39). When Peter, somewhat later, evangelized the family and staff of Cornelius, a Roman centurion, and when his message was accepted, "the Holy Spirit came on all who heard the message." The believers of Jewish extraction were "astonished" that this happened, but they had yet to understand that the Spirit does not regard any of the boundaries that they had considered sacrosanct (Acts 10:44-46; 11:12, 15-17).

And so the story continues. The Holy Spirit is the motor of the church, the divine source of energy that is the only credible explanation for the success of the new Christ movement. No wonder that, when Paul came to Ephesus and met church members (or at least people who attended church) who had never heard of the Holy Spirit, he made it his top priority to impress the importance of the Holy Spirit on them (Acts 19:1-7).

Sometimes the reception of the gift of the Holy Spirit is described as "baptism" with the Spirit. Often it is suggested that this is a kind of "second blessing"—one may have the Spirit to some degree but not as yet have the experience of being totally immersed in the power of the Spirit, often having the ability of speaking in tongues or being able to exercise gifts one did not have previously. The biblical evidence does not allow for that interpretation. It is clear that sometimes the reception of the gift of the Spirit was accompanied by the laying on of hands (Acts 8:17) and sometimes it was not (Acts 10:44).[12] Also, there is a definite link between the rite of baptism and the reception of the Spirit. That was the case when our Role Model, Jesus, was baptized. Repeatedly also in the book of Acts, in particular, the gift of the Spirit is linked with baptism. Yet believers are supposed to grow to spiritual maturity, and, as growth takes place, the Spirit will be more strongly present and will further equip them for ministry.

The more we *empty* our lives of nonessential or harmful things, the more room there will be to be *"filled"* with the Spirit (Eph. 5:18). Once again, this applies to any believer individually and to the church community as a whole. And what a difference it would make! Said Ellen White: "The Lord did not lock the reservoir of heaven after pouring His Spirit upon the early disciples. We also may receive of the fullness of His blessing. Heaven is full of the treasures of His grace, and those who come to God in faith may claim all that He has promised."[13]

Adventists have always recognized their need of "a greater portion of the Spirit" and believe that before this world comes to its end, Pentecost will be repeated in a "latter rain" that is to be poured out over the earth. The imagery comes from the Old Testament, which repeatedly pictures divine blessings as the falling of the rain—the *early* rain that made the seed sprout and the *latter* rain that prepared the harvest (see, for example, Hosea 6:3; Joel 2:23; Jer. 5:24; cf. James 5:7). The Spirit was needed in a spectacular manner when the work of preaching the gospel started. It will be needed in no less a spectacular way in the final phase of the "finishing" of the gospel commission (Matt. 24:14). "The outpouring of the Spirit in the days of the apostles was the beginning of the early, or former, rain. . . . But near the close of earth's harvest, a special bestowal of spiritual grace is promised to prepare the church for the coming of the Son of man."[14]

The Gifts of the Spirit

The *gift* of the Spirit is not fully synonymous with the *gifts* of the Spirit. The first term is broader than the second. The gifts, or *charismata*, as they are often called (literally, gifts of grace), are, however, an important part of the gift. The charismata are given to the church, through its members, for ministry in the church and to the world. The gifts are diverse in nature, and answering the question as to how many gifts there are is not easily done. The different passages that refer to the gifts show many similarities but also significant dissimilarities (1 Cor. 12:8-12; 1 Cor. 12:28; Rom. 12:6-8; and Eph. 4:11).

The letter to the Ephesians mentions gifts that are entrusted to leaders in the church: apostles, prophets, evangelists, pastors, and teachers. The list sent to the Corinthian believers omitted pastors but added being endowed with extraordinary wisdom, or knowledge, the exercise of faith in a special way, performance of miracles, the gift of healing in particular, a special ability to help others, the gift of administration, the gift of prophecy, the gift to distinguish between what is of divine origin and what is not, the ability to speak in tongues, and interpreting what others say when they exercise that gift. We might classify the gifts under three headings: (1) teaching/leadership gifts; (2) service gifts; and (3) "sign" gifts, given to authenticate the work of apostles and prophets particularly at the time when God wanted the early church to be established and grow.

Can we say that some gifts are more important than others? It would be wrong to consider any of the gifts as unimportant. There is no such thing as a minor gift. "Some of the least impressive gifts, in fact, may be downright vital to the life of the church."[15] First Corinthians 12:28 suggests, however, that there is a certain hierarchy in the gifts, and the manner in which the apostle Paul speaks of the gift of tongues certainly does not suggest that this gift should be given a place of honor.

The Bible does not tell us what the exact difference is between talents and gifts. It appears that they overlap to a considerable extent. Perhaps "talent" refers in particular to the genetic aspect, and to the natural process of learning and developing certain skills, whereas "gift" emphasizes the divine grace of bestowing certain possibilities on us, even when we lack a natural giftedness in these areas.

Why does God bestow a cocktail of gifts on some believers, whereas He seems to treat others much more frugally? We need to remember that it is God's absolute prerogative to distribute the gifts as He sees fit: "He gives them to each one, just as he determines" (1 Cor. 12:11). He gives the charismata for one reason: "The manifestation of the Spirit is given for the common good" (verse 7). The passages in Ephesians 4 are just as clear. The gifts have the singular purpose "to prepare God's people for works of service, so that the body of Christ may be built up until we all reach unity in the faith and in the knowledge of the Son of God and become mature, attaining to the whole measure of the fullness of Christ" (Eph. 4:12, 13).

In some circles the gift of speaking in tongues is singled out as the gift par excellence that demonstrates whether or not one has been filled with the Spirit. There is no ground for doing so. The believers are warned that this gift, if it were to manifest itself, must be exercised with great care.

Speaking in tongues when no one can understand what is being said can easily lead to disorderly conduct or worse (1 Cor. 14). There continues to be uncertainty as to what the gift of tongues exactly is. What occurred at Pentecost (Acts 2) seems to be a dramatic reversal of what happened when mankind opted to go its own way by staying in one place and building the tower of Babel and God "came down" and "confused the language of the whole world" (Gen. 11:5, 9). These language barriers were now, albeit temporarily and partially, removed as a powerful sign that world history had entered into a new phase.[16]

But what exactly is this gift of tongues? Is it the ability to speak and/or understand a foreign language without taking language classes? This would, no doubt, in some instances be very practical for communicating the gospel, and there have been reports, even quite recently, of incidents in "mission fields" where this has occurred. Or is speaking in tongues rather the gift to speak in some ecstatic prayer language that seems to lift the speaker to a higher spiritual level but remains gibberish for everyone else as long as no one can "interpret"?

There is no doubt that the miraculous occurrence on the day of Pentecost included the speaking and understanding of foreign languages by the people who had gathered from far and near, with the result that each person present heard the apostles in their "native language" (Acts 2:8). In 1 Corinthians, however, we seem to be confronted with quite a different phenomenon. The gift of tongues in this context appears to be a kind of ecstatic, unintelligible speech that obstructs rather than assists direct communication, and Paul counsels the church that there is a danger that "speaking in tongues" may lead to disorderly conduct. Therefore, he reasons, restrictions should apply (1 Cor. 14:2-25). When we read of speaking in tongues in some other passages, it is less clear whether the gift resembled what happened at Pentecost or was like the gift discussed in 1 Corinthians. It should, however, be remembered that whatever this gift of tongues was, there is no way to prove that it originally resembled the gift that many charismatic Christians today claim to possess.

One has some reason to wonder whether the traditional Adventist view, which interprets the gift of tongues exclusively as the supernatural ability to speak and/or understand a foreign language, was primarily inspired by a careful study of the biblical material or was at least in part influenced by a solid fear of charismatic manifestations. It should be remembered that extremism and fanaticism constantly threatened the early Adventist pioneers and that a growing interest, or even obsession, with occult and paranormal phenomena (and speaking in tongues was regarded by many as such) was seen as a threat to a sound Christian experience. In his 1991 book on speaking in tongues, Gerhard Hasel, a prominent Adventist theologian, defended this traditional view in particular on linguistic grounds.[17] Some other Adventist scholars today, however, support the view that the tongues referred to in 1 Corinthians did not reflect the gift of languages as manifested in Acts 2. Richard Rice suggests that we may never know exactly what this gift that was manifested (and abused) in the church in Corinth exactly was and warns us to be cautious.[18] William E. Richardson, a theologian who teaches at Andrews University, has analyzed the issue in considerable depth and comes to the same conclusion.[19]

Another gift that warrants further comment is the gift of prophecy. On the one hand, there is no reason to think that all who have received this gift were inspired in the same sense as the writers who have contributed to the Bible. The gift refers more generally to any exhortation that communicates a clear message to its hearers.[20] It is a gift that is not just reserved for a minute group of people but may be "eagerly desired" by all (1 Cor. 14:1-4). After all, a prophet is not always a person who speaks about the future but is one who speaks on behalf of God (Ex. 7:1). On the other hand, some people in particular have this gift in such a way that they are identified as prophets. The book of Acts mentions a prophet by the name of Agabus (Acts 11:27, 28) and also refers to the four daughters of Philip (one of the seven "deacons") as prophets (Acts 21:9). However, not everyone who claims to be a prophet must however be accepted as such. The Bible repeatedly refers to "false" prophets (for example, 2 Peter 2:1) and tells us to "test" those who claim to have the gift of prophecy (Isa. 8:20; Matt. 7:20; Jer. 28:9; 1 John 4:2).

The gift of prophecy remains an important gift for the church in our time, when more than ever people need to speak on behalf of God and proclaim His Word in powerful, creative, and convincing ways without any scruples and without compromising any of its truths (Rev. 12:17; 19:10). Therefore, it is important that twenty-first-century Christians eagerly pray for this gift. A very special manifestation of this gift was, however, early recognized by Adventist believers in the ministry of Ellen G. White. When she is put to the biblical test, it becomes clear that she did not simply posses the gift in its general sense but served as a messenger who may, in many respects, be classified as a prophet on a par with Old Testament and New Testament prophets.[21]

The Church at Worship

The theology of worship is a subdiscipline in itself, and in this book we cannot do full justice to this topic. In addition to regular articles in denominational journals, only a few major Adventist publications deal in any systematic way with this topic. Worship is, however, an important aspect of the praxis of the church and is, therefore, closely related to ecclesiology and, in particular, to the role of the Holy Spirit in the church. We are to worship in truth and "in Spirit" (John 4:24). Worship is a source of life for the believer. In John's statement that God is Spirit and must therefore be worshipped "in Spirit," the apostle is not so much combating an "unspiritual view of God" as he is asserting God's creative and life-giving power.[22] It is highly significant to see this link between worship and the life-giving Spirit. Paul underlines this by stating that we "worship by the Spirit of God" (Phil. 3:3).

The word "worship" derives from the Old English roots *weorth*, meaning "honor" and "worthiness," and *scipe*, meaning "to create." So to worship is to seek ways to honor God that bespeak of His worthiness. We worship God because He is our Creator (Rev. 14:6-12). Worship must be God-centered. *The first question is not whether our worship is attractive to us, but whether it is pleasing to God.* Worship is not a prime occasion to display our talents. Everything that is done must be done to the glory of God (1 Cor. 10:31). Yet true worship is also a highly satisfying and spiritually rewarding activity for the Christian believers themselves, whether this worship is in private, in the home, or in church. It is important that we worship actively as participants and not merely as spectators (1 Cor. 14:26). Wherever we are, when we open our hearts to Him in loving adoration, God in turn pours His love into our hearts by the Holy Spirit.[23]

Worship may take many different forms, but it will consist of at least six elements: (1) Scripture reading, (2) preaching, (3) prayer, (4) singing, (5) the Lord's Supper, and (6) the bringing of gifts. There is, however, insufficient scriptural evidence to reconstruct any prescribed order of service (if there ever was one). Christ and the earliest Christian congregations worshipped in the Jewish context of Temple and synagogue, and on that basis, ever since, Christians have tended to adopt forms of worship that were culturally relevant to them. There is, therefore, nothing intrinsically new about contemporary renovations in worship styles, in particular in the use of music, which is easily the most controversial aspect of contemporary worship. It is certainly legitimate to praise God in "new" forms that are culturally relevant, and it is hardly defensible to exclude, as a matter of principle, certain musical instruments from use in worship. In October 2004 representatives of the Adventist world church voted a document entitled "A Seventh-day Adventist Philosophy of Music," which was offered to the church as a guideline, rather than a prescriptive policy. It concludes with this statement: "We should recognize and acknowledge the contribution of different cultures in worshiping God. Musical forms and instruments vary greatly in the worldwide Seventh-day Adventist family. . . . Seventh-day Adventist music-making means to choose the best and above all to draw close to our Creator and Lord and glorify Him."[24] Yet, on the other hand, we must realize that much of the content of what nowadays is called "praise" may at times have to do more with human feelings and fashions than with a prayerful recognition of the character of God.

Some contemporary authors have expressed doubt about the kind of God who is interested in constant uninterrupted praise. They claim that postmodern people no longer wish to spend their time praising and worshipping Someone Else.[25] This view hardly corresponds with today's reality, when praise and worship for human "stars" has risen to strange and often extremely disturbing levels. In his beautiful book *Reflections on the Psalms* C. S. Lewis counters the validity of such statements about the rejection of praise by making some important observations. God demands the praise of His church, he says, first of all because of His unfathomable love. He was willing to enter this world. That makes Him the One who is to be admired and praised more than anyone else. God also is entitled to our worship because He is our lawgiver and has provided us with guidelines to live happy and fulfilling lives. But more than all this, we will want to praise Him because that is how human beings express their love. They do so when they truly love another human being, and they will want to do this even more when they have entered into a close relationship with God.[26]

The "Ordinances"

This chapter concludes with some brief comments on a few prominent aspects of worship. These are often referred to as the "sacraments," or, by those who are reluctant to use that term because of its supposedly Roman Catholic connotation, as the "ordinances." Most Protestants do not like to use the words "Eucharist" or "sacrament."

Catholics view the sacraments as instruments that convey grace in a very direct manner. The technical term *ex opere operato* expresses the fact that the act of giving the sacrament is, of and in itself, significant.

Protestants, however, deny any causal effect and maintain that no rite can truly convey grace if the recipient does not approach it in faith. The old Latin word *sacramentum* translated the Greek word *mysterion* (mystery). The word had the connotation of initiation (for example, in the ancient mystery religions). In the Roman world the term *sacramentum* was used in a military context for the oath of allegiance. The church adopted the word to signify a few of its important rituals. As sacramental theology developed, it ultimately led to the Roman Catholic view that there are seven sacraments—church rituals that convey grace: baptism, the Eucharist, auricular confession, confirmation, holy orders (ordination), marriage, and anointing of the sick.

The word "ordinance" also has a Latin origin—*ordo* (order). Protestants single out baptism and the Eucharist (usually referred to as the Lord's Supper or the Communion service) as the two ordinances in a class of their own. The practice of confession (often linked with doing penance) is a separate rite found in Catholicism and some other "high church" circles. The anointing of the sick (James 5:14, 15) is practiced by a few denominations—as, for instance, the Adventist Church—but is steadily receiving more attention in many Protestant circles. Confirmation is a common practice in those churches that administer infant baptism. In addition, a few denominations—among them Adventism—have retained the practice of footwashing, based on Christ's instructions recorded in John 13:14, 15.

Protestant theology considers the ordinances as *symbols*. It would, however, be wrong to refer to them as *mere* symbols, as if symbols are not of great importance. Symbols often communicate in ways that verbal communication cannot. They provide access to a reality that can be opened up only by symbols.[27] We use symbols all the time: a kiss, a handshake, a bouquet of flowers, a wedding ring. We recognize the graphic symbols that point to our favorite gasoline station or to one of the various fast-food chains. Without symbols (traffic signs, lights, etc.) modern traffic would be unthinkable. Religion cherishes many symbols: kneeling, folding our hands, the cross, the fish, etc.). The symbols of baptism, Communion, and footwashing are at the absolute top of the list of meaningful symbols, because the Lord Himself ordered them. They speak to us in a mysterious but powerful manner. They fortify our faith, confirm God's promises to us, and strengthen and unify the church.[28] Ellen White rightly says: "The ordinances of baptism and the Lord's supper are two monumental pillars. . . . Upon these ordinances God has inscribed the name of the true God."[29]

Baptism

Even a quick scanning of the New Testament will tell us that baptism is an important ceremony. All four Gospels record the fact that Jesus Himself insisted on being baptized (Matt. 3:13-17; Mark 1:9-11; Luke 3:21, 22; John 1:31-34). He felt it was "proper" for Him to submit to baptism, since He wanted to "fulfill all righteousness" (Matt. 3:15). There is no question that in the New Testament baptism was the baptism of believers by immersion (John 3:23; Acts 8:36-39). The book of Acts leaves us in no uncertainty that adult baptism was clearly the apostolic practice. Baptism constituted an intrinsic part of the Gospel Commission: "Go, make disciples, and baptize them in the name of the triune God!" (see Matt. 28:19). The order is significant: "Whoever believes and is baptized, will be saved" (Mark 16:16). There is abundant historical and archaeological evidence that it was not until several centuries later that infant baptism became common in the Christian church, though adult baptism was never completely eradicated.[30] As we noted above, there is a close link between the Spirit and baptism. A person who is born again is reborn in water and Spirit (John 3:5). Baptism implies the beginning of spiritual growth as a member of the body of Christ. It marks one's entrance into the church (Acts 2:41-47; 1 Cor. 12:13).

The fullest explanation of the significance of this beginning of a new kind of life is provided by the apostle Paul in Romans 6:1-5. Through baptism the believer identifies in a unique way with Christ. As Christ died, went into the grave, and rose from death, so His followers in their baptism testify that they have died to their old lives but are now, through the power of the Spirit, raised from death in sin to a new life in Christ. In principle, baptism is a one-time event, not to be repeated. The rather weak biblical and theological basis for the practice of rebaptism has prompted the Adventist Church to recommend that any desire for rebaptism should be carefully evaluated and that rebaptism is only to be administered in special circumstances.[31] Adventists recognize the baptism of those who have been immersed in other religious communities, but it is not uncommon for such individuals to request rebaptism when they want to join the Adventist Church.[32]

The Lord's Supper

Hours before Christ was arrested and the dramatic events of His passion began, He instituted the Communion service with the bread and the wine that had in part been used for the Passover meal (seder). The event in the "upper room" is recorded in the three Synoptic Gospels (Matt. 26:36-39; Mark 14:22-26; Luke 22:14-20). Jesus took of the bread that was on the table, blessed it, broke it, and gave it to His disciples. Likewise He took one of the cups that had been used for the Passover meal, gave thanks over it, and shared it with His disciples. The emblems of the bread and the wine, Jesus said, represented His body and His blood that were "broken" and "poured out" to atone for the sins of the world. Although the Gospel of John contains a very clear reminder of the Communion service (John 6:53), and though it can be no coincidence that so much attention is given to statements of Christ with "Eucharistic overtones" (for example, John 6:35; 15:1-8), this Gospel does not provide a parallel to the Synoptic account of how the Communion service was instituted. Paul, on the other hand, "received from the Lord" the sacred commission to exhort the believers to eat of the bread and drink of the wine, thereby proclaiming "the Lord's death until he comes" (1 Cor. 11:26).

Christ's words "this is my body" and "this is my blood" have caused great disharmony among Christians. Roman Catholic theology takes these words literally. When the blessing is pronounced, in some miraculous way the bread and wine *in reality* become the body and blood of Jesus Christ. Protestants have rejected this view. It would, they feel, imply that at every Eucharistic celebration Christ is sacrificed anew. They consider this as unbiblical and refer to Hebrews 10:10, which stresses that Jesus died "once for all." The Catholic position is referred to as transubstantiation, which means that the substances of the bread and wine are changed. Lutherans take a position that does not fully abandon the Catholic viewpoint. Their theory is called consubstantiation, which means that the body and blood of Christ are somehow present "alongside" the bread and wine. Other Reformers and many Christian believers after them (as, for instance, Adventists) believe that when Christ said "this is," He meant "this represents" or "this symbolizes." There are other instances when Jesus used the verb "to be" in the sense of "to represent," as, for instance, in John 14:6, where He states, "I am the way" or in John 10:9, where He says of Himself, "I am the gate."

The Communion service helps us to "remember" in the most intense possible manner what Christ did for humankind. Christian believers are to eat and drink "in remembrance" of Christ. At the same time the service looks forward, because it is to be repeated "until He comes." The Bible gives no indication about the frequency of celebrating the Communion service. Paul simply says, "*Whenever* you eat . . ." and "w*henever* you drink.

. . ." Adventists follow a tradition (inherited from the denominations from which the early Adventist pioneers came) of holding the Communion service once every quarter.

Although the apostle John does not give an account of the institution of the Lord's Supper, he records at considerable length how Christ, just prior to the Passover meal and the Communion service, washed the feet of His disciples (John 13:1-17). A careful reading of this impressive story indicates that this was far more than a habitual Near Eastern display of hospitality or a one-time lesson in humility and servant leadership. Jesus said, "I have set you an example that you should do as I have done for you" (verse 15).

Footwashing has a long history in the Christian church. It was reintroduced on a major scale by the Anabaptists. It took early Sabbatarian Adventists some time before they united on the need of practicing footwashing, but eventually it was universally accepted in the Adventist Church.[33] Relatively little has, however, been written by Adventist authors about the theology of footwashing. In what has been written, two emphases usually emerge: (1) the opportunity to effect reconciliation when relationships between church members have become strained and (2) footwashing as a kind of mini-baptism and a recommitment in line with one's baptism. Mindful of the fact that Christ did not set particular requirements for participation in the Communion service (even Judas was there!), Adventists have always held that church membership is no prerequisite for participation in the Lord's Supper. Adventists therefore practice "open" Communion.

---

[1] Veli-Matti Kärkkäinen, *An Introduction to Ecclesiology: Ecumenical, Historical and Global Perspectives* (Downers Grove, Ill.: InterVarsity Press, 2002), p. 19.

[2] David G. Bloesch, *God the Almighty: Power, Wisdom, Holiness, Love* (Downers Grove, Ill., 1995), p. 191.

[3] *The SDA Bible Commentary,* vol. 5, p. 1037.

[4] Jon Paulien, *The Abundant Life Bible Amplifier: John* (Boise, Idaho: Pacific Press Pub. Assn., 1995), p. 231.

[5] C. K. Barrett, *The Gospel According to St. John* (London: SPCK, 1967), pp. 385, 386.

[6] David Watson, *I Believe in the Church* (Grand Rapids: William B. Eerdmans Pub. Co., 1985), p. 166.

[7] Rice, *Reign of God,* p. 294.

[8] *Ibid.*

[9] George Eldon Ladd, *A Theology of the New Testament* (Guildford and London: Lutterworth Press, 1975), p. 343.

[10] Watson.

[11] Norman Gulley, *Christ Is Coming: A Christ-centered Approach to Last-Day Events* (Hagerstown, Md.: Review and Herald Pub. Assn., 1998), p. 496.

[12] Ladd, pp. 245-248.

[13] *The SDA Bible Commentary,* Ellen G. White Comments, vol. 6, p. 1055.

[14] E. G. White, *The Acts of the Apostles,* pp. 54, 55.

[15] Rice, p. 217.

[16] C. Norman Kraus, *The Spirit of the Community: How the Church Is in the World* (Scottdale, Pa..: Herald Press, 1994). p. 19.

[17] Gerhard F. Hasel, *Speaking in Tongues* (Berrien Springs, Mich.: Adventist Theological Society, 1991), pp. 150-154.

[18] Rice, p. 219.

[19] William E. Richardson, *Speaking in Tongues: Is It Still a Gift of the Spirit?* (Hagerstown, Md.: Review and Herald Pub. Assn., 1994).

[20] W. Larry Richards, *The Abundant Life Bible Amplifier: 1 Corinthians* (Boise, Idaho: Pacific Press Pub. Assn., 1997), p. 230.

[21] Several good books can guide us to a better understanding of the various issues involved. Several concise books by George R. Knight, which have recently been published by the Review and Herald Publishing Association (*Meeting Ellen White*; *Reading Ellen White*; *Ellen White's World*; and *Walking With Ellen White),* are very informative and provide a lot of balanced, easily accessible information. This is also true of a much larger book by Herbert E. Douglass, *Messenger of the Lord* (Boise, Idaho: Pacific Press Pub. Assn., 1998).

[22] Barrett, p. 199.

[23] Watson, p. 183.

[24] *Statements, Guidelines and Other Documents of the Seventh-day Adventist Church,* (Silver Spring, Md.: Communication Department, General Conference of SDAs, 2005), pp. 147-150.

[25] Richard Harries, *God Outside the Box* (London: SCPK, 2002), p. 30.

[26] C. S. Lewis: *Reflections on the Psalms* (London: Collins-Fount, 1961), pp. 78-83.

[27] William G. Johnsson, *De Doop—Oorsprong en Betekenis* (Alphen a/d Rijn: Uitgeverij Veritas, 1983), pp. 78-82.

[28] Alistair McGrath, *Christelijke Theologie* (Kampen, Netherlands: Uitgeverij Kok, 1997), pp. 441-462.

[29] E. G. White, *Evangelism,* p. 273.

[30] For a condensed history of baptism, see Henry F. Brown, *Baptism Through the Centuries* (Mountain View, Calif.: Pacific Press Pub. Assn., 1965), pp. 6-90.

[31] *Seventh-day Adventist Church Manual* (Silver Spring, Md.: Secretariat of the Seventh-day Adventist Church, 2005), pp. 42-44.

[32] Herbert Kiesler, "The Ordinances," in R. Dederen, ed., *Handbook of Seventh-day Adventist Theology,* pp. 587, 588, 591; *Seventh-day Adventist Church Manual* (2005), pp. 42-44.

[33] Reinder Bruinsma, "Christ's Commandment of Humility," *Ministry,* July 1966, pp. 24-26.

Chapter 7

The Government of the Church

Where is the true church of Christ to be found? In one visible organization? Or in several or many visible communities that, to a sufficient degree, possess the "marks" of the church? Or is the church not to
be identified with any specific visible organizations at all, but is rather to
be defined as "the communion of saints, the total number of those who
believe in Christ"?[1] There are two positions at the extreme ends of the
spectrum. One holds that the idea of an invisible church is a human inven-
tion that cannot be supported by solid biblical evidence. The other maintains that only the concept of an invisible church captures the biblical view
of the people of God.

It is impossible, the proponents of the latter view state, for human beings to determine who truly belongs or do not belong to God's people.
Only God knows who are His. The issue is further complicated, they say,
by the fact that the concept of the invisible church has two different dimensions. It relates to the question as to who are, at this very moment in
time, part of God's church. However, the focus can also be broader. God's
invisible church, it is often suggested, is comprised of all those in past, present, and future who were, are, and will be disciples of the Lord Jesus
Christ. It is not only comprised of those who in today's world—whether
they are actually members of a visible church organization or not—belong
to Christ, but also of those who in centuries past were His children, and
even of those who are as yet unborn but will make the choice to trust in
God.

As we will see, this is one of the areas in which Roman Catholic and
Protestant ecclesiology clash most vehemently. Roman Catholic theology
has rather consistently emphasized the role of the visible church and has
often been unclear as to what extent Protestant denominations may be also
considered as "church" in the full sense of the word. It should, in all fairness, be admitted that some Protestant denominations have at times also

tended to identify the true church with their own particular visible structure. Yet, by and large, Protestants have defended the view of the invisible church as a reality that far extends beyond any temporal, national, regional, or denominational entity.

The biblical facts underline that the idea of an invisible church is in some sense sound. The apostle Paul wrote to the Romans that there were some in his day who had not yet had the opportunity to hear and respond to the preaching of the gospel but who had responded to the inner urging of the Spirit and "do by nature" what God wants them to do (Rom. 2:14) and thus belong to God. Although the opportunities to hear the gospel have greatly increased in today's world, even now there are men and women who fall into this category. God has children who are still anonymous and who have not (yet) united with His visible family, just as in Christ's days there were those who were already part of His flock while there were other sheep also, whom He counted as His but who would only at some future time be united with His visible flock (John 10:16).

On the one hand, toward the time of the end there will be true believers in all kinds of ecclesiastical structures and who will eventually separate from Babylon and at long last join the visible church that bears the marks that identify the end-time church. But that does not mean they may not already at present constitute part of His invisible church. On the other hand, there are those who are members of the visible church who may have been baptized but who, in actual fact, have never become true disciples of Christ. In fact, therefore, they have not really become part of His church. Christ said that as long as the church would exist, there would be "wheat" and "weeds," and the final distinction must not be left to human eyes but with the Judge who will deal with this problem at "harvest" time (Matt. 13:24-30; 36-43).

A passage in Ephesians 1 also seems to imply that the church is a concept wider than a recognizable collection of human beings on earth at one particular time and that, in a certain sense, God's church is made up of heavenly beings as well as the redeemed from the earth (verses 22, 23). The book of Revelation contains several pointers to the fact that those who have in ages past remained loyal to their Lord, even in the midst of persecution, are not to be forgotten by God but will continue to be counted as part of His church. As the fifth seal was opened, John the revelator saw "the souls of those who had been slain because of the word of God and the testimony they had maintained" (Rev. 6:9). They were told to wait until the great controversy would be over, "until the number of their fellow servants and brothers . . . was completed" (verse 11). John also saw how the church (symbolized by a woman) was kept in hiding by God during a 1260-day period (symbolizing the long period when true Christianity was almost destroyed by religiopolitical powers that aimed at raw power rather than piety [Rev. 12:6, 14]).

Yet there is reason to be careful with regard to the idea of the invisible church and not to overemphasize it—but not, as some would argue, because the term itself is not found anywhere in the Bible or because the concept does not have biblical support. We must be aware that other concepts that are clearly unbiblical may enter our thinking. When we refer to those unborn who are already, in a sense, part of God's people, we must be on guard against the predestinarian suggestion that we are dealing with those who in God's sovereign plan have from all eternity been predetermined to be among the elect, as if the human response were not a vital element in this process. And there is another caveat. The fact that those who have died in full recognition of the Lordship of Christ are safe in God's memory and may therefore be counted as part of God's invisible church should not be understood to support the belief that they are already in heaven enjoying God's presence and living as "saints" who are interceding for us who are still on earth.

The Church as a Visible Institution

The invisible aspect of the church is not to be ignored. Indeed, God only knows the hearts of people and knows who are His (2 Tim. 2:19). But the New Testament leaves no doubt about the importance of the visible church in the here and now. In fact, those passages that refer to the invisible aspect of the church are only few, whereas there is a constant referral to the visible church, the local church in specific places and the conglomerate of all local churches united in following the Way (Acts 9:2). This visible church manifested itself in apostolic time in (mostly) small groups of Christians in (mostly) cities spread over the Roman Empire, with a developing local organization and a growing supralocal network that provided leadership, theological guidance, and direction for the mission. Today the church manifests itself visibly in different traditions and hundreds of "churches" or denominations.

The word "denomination" comes from the Latin *denominare,* "to name." A denomination may be *a* church, but it is never *the* church in its fullness. The *Dictionary of Christianity in America* gives this definition, which appears to be quite satisfactory: "A denomination is an association or fellowship of congregations within a religion which have the same beliefs or creed, engage in similar practices and cooperate with each other to develop and maintain shared enterprises. Similar religious groups, such as the many Baptist bodies in the United States, constitute a 'denominational family.' "[2] American Protestantism has probably experienced a greater proliferation than is seen anywhere else, but denominational splits are certainly not an exclusively American phenomenon. The reasons for this unfortunate proliferation are many: theology and culture play an important role, but one may also often detect a thinly disguised desire for power, hegemony, or independence.[3]

In addition to the denominations, there are many so-called parachurch organizations, which focus on particular functions or target specific population segments for mission outreach. Often they emerge out of discontent, when the initiators feel their denomination neglects a certain aspect of its God-given task. These organizations tend to flourish particularly in a pragmatically oriented, entrepreneurial society such as found in America, or in any case, in an environment of "free" churches, rather than in the context of state churches or "established" churches. Recent research indicates that worldwide the monetary power of the parachurch movement has surpassed that of the traditional churches, with some $100 billion being given by Christians annually to parachurch organizations.[4] Many questions can (and should) be asked regarding this remarkable parachurch phenomenon. Can these organizations be viewed as part of the church? Do they exhibit the biblical characteristics of the New Testament church? Or are they, in actual fact, no more than "clubs" of church members and other supporters (that may or may not operate in support of the church)? These are also important questions for the Adventist Church, in which "independent" organizations, which often are very supportive of the church's goals and regular activities, play an enormously important role.

In many denominations distinct (and sometimes opposite) theological trends can be noticed, with varying degrees of formal organizational status. Often there is a distinction between more "liberal" and more "conservative" factions. These currents of thought are often referred to as "modalities." The phenomenon is more widespread in the traditional, older churches than in the younger denominations, which tend to split more easily into new denominations, each catering to a specific segment of the public. Some state churches in Europe have aimed to serve an entire nation and have consciously provided space for various modalities (for example, the Anglican community in the United Kingdom, with its "low church" and "high church" modalities, but also the Protestant state churches or former state churches in Scandinavia). However, we also find these modalities in worldwide movements, which do everything they can to preserve their global organizational unity but nonetheless do face significant internal theological diversity. The Adventist Church, again, is an example. Of course, problems arise, even leading to schisms, when some are convinced that a particular modality has stretched certain doctrinal convictions or lifestyle issues to the point that it has, in fact, in their view apostatized.

All this relates to the visible church in today's world. But the local communities of Christians are the real centers of the visible church. They are not the only manifestation of the church, but it would be correct to say that they are the foundational layer. Nonetheless, it is clear that the New Testament does not support unmitigated congregationalism, in which there is no interest in any supralocal form of authority, and no, or hardly any, formalized bond or relationship of authority exists between the various congregations.

In many evangelical churches small groups—or "cells"—are increasingly considered as the lifeblood of the church. There is certainly biblical support for this. Some point to the time of Moses, when the nation was divided into small groups of hundreds, fifties, and tens (Ex. 18:25). Others point to the small group of disciples around Christ (Mark 3:13-15; Luke 6:12, 13). Small house churches operated in the early church (see, for example, Rom. 16:5). There have been times in the post-Reformation history of the church that small groups flourished—particularly in circles of continental European Pietism and also in early Methodism. It would seem that participation in a "small group" increasingly meets the social needs of many people. Some have argued that small groups are definitely part of God's plan for His church.[5] Again, a word of caution may need to be sounded. The role of the small groups must by their very nature be limited. The activities that take place in the congregation—the communal worship in its various forms and the celebration of the Lord's Supper—must remain primary, and the primary loyalty of the members of the small group must lie with the local church. If not, the question should, once again, be asked whether we have ended up with a "club" of like-minded individuals (a kind of spiritual support group) rather than with a vital part of the church.

The church has, in particular, become visible in its various institutions. It has often been a temptation for the church to overemphasize visible, institutional structures, and, in connection with this, to stress the powers and rights of church leadership. During the Second Vatican Council the Belgian bishop De Smedt made some powerful speeches against the dangers of institutionalism. He signaled three main dangers: clericalism, juridicism, and triumphalism.[6] These dangers, he said, had done much harm to his church, but they have at times clearly also affected other denominations. Clericalism leads to overvaluing the role of the paid ministry, whereas the laity and their gifts are undervalued. Juridicism amplifies unduly the place of church law and policies. Triumphalism is at odds with the biblical notion of the "little flock" following the humble Lord Jesus.[7]

But not only has the Catholic Church at various times succumbed to these temptations! When institutionalism prevails, the church easily becomes an institution that exists for its own sake and aggrandizement. One of the deplorable results is passivity among the members. It also destroys fresh thinking, as there is but little or no room at all for renewal beyond the traditional positions. So while the visible church will need to have an institutional form, an overemphasis on the institutional element runs contrary to the essence of the church as a gathering of individuals who are united in Christ.

Church Authority

We continue to return to the question whether or not particular segments of the visible church have retained the qualifying "marks" of the church to the extent that they are indeed entitled to carry the designation "church." Implied in this question is the matter of how the church deals with the issue of authority. Most important is, of course, how the church has maintained and practiced a Christian view of authority. Christ taught us that having and exercising authority is not the same as wielding power or—still worse—as being authoritarian and that any kind of Christian leadership, at whatever level, must be "servant leadership."[8]

The ultimate authority in the church rests not with church leaders of ecclesiastical bodies or gatherings (as, for example, an annual church synod or a quinquennial General Conference session), but with the Head of the church—Jesus Christ. The church is Christ's body. Christ has been given all authority in heaven and on earth (Matt. 28:18). God has "exalted" Christ and given Him "the name that is above every name," and thus it is God's wish that "every tongue confess that Jesus Christ is Lord" (Phil. 2:9-11).

The Word of God is the primary instrument by which the Lord of the church exercises His authority. The Spirit, who is the divine person responsible for the inspired nature of the biblical writing, is also the one who directs human beings—individually and collectively—to apply those writings in any leadership process. Human beings are enlisted in the exercise of divine authority, just as the human authors of the Scriptures allowed themselves to be used as channels of communication. All human authority is derived or delegated authority. Even though the New Testament clearly indicates that from the beginning an umbrella structure that encompassed all local churches held a measure of administrative authority that was recognized by all, it is also abundantly clear that this delegated authority primarily rests with the members of the local church, with a special role for its duly elected leaders.

Local Church Leadership

The New Testament does not provide us with a clear picture of church organization at the local or supralocal level. Reading the New Testament, we do, however, discern the beginnings of a gradually developing pattern. As long as the apostles were still actively involved with the mission of the church, they continued to play a major role, in particular at the supralocal level. But we also discern the gradual development of a local leadership pattern, with two categories of leaders emerging as predominant: elders and deacons.

The word "elder" translates the Greek *presbyteros*, the term that was also used for the rulers of the synagogues and appropriated by the early Christians to designate their local leaders. From early on, Bible exegetes have recognized that in the New Testament the term *episkopos* (bishop; literally, overseer) is interchangeable with the word *presbyteros* (see Acts 20:17, 28; Titus 1:5, 7). The English translation "elder" reflects the connotation that the Greek word originally had. It reflected the great respect that in the ancient world was usually paid to the older generation, since age was considered a prerequisite for wisdom.[9] The word *presbyteros* was also frequently applied in the Greek translation of the Old Testament to people in leadership positions. The earliest biblical occurrence of the term is found in the Septuagint rendering of Exodus 12:21-27. The word *episkopos* also had its Old Testament parallels, and the Greek word appears regularly in the Septuagint. The word carries, in particular, the connotation of supervision.

It would appear that quite soon after the establishment of the church a group of "elders" in the Jerusalem church (Acts 11:30) operated in close accord with James, the brother of the Lord (Acts 15:2; 21:28). Acts 14:23

95

indicates that Paul and Barnabas appointed elders in the churches they founded. Other New Testament texts confirm that elders soon came to play an important role in the church. See, for instance, James 5:14, where we read that elders pray for and anoint the sick, and 1 Peter 5:1-4, where Peter refers to himself as a fellow elder and calls the elders "shepherds of God's flock."

Like Peter, the author of 2 and 3 John refers to himself (in both cases in verse 1) as "the elder." If these letters were written by the apostle John, as the traditional view holds, this again shows how valued the term was. Here, also, one of the key apostles gladly used the term to refer to himself, which was quite fitting considering his advanced age at the time of writing.[10] That the presbyters were persons of distinction is further underlined in a special way by the fact that the Revelation refers 12 times to their heavenly counterparts, the 24 elders who give praise to God (for example, Rev. 4:4ff.; 7:11).

Two passages (1 Tim. 3:1-7 and Titus 1:7-9) provide in some detail a list of qualifications for the "noble task" of overseer. Those who want to serve in this capacity must be "above reproach" and have a good reputation. First Timothy stresses the importance of a responsible lifestyle and a harmonious family life. The passage in Titus adds that an elder must "hold firmly to the trustworthy message as it has been taught, so that he can encourage others by sound doctrine and refute those who oppose it" (verse 9).

Whether or not the office of the elder was reserved exclusively for men or whether there may also have been female elders in the early church is still a debated issue. We will have to come back to the question whether women in principle have the same leadership status as men when we discuss ordination. It should be noted that in his list of greetings to the church in Rome, Paul includes the name of a certain Junias and that this person is referred to as an "apostle" (Rom. 16:7). This name was in ancient times used for males as well as for females, and there are some strong arguments for the likelihood that this Junias (or Junia) was actually a woman.[11] If this is true, it clearly has some significant implications.

The "deacons" form the second category of local church leaders. The Greek word *diakonos* is derived from the verb *diakoneo* (to serve), which the New Testament uses in the meaning of serving at the table (for example, Matt. 8:15) or in a wider sense of taking care of (for example, Matt. 27:55) and in connection with the service of the *diakonoi* (deacons). There is the same spread of meaning for the related word *diakonia* (service) and for the word *diakonos* (the one who provides *diakonia*). The *diakonos* can thus be someone who waits at the table (for example, John 2:5, 9) or can be a servant in the wider sense (for example, Matt. 20:26). The word receives a specifically Christian meaning when used to denote the followers of the Lord as servants of Christ (for example, 2 Cor. 11:23) and in the few cases where it refers to someone holding the office of deacon in the local church, as in 1 Timothy 3:8-13. There the qualifications for this office are spelled out, as in the previous paragraph for the elders.[12]

The seven men who were elected to assist with the social functions in the Jerusalem church (Acts 6) are popularly referred to as "deacons." Even though their original assignment may have included some of the traditional diaconal tasks, Luke avoids referring to these seven men or to their work by using such terms, and two of them (Stephen and Philip) are pictured in roles that suggest that this group had a special status.

Again the question may be raised whether women should serve as deacons. Much hinges on whether the word *diakonos* in Romans 16:1, where it is applied to Phoebe, the carrier of the letter, is used in a general sense as "servant," or in the technical sense of "deacon." Many commentators argue that the latter is very possible but that it is impossible to be certain.[13] Others, like Tübingen professor Peter Stuhlmacher, think that the context makes it probable that Phoebe indeed was a deaconess, even one with a special status.[14] The *SDA Bible Commentary* states that the use of the term *diakonos* suggests that the office of deaconess may already have been established in the early Christian church.[15]

It has often been suggested that there also was a category of widows that may have played a special role in the early Christian communities, possibly exercising some diaconal tasks. First Timothy 5:9, 10 seems to point in that direction when discussing the role of "real widows."[16] Yet it is clear that the New Testament focuses on two main groups of leaders in the local church: elders and deacons. Having stated this, we must immediately add that (1) these *leaders* were to be *servants* in all aspects of their ministry; (2) their ministry did not exclude the ministry of others (on the contrary, as we already saw, all members of the church received their own Spirit-driven ministry); and (3) as time progressed this original model would be adapted to changing circumstances—unfortunately sometimes beyond the original principles on which they were based.

A Biblical Model of Church Governance
The individual churches were not founded and did not grow in a vac-

uum or without close ties with one another. In apostolic times the apostles were the glue that held the churches together. We already noted in chapter 3 that although the New Testament applies the word *ekklesia* (church) mostly to the local congregation, it is also used in a more generic sense and at times points to the universal church in ways which suggest that the local church is part of a larger structure, geographical and historically, however undefined that may at first have been (see, for example, Eph. 1:22; 3:10, 21; 1 Cor. 10:32).

From the outset it is clear that the apostles and some other leaders (such as Stephen and Philip, and, a little later, Timothy and Titus) served the church in a supralocal role. They established new churches and stayed in contact with these churches, providing some general oversight. Some of them wrote general letters to the churches (John, Peter, James, and the author of the letter to the Hebrews). While in his place of exile, John felt a pastoral responsibility for a group of churches in Asia Minor. It is clear that the apostle Paul in particular had a leadership role that extended far and wide. George Knight aptly suggests that their role may best be compared to that of the so-called circuit riders in early Methodism.[17] The clearest evidence that important church matters were solved in a corporate way is the council in Jerusalem, as reported in Acts 15 (see chapter 3).

That a more formal manner of coordinating the church's mission and maintaining its unity of belief and purpose would be needed as the apostles grew old and died and as the church extended further and further stands to reason. After all, God is presented in the Bible as a God of order (1 Cor. 14:33, 40). In the following chapters we will look at the main historical developments that took place in postapostolic times.

Here we need to note that over time three main models of church government emerged. Most denominations have opted for one of these three types of church governance, while others have developed a model that combines elements from several of these.[18]

In the first place we find the episcopalian form of church government. The most important representatives of this form of government are the Roman Catholic Church and the Anglican and Episcopalian communities. But it has also been adopted by other religious groups, as for instance in the various Orthodox churches and the United Methodist Church. In this system the bishop (*episkopos*) is the key person in the hierarchy of authority. Local churches are to a large degree subject to the authority of the bishop. The hierarchy usually extends upward to archbishops and other dignitaries such as cardinals. In Roman Catholicism the bishop of Rome stands at the top of the hierarchical structure. The bishops receive their special authority through ordination, as the powers of the episcopal office are supposedly transferred from one generation to the next. Denominations that employ the episcopal form of government differ with respect to the process that determines the selection of new bishops and of the various persons in higher echelons of the hierarchy.

Second, there is the presbyterian type of church government, which has as its distinguishing element "a graduated series of councils from the congregational to the national level."[19] Denominations governed in this way recognize a fundamental equality among the pastors and the elders (*presbyters*) and also give a major say to the church members. Churches that have adopted this polity (as, in particular, many denominations in the Calvinist tradition have) do not operate through a hierarchical system of bishops but rather through a hierarchy of councils, which are representative bodies based ultimately on popular election.[20]

The third form of church government is the congregationalist model, which enjoys great popularity with the "free" churches of, among others, the Baptist and Pentecostal tradition. Those who have adopted this model are convinced that it corresponds most closely to what is found in the New Testament. In this model the local congregation exercises the final (human) authority in the church. It emphasizes more than the other models the local nature of the church.

The various models each have their strong and weak points. The Bible does not spell out every aspect of church organization, and considering the fact that even in New Testament times variations occurred and various aspects of civil life were borrowed and adapted to fit the needs of the church, there is every reason to accept that as time wore on, the church was called upon to be innovative and creative and to adapt organizational patterns to changing needs, as long as the fundamental principles of church governance were not compromised and the New Testament would continue to serve as the church's inspiration.

Seventh-day Adventists have adopted a model of church governance that has elements of all three traditional models. This composite model steers away from an undue emphasis on a hierarchy with a clergy that differs fundamentally from the other people of God and from the congregationalist option that shortchanges the importance of the interconnectedness of congregations. Though at first hesitant to adopt any formal type of church governance, before too long the Adventists understood the importance of organizing for mission.[21]

An analysis of the Adventist organizational pattern will show how, while taking care to be in line with the biblical data, various influences have been at work. Underneath the ecclesiastical influences, in particular from the "free" church tradition, there is no doubt that the Adventist organizational model received a strong American flavor. The church's presidential system was clearly inspired by the American political system, and the American influence also continues to be noticeable in the nomenclature. On the one hand, the Adventist thought leaders based their conclusions on their understanding of the Bible. But on the other hand, to a major degree the organizational developments—certainly on levels above the local church—were need-driven. This is not a uniquely Adventist phenomenon or specifically American. But there is no doubt that denominations that originated or developed in an American context have tended to have a more pragmatic approach to organization and other aspects of church life than churches in, for example, Europe would tend to manifest. It would be fair to say that much of the development of the organizational model of Adventism was mission-driven. As the church moved into "all the world," it struggled and succeeded to find a structure that would best fit its ever more complex needs. While in its early years all church business was directed from one central point, as time went on and the church expanded, a union and division structure was developed to bring the decision-making and planning processes closer to various regions of the world and countries. Increasingly the leadership of the church has been internationalized, while also substantial lay participation at all organizational levels has strengthened the democratic nature of the church and has testified that the church is serious when it confesses the priesthood of all believers![22]

Discipline

One of the main issues the church as an organization has to deal with is that of discipline. Every denomination needs to determine how it will deal with disciplinary issues, though Protestants have always maintained that the actual application of church discipline, in terms of how it affects a person's membership in the church, lies in principle with the local congregation. Church discipline centers on two important areas: (1) purity of doctrine and (2) purity of life.

The New Testament is clear about the importance of correct doctrine and about the ugly reality of apostasy. There are situations, then and now, when false doctrine is taught and "false prophets" lead people astray. When one no longer worships Christ as Lord, this is serious apostasy (1 John 4:1-

6). One can no longer claim to be a member of the body of which Christ is the head if one denies the Lordship of Jesus. Passages such as 1 Timothy 4:1-5 and 2 Timothy 3:1-9 are among the most outspoken regarding the reality of apostasy, in particular during "the last days." The New Testament also does not mince words regarding the reality of the presence of gross immorality and other flagrant transgressions of God's holy law. The apostle Paul refers to a kind of conduct in the church in Corinth that "does not occur even among pagans" (1 Cor. 5:1). When there are serious deviations from biblical doctrine and when serious offenses against God's moral law are committed, the church cannot turn a blind eye but must deal with the issue. It will bring reproach upon the church if it appears that the church ignores persons, doctrines, actions, and events that seriously compromise the basic teachings of the church or flagrantly contradict the ethics that Christians believe in.

How to deal with backsliders, apostates, or people who indulge in immoral behavior has been a thorny problem in much of past church history. It has led to major schisms, as for instance when the fourth-century Donatists separated from the church. It has led to rather extreme "shunning" practices among certain sixteenth-century Anabaptists,[23] while both Catholics and various Protestant churches have often enlisted state authorities who, on behalf of the church, brutally punished and even executed those whom the church had decided needed to be disciplined. In more recent times, many are the examples of the administering of discipline in ways that have hurt or even destroyed people and that have ruined relationships between people and have caused the creation of factions in local churches that have continued for many years. In recent decades, however, many denominations have tended to err on the other side, and as a result many traditional believers feel that discipline has become a seriously neglected area. However, many people in the Western world with a post-modern outlook, including church members, insist that everybody has their own truth and should decide for themselves what lifestyle to adopt, without being judged by others—let alone by an institution.

The fact that discipline can indeed be politically motivated or cause great psychological harm and the reality that many people do not like the idea of discipline does not mean that there is no place for discipline in the Christian church. After all, one of the "marks" of the church is its holiness! A concern for holiness will almost automatically result in a determination to use discipline where and when needed. The Bible certainly does not allow for a rejection or downplay of the concept of discipline. It neither promotes an approach of legalistic sternness nor one of irresponsible laxity. It does, however, directly and indirectly teach that discipline must always be embedded in love and care and should be redemptive and corrective rather than punitive.

The biblical data point in two directions.[24] Something must be done when serious apostasy or serious misconduct occurs. "Make a right judgment" (John 7:24). The church has the power to "bind" and "loose," and what the church, led by the Spirit, will bind on earth will remain bound forever (Matt. 16:19). This does not mean that the church can "bind" and "loose" at its own discretion and has the authority to dictate what members should believe or practice even if there is no clear "thus says the Lord." The church may require only what Heaven requires and will prohibit only what Heaven prohibits and must, therefore, always be guided by what Inspiration has clearly revealed.[25] However, when it follows Scripture, the church can indeed speak with authority.

There are, unfortunately, rebellious people, "mere talkers and deceivers," as we read in Paul's letter to Titus (1:10). These people, the apostle says, "must be silenced, because they are ruining whole households by teaching things they ought not to teach" (verse 11). He continues with additional sharp warnings toward the end of the short epistle: "Avoid foolish controversies and genealogies and arguments. . . . Warn a divisive person once, and then warn him a second time. After that, have nothing to do with him" (Titus 3:9-11). Similar stern language is found also in 1 John 2. Obviously, when people have strayed from the truth of the gospel to the extent that they have become a "liar," this simply cannot be tolerated. When the fundamentals of the gospel are denied, for instance, by stating that Jesus is no more than an ordinary human being rather than "the Christ," the people who do so belong in fact to the realm of the antichrist (verse 22).

Referring to an abominable case of immorality in the church of Corinth, Paul concluded that when the church is "assembled in the name of the Lord, and the power of our Lord Jesus is present," the perpetrator must be handed over to Satan (1 Cor. 5:4, 5). "You must not associate with . . . sexually immoral" people in the church or with a church member who is "an idolater, or a slanderer, a drunkard, or a swindler" (verse 11). There are a great many of such people outside the church, and God will eventually judge them. But the church must deal with such people who profess to be members. Therefore, Paul concluded, "Expel the wicked man from among you" (verse 13).

It is clear that the church ought to have a disciplinary system. Not everything goes. Certain moral standards must be maintained in the church, Paul says.[26] Any denomination must decide how the issue of discipline will be handled in real life, and any local church board must take its disciplinary task seriously. After all, it often takes just one rotten apple to ruin the entire barrel of fruit. The influence of those who propagate heretical notions has the tendency to "spread like gangrene" (2 Tim. 2:17). It takes no more than one undisciplined sinner in a local church to harm or even partly nullify its united testimony.[27]

In whatever way the disciplinary system is structured, it must be based on the fundamental biblical principles that apply. Matthew 18:15-19 fixes the ground rules: "If your brother sins against you, go and show him his fault, just between the two of you. If he listens to you, you have won your brother over. But if he will not listen, take one or two brothers along." Then follows a quotation from Deuteronomy 19:15 about the need to have trustworthy witnesses. If this discussion in the presence of witnesses does not produce any result, then "tell it to the church." If the perpetrator refuses to listen to the church, disciplinary action cannot be avoided. Clearly the underlying principle is that admonition and the sorting out of problems needs to happen at the lowest possible level, and any unnecessary escalation must be avoided.

Another point to keep in mind is that the need for discipline does not presuppose a constant measuring of the orthodoxy, or alleged lack thereof, of fellow believers or an untiring preoccupation with what others in the church do and eat or how they dress, etc. There is abundant evidence that this was not the way Christ treated the people He associated with, and there is likewise no evidence whatsoever that the apostles encouraged such attitudes. Rather, those who are "strong" in their faith ought to lovingly "accept" those who are "weak" (Rom. 14; 15). A judgmental attitude is wrong. There is always the real danger that we see the relatively small problems in the lives of other people while remaining blind to our own serious shortcomings. Jesus therefore asks us to consider whether we see the speck of saw dust in the eye of others while we ignore the plank in our own eyes (Matt. 7:3). It is against this background that we are told, "Do not judge, or you too will be judged" (verse 1). To make a division between what is "true" and what is "false" can be a very hazardous undertaking for sinful humans beings, as our human judgment will never be fully trustworthy (Matt. 13:24-30, 36-43).

The instruction to exercise discipline can never be severed from the command to forgive. Note the context of the passage in Matthew 18 about the way discipline is administered. It is preceded by the parable of the lost sheep, which in a sublime way underlines that God will do anything to keep His flock together, even if a sheep has been willfully erring. And it is followed by the parable of the unmerciful servant, which also stresses the golden rule of forgiveness, however large the debt is. One might sum it all up by saying that discipline can never be a mere legal action or only a political signal to the outside world that the church sets limits to what it allows. It can certainly never be vindictive or purely administrative. Those who administer discipline will always need to do so in humility, keenly aware of their own failings. Any sense of spiritual or moral superiority is misplaced.

Discipline must always and only be administered in a context of love. The aim is never just to see to it that justice is done, but rather to restore the person who is disciplined. Even excommunication, as a last resort, is designed for ultimate restoration.[28] In other words, true Christian discipline must be genuinely redemptive. It must be for the people's good (Heb. 12:10).

The church must take the biblical data as its point of departure. Based on that, it will develop practical procedures that will also take cognizance of circumstances of time and place and cultural environments. In line with these principles, the Adventist Church has developed its approach to church discipline, which it considers it a "solemn responsibility that rests upon the people of God in maintaining the purity, the integrity, and the spiritual fervor of the church."[29]

Closely connected with the topics discussed in this chapter about governance and discipline is, of course, the question how the biblical principles are translated in the life of the church today. Most denominations have developed a system of canon law or other bodies of ecclesiastical rules or laws on the basis of which they operate. Sometimes these have become so complex that it takes legal experts to interpret them, and these "laws" often begin to lead a life of their own.

The Adventist Church, with its fast-growing worldwide structure and its many institutional entities, has also felt the need to develop clear policies and guidelines for the governance of the church on all its administrative levels, as well as for the way local churches are organized for their mission. These have been brought together in two major publications, which are subject to a constant process of revision. These publications are available to every church member. The *General Conference Working Policy* was first published in 1926 as a digest of former church actions. An updated version is now published annually. Over time this document—a kind of Adventist canon law—has grown into a very substantial book of almost 1,000 pages. It is "the authoritative voice of the church in matters relating to the administration of the work of the Seventh-day Adventist denomination in all parts of the world. It is to be adhered to by all denominational organizations."[30] The Annual Council of the General Conference (the yearly meeting with major representation from all over the world) usually votes a number of new policies and many policy revisions as circumstances have changed or new developments dictate. These are incorporated in the new edition that is published subsequent to each Annual Council. The *Working Policy* also contains model constitutions and model operation policies for the various administrative levels of the church.

The *Seventh-day Adventist Church Manual* dates back to 1882, when a first attempt was made to spell out the rules for how the church operates, in particular at the local level. There is a very careful process in place that is followed when revisions and additions are deemed necessary.

Church and State

Another issue closely tied to the question of authority in the church and the governance of the church is that of its relationship to the state. The church's origin and early development was mainly within the confines of the Roman state, and the relationships between the church and the state were mostly quite strenuous. At times the Christian church was tolerated, but often the degree of tolerance or intolerance depended upon the decisions of local and regional authorities, some of whom even protected the church.[31] There were also periods of outright persecution, as is reflected in the book of Revelation. A drastic turnaround of events took place when in A.D. 313 Emperor Constantine decided to command official tolerating of Christianity. In 380 Emperor Theodosius made Christianity the official religion of the state. This brought momentous changes to the Christian church—not all of them positive. In the Middle Ages the roles of church and state vis-à-vis each other could fluctuate significantly from time to time and region by region.[32] The Church of Rome often claimed prerogatives and exerted political and even military pressures that were not appreciated by civil rulers, whereas the civil authorities, on their part, would often try to unduly influence or direct the affairs of the church—including the appointment of church leaders and the settling of theological controversies. In Europe for centuries a close relationship between the church and the state was the rule rather than the exception, and the phenomenon of a Protestant state church has still not fully disappeared. (In Islamic countries there, of course, also tends to be a very close tie between the state and the dominant religion.)

Adventists have traditionally advocated a strict separation between church and state. This follows the Anabaptist and "free" church tradition much more closely than the Lutheran or Calvinist tradition. The fact that Adventism developed in the United States is certainly also a factor that comes into play. The principle of full separation between church and state became enshrined in the American Constitution. A major factor was, of course, the vivid memory of religious intolerance and persecution during the previous centuries in Europe, from which the Pilgrims had fled. The Adventist stance toward the state no doubt was further determined to a major extent by the fear of state interference in their Sabbathkeeping. A number of incidents toward the end of the nineteenth century made this appear a very concrete possibility,[33] while also the Adventist end–time scenario gives further emphasis to the dangers of dangerous state involvement in religion.

The New Testament does not reflect the close ties between religion and state that were evident with respect to Old Testament Israel, where the ideal was a theocracy in which God ruled though His appointed servants. Although the New Testament is positive with regard to the principle that there is a definite need of civil power and even points out that it is "established" by God (Rom. 13:1-4), it also underlines that the respective realms of the church and state are quite distinct. "Give to Caesar what is Caesar's, and to God what is God's" (Matt. 22:21). Jesus Himself focused on His mission of spreading His spiritual message and stayed clear from any political involvement. One does not need to conclude from this, however, that a Christian cannot exercise his democratic rights and be involved in any government position, but it does seem safe to conclude that the Christian mission and the assignments of the state should not intermingle. The very fact that the followers of Christ are to be the salt of the earth (Matt. 5:13) would, however, suggest that individual Christians may consider it a calling to enter into politics and work for the good of society from a position of influence.

The principle that church and state should remain separate does not mean that the church should not try to let itself be heard in the public domain. It definitely belongs to the prophetic responsibility of the church to speak out on major ethical and moral issues and not to remain silent for fear that speaking out on matters that are also discussed in politics would necessarily constitute political meddling. And most certainly Christians who exercise their God-given right to worship God as they believe they should must unwaveringly show their support for any effort to grant all citizens of the world that same right—even if not all will make the same religious decision as they have made.

---

[1] *Catechism of the Lutheran Church—Missouri Synod* (1986), pp. 153.

[2] Daniel G. Reid et al., eds., *Dictionary of Christianity in America* (Downers Grove, Ill.: InterVarsity Press, 1990), p. 350.

[3] For a good overview of the denominational proliferation in the United States, see Frank S. Mead and Samuel S. Hill, *Handbook of Denominations in the United States* 11th ed. (Nashville: Abingdon Press, 2001).

[4] Wesley K. Willmer et al., *The Prospering Parachurch: Enlarging the Boundaries of God's Kingdom* (San Francisco: Jossey-Bass Publications, 1998), p. 10.

[5] David Cox, *Think Big, Think Small Groups* (Watford, U.K.: Personal Ministries Department, South England Conference of SDA, 1998), pp. 14-18.

[6] Avery Cardinal Dulles, *Models of the Church* (New York: Doubleday, 2002), p. 31.

[7] *Ibid.*, p. 32.

[8] The phrase "servant leadership" became popular after the publication of the influential book by Robert K. Greenleaf: *Servant Leadership* (New York: Paternoster Press, 1977).

[9] Colin Brown, ed., *Dictionary of New Testament Theology* (Exeter, U.K.: Paternoster Press, 1975), Vol. I, pp. 192, 193.

[10] *The SDA Bible Commentary*, vol. 7, p. 685.

[11] Robert M. Johnston, "Ministry in the New Testament and the Early Church," in Nancy Vyhmeister, ed., *Women in Ministry: Biblical and Historical Perspectives* (Berrien Springs, Mich.: Andrews University Press, 1998), pp. 47, 48; Stanley J. Grenz and Denise Muir Kjesbo, *Women in the Church: A Biblical Theology of Women in Ministry* (Downers Grove. Ill.: InterVarsity Press, 1995), pp. 92-97.

[12] Brown, ed., *Dictionary of New Testament Theology* (Exeter, U.K.: Paternoster Press, 1978), Vol. III, pp. 544-553.

[13] See, e.g., Herman Ridderbos, *Commentaar op het Nieuwe Testament: Romeinen* (Kampen: Uitgeversmaatschappij J. H. Kok, 1959); Kenneth Boa and William Kruidenier, *Romans* (in series of *Holman New Testament Commentaries*) (Nashville: Broadman and Holman Pub., 2000), p. 458.

[14] Peter Stuhlmacher, *Paul's Letter to the Romans: A Commentary* (Edinburgh, U.K.: T. & T. Clark, 1994), p. 246.

[15] Vol. 6, p. 649.

[16] See Everett Ferguson, *The Church of Christ: A Biblical Ecclesiology for Today* (Grand Rapids: William B. Eerdmans Pub. Co., 1996), pp. 339-341.

[17] George R. Knight, *If I Were the Devil* (Hagerstown, Md.: Review and Herald Pub. Assn., 2007), p. 189.

[18] For a good summary of these forms of church government, see Reid, pp. 269-271; also useful is J. S. Hammett, *Biblical Foundations for Baptist Churches,* pp. 137-146. I do not, however, agree with the author's emphasis on congregationalism as the form that has the strongest biblical support.

[19] Reid, p. 270.

[20] F. L. Cross., ed. *The Oxford Dictionary of the Christian Church* (London: Oxford University Press, 1963), p. 1101.

[21] The focus is on this aspect in the book by George R. Knight that gives a succinct overview of the development of the Adventist organization: *Organizing for Mission and Growth* (Hagerstown, Md.: Review and Herald Pub. Assn., 2006). An important study in this area remains Barry D. Oliver, *SDA Organizational Structure: Past, Present and Future* (Berrien Springs, Mich.: Andrews University Press, 1989).

[22] For a survey of the Development of Adventist church structure, see Walter R. Beach and Bert B. Beach, *Pattern for Progress* (Hagerstown, Md.: Review and Herald Pub. Assn., 1985) and George R. Knight, *Organizing to Beat the Devil* (Hagerstown, Md.: Review and Herald Pub. Assn., 2001).

[23] George H. Williams, *The Radical Reformation* (Philadelphia: Westminster Press, 1962), pp. 396-398.

[24] Informative studies of the topic include Roy E. Knuteson, *Calling the Church to Discipline* (Nashville: Action Press, 1977), and Thomas C. Oden, *Corrective Love: The Power of Communion Discipline* (1995).

[25] *The SDA Bible Commentary*, vol. 5, p. 433.

[26] For a full list of examples of discipline in the apostolic church, see Mal Couch, ed., *A Biblical Theology of the Church* (Grand Rapids: Kregel Publications, 1999), pp. 231-234.

[27] Knuteson, p. 81.

[28] *Ibid.*, p. 82.

[29] *Seventh-day Adventist Church Manual* (2005), p. 185.

[30] *General Conference Working Policy* B 10.

[31] H. Chadwick, *The Early Church* (Penguin Books, 1967), p. 29.

[32] For a detailed survey of relationship between the state and the church from the seventeenth century onward, see J. F. Maclear, *Church and State in the Modern Age: A Documentary History* (New York/Oxford: Oxford University Press, 1995). For a survey of recent views in various European countries, see Gerhard Robbers, *State and Church in the European Union* (Baden-Baden, Germany: Nomos Verlagsgesellschaft, 1996).

[33] Eric Syme, *A History of SDA Church-State Relations in the United States* (Mountain View, Calif.: Pacific Press Pub. Assn., 1973), pp. 20-33.

Chapter 8

Ordination

The ongoing debate in many denominations about women's ordination has in recent decades highlighted the topic of ordination in general. The question of who may receive ordination is, of course, not unimportant and will also receive attention below. But let's begin with the basic question as to what ordination is. What happens when a person is ordained? Why do some church offices require that one is ordained?

The Biblical Data Regarding Ordination

Ordination by laying on of hands has Old Testament precedents. Various functionaries in Old Testament times were anointed before they assumed their tasks. Several instances are reported in considerable detail about priests, prophets, and kings who were installed with a ritual that included anointing.[1] For some examples, see Exodus 28:41 (the high priest Aaron and his sons), 1 Samuel 10:1 (King Saul), and 1 Kings 19:16 (the prophet Elisha). However, this was not carried over into New Testament times, whereas another ritual, that of the laying on of hands, was.

The Hebrew term for "laying on of hands" (either in the plural or in the singular) occurs some 25 times in the Old Testament. We find it sometimes in a sacrificial setting, as for instance when the person who came to bring a burnt offering (Lev. 1:4), a peace offering (Lev. 3:2) or a sin offering (Lev. 4:4), placed his hand on the head of the animal that was to be sacrificed. It also occurs in the context of the Azazel ritual on the Day of Atonement, when the high priest was to "lay both hands on the head of the live goat" (Lev. 16:21), while confessing all the sins of the people and symbolically transferring them to the goat. It could be argued that the laying-on-of-hands ceremonies to consecrate Aaron and his sons to the priesthood (Ex. 29:10, 15, 19; Lev. 8:14, 18, 22) were of a sacrificial nature. The laying on of hands, however, also occurs in non-sacrificial settings, as for instance when Jacob laid his hands on the heads of Ephraim and Manasseh and blessed them (Gen. 48:14).

Two instances of laying on of hands in the Old Testament can be specifically classified as a kind of ordination ritual.[2] The first of these is the ordination ceremony of the Levites, recorded in Numbers 8:5-26. Analyzing the significance of this ritual, Keith Mattingly, a theology professor at Andrews University who wrote his Ph.D. dissertation on this topic, recognizes five elements: (1) the Levites were identified as the specified ones who become an offering of the whole congregation of Israelites; (2) the Levites were set aside from the people to perform a special task; (3) the people symbolically transferred to the Levites their obligations in connection with the tabernacle service and to act on behalf of them; (4) it included an act of substitution: the Levites substituted for and represented their people, in particular the firstborn; and (5) it marked the appointment to a particular office.[3]

The second instance in the Old Testament—and the clearest—in which the laying on of hands is connected with "ordination" to a spiritual office among the people of God is Joshua's receiving the laying on of hands from Moses (Num. 27:12-23; Deut. 34:9). This ritual was a public act of confirming and ratifying the spiritual gifts God had already given Joshua. Moses was told by God, "Take Joshua son of Nun, a man in whom is the spirit, and lay your hand on him. Have him stand before Eleazar the priest and the entire assembly and commission him in their presence. Give him some of your authority so the whole Israelite community will obey him" (Num. 27:18-20). The ceremony identified Joshua as the new leader and was associated with a commission given to him. It also symbolically transferred some of the honor and authority from Moses to him, even though that authority was rooted not in Moses but in God. This, one commentator states, may best be understood as a charisma that induced in the people a readiness to listen to him with trust and confidence.[4] Also, it is to be noted that Joshua already possessed the spirit of God but that this ordination reinforced that gift in him.

The New Testament in the English language (in particular in the KJV) regularly uses the word "ordain" and related words. The English word "ordination" comes from the Latin *ordinare,* meaning to regulate. It translates various Greek terms that carry a broad spectrum of meanings and tends to be much more general than the English word "ordain" suggests. In Acts 14:23 (KJV), for example, we are told that Paul and Barnabas "ordained" elders in every city in which they had established a church. Other translations render the word *cheirotoneo* (literally, stretching out a hand in voting) simply as "appoint." The use of this particular word and the context may suggest that reference is indeed in this instance to some form of ordination ceremony, as they were "committed" to the Lord "with prayer and fasting." Titus 1:5 in the KJV also has the word "ordain" in the statement that Paul appointed elders in the cities where he founded churches. Here the Greek word *kathisthemi* is used, which literally means "to arrange for." Again, this may or may not imply some formal ordination ritual. But in other instances, as in Mark 3:14 in the KJV, the word "ordain" does not seem to be used in any sense that is associated with ordination as we understand it, even though Ellen White in *The Desire of Ages* does explain the text in such terms.[5]

The New Testament refers some 25 times to the laying on of hands and does so in different ways. The hand appears to symbolize power, and the laying on of hands symbolizes that a process of power transfer or of empowering takes place. Most of the use of this term occur in the context of blessing or healing (for example, Mark 6:5; Luke 13:13; Acts 9:12; Matt. 19:13-15) or are related to the reception of the Holy Spirit (Acts 8:17-19) or spiritual gifts (1 Tim. 4:14). In Acts 19 we find Paul in Ephesus, confronted with a group of believers who possessed only a partial knowledge of the Christian teachings. After that was remedied, Paul laid his hands on these 12 men, and "the Holy Spirit came on them" (verse 6). Here the laying on of hands is clearly unrelated to any commissioning for a church office. But a few other New Testament passages that mention the laying on of hands (Acts 6:1-6; 13:1-3; 1 Tim. 4:14; 5:22; 2 Tim. 1:6) have traditionally been tied to ordination to a spiritual office. Bible scholars have noted that the laying on of hands is the only ceremony taken over from the Old Testament by the New Testament church for the consecration and ordination of its ministry.[6]

In Acts 6:6 we read about the laying of hands on the seven men who had been chosen to assist the apostles. They were set apart because they had been found to be "full of the Spirit and wisdom" (verse 3). Acts 13:3 refers to Barnabas and Saul, who were sent off for further missionary work by the church of Antioch, after the Holy Spirit had indicated to the church that they should do this. In 1 Timothy 4:14 Paul reminds Timothy of the important moment "when the body of elders laid their hands on you," while it is clear from 2 Timothy 1:6 that Paul himself also participated in this ceremony (assuming that both passages refer to the same occurrence). In this second brief reference to this ceremony, emphasis is again placed on the gift of the Spirit, which Paul tells Timothy "is in you through the laying on of my hands."

First Timothy 5:22 contains one final brief reference to the laying on of hands: "Do not be hasty in the laying on of hands." In this case the phrase is more or less used as a technical term and no doubt refers to the moment when new local leaders are initiated into their office.

The question may be asked whether the New Testament data are of sufficient weight to justify the emphasis most churches place on the ordination of men and, in many cases, also women to the gospel ministry and to the offices of elder and deacon. When hands were laid on Paul and Barnabas in Antioch, it was certainly not to mark the beginning of their apostleship. Rather, they were commissioned by the church to undertake a new mission tour. The passage in Acts 13 does not give much support for the rite of ordination through the laying on of hands as a prerequisite for holding one of the major church offices. And were "the seven" in Acts 6 ordained in the sense as we currently understand ordination? Some feel that the incident rather appears to refer to an ad hoc blessing on these men but falls short of providing proof for the existence of a formal ordination ritual at this early stage in the history of the church. Others disagree. F. F. Bruce, for instance, sees a clear parallel with the ordination of officials in contemporary Judaism and is, therefore, of the opinion that the seven were, in fact, ordained.[7]

The two passages in 1 Timothy and 2 Timothy respectively have also provided grounds for debate. Was Timothy here formally commissioned (ordained) for his tasks or did the laying on of hands have a much more restricted meaning, marking the receipt of an extra blessing to better equip him for his work? *The Seventh-day Adventist Bible Commentary* states that this "ordination service" recognized Timothy's abilities and commitment and "expressed the church's approval of his appointment as a church leader."[8] The position that in the letters to Timothy the laying on of hands is to be understood in terms of an ordination ceremony is strengthened by the short reference in 1 Timothy 5:22, where Timothy is warned not to proceed too hastily in ordaining people.

The Meaning of Ordination

The laying on of hands as a central feature of church praxis points to the fact that the church believes that God has special blessings in store for those who serve the church in a special capacity, and is willing, at the request of the church, to bestow this on the ordinands. It is not that those who are ordained will thereby receive "the gift of the Spirit," as if they were not already led by the Spirit. Rather, the ordinands are selected by the church because they are "filled" with the Spirit, but it is also recognized that they will need additional Spirit power as they are inducted into their specific roles in the church.

Ordination must always be seen against the background of the fundamental truth of the priesthood of all believers. Unfortunately, church history teaches us that this balance has not always been retained. In fact, in major parts of the Christian church a wide chasm soon evolved between the ordained clergy and the "ordinary" believers, and ordination came to be regarded more and more as a sacrament. Instead of the biblical model of representatives of the church praying for a special blessing for some who would be solemnly set apart for a special assignment, ordination evolved into a sacrament whereby particular human beings—because they supposedly are no longer just "ordinary" believers—are able to confer a measure of grace and authority on some other human beings, with the understanding that this will give them also a status beyond that of "ordinary" believers. Protestants have "protested" against this sacramentalized view of ordination and all that it entails.

Seventh-day Adventists began ordaining their leaders and local elders without much in-depth study or discussion. Some of the leaders in early Adventism had already received ordination in other denominations. From 1852 onward we note the first instances of ordination of ministers. The ordaining of elders and deacons soon followed suit after some articles on the issue were published in the Adventist press.[9]

But Adventists have traditionally not paid much attention to the theological meaning of ordination. They have often more clearly expressed what they believe it is not than what they think it actually *is*. Ellen White's remarks on Acts 13 illustrate this point: "The ceremony of the laying on of hands [on Paul and Barnabas] added no new grace or virtual qualification. It was an acknowledged form of designation to an appointed office and a recognition of one's authority in that office. By it the seal of the church was set upon the work of God." She added that "at a later date" this rite "was much abused; unwarrantable importance was attached to the act, as if a power came at once upon those who received such ordination." However, it should be clear from the Scriptures, she says, that no "virtue was imparted by the mere act of laying on of hands."[10] Ellen White thus reacted against the understanding of ordination that over the centuries developed in Roman Catholic theology, namely, that ordination marks "the

113

conferral of a grace that effects an indelible, lifelong change and empowers the ordinand to celebrate the sacraments."[11] Ordination is rather "the church's setting apart a person whom it believes God has called. . . . This setting apart is not to a superior status, *above* the rest of the church, but rather to service *within* the church."[12]

I agree with Russell L. Staples, a prominent Adventist missiologist, who remarked in an essay he wrote on the Adventist theological understanding of ordination, that "it is extremely difficult to delineate understandings of ministry and ordination within the Adventist Church with exactitude and clarity. For the greater part, patterns of church organization and ministry have been developed pragmatically."[13] Raoul Dederen, an emeritus Adventist scholar who has probably written more on the doctrine of the church than any other Adventist theologian,[14] admits that the Adventist Church has "no elaborate doctrine of . . . ordination."[15] Most of the little that has been written about ordination refers to ordination to the ministry and much less to that of elders and deacons. Dederen believes the Adventist concept of ordination can be summarized in four points: (1) "Adventists believe in a personal, divine call to the Christian ministry and have historically insisted on an ordination procedure for those thus called"; (2) through the ordination ceremony the church "confirms the call by publicly recognizing its validity"; (3) the individual who is set apart is "a representative of the church"; and (4) "as part of the act of ordination, the church engages in intercessory prayer for the continuation of the gift of the Holy Spirit upon those fulfilling the ministry committed to the church."[16]

These and other statements from Adventist theologians point to a consensus that ordination must not be sacramentalized. It does not convey a special authority, but is a symbolic act to demonstrate that the church has recognized the calling of an individual. It is a symbol just as the ordinances of baptism and Communion are symbols and are not to be interpreted as sacerdotal acts that in and of themselves confer status or authority.

But what about the fact that in the Adventist Church certain acts are restricted to persons who have been ordained and that there are differences in authority between the various groups of ordained persons? Ordination to the gospel ministry and to the office of elder or deacon is intrinsically identical, yet the church has decided to limit particular functions to ordained ministers. Hence, the difference between ministers, on the one hand, and elders and deacons, on the other hand, is not theological but lies rather in the degree of authority that the church has decided to grant to them. Why are elders allowed certain tasks that deacons cannot perform and why are, in principle, certain acts restricted to the ordained pastor? This relates to not only the prerogative of baptizing people and of officiating at the Lord's Supper but also certain organizational functions, such as organizing or dissolving a church. And why can, according to Adventist policy, only an ordained minister become the president of particular organizational units (a conference, a union, or the General Conference)?

These restrictions are a matter of church policy and are not dictated by theological considerations. On the one hand, Adventists have followed the general tendency within Protestantism to reserve the rights to administer baptism and the Lord's Supper to those who are ordained, but it is recognized that there is no clear biblical "thus says the Lord" that mandates this policy. On the other hand, it is reasonable that a community establishes rules, and there is no problem with this as long as these rules do not contradict fundamental biblical principles, of which the priesthood of all believers is foremost.

Several early Adventist leaders had their roots in other Christian communities, such as Methodism, and it should therefore not surprise us to find parallels between Adventists and Methodists regarding certain patterns of ministry. In both cases a system of an appointed rather than congregationally called ministry has been maintained.[17] And again, we notice a major degree of pragmatism in the way in which ordination is understood and practiced in the Adventist Church. Ordination in the Adventist Church has by and large been limited to the church offices mentioned in the New Testament (pastors, elders, deacons) and has not been extended to other church leaders (church clerks, church treasurers, youth leaders, etc.). In recent times the concept of "commissioning" has been introduced to provide for an ordination-like ceremony in which the setting apart of people for nonpastoral roles is celebrated.

The Ordination of Women

The question of whether women can be ordained to the priesthood or to the pastoral ministry or as elder or deacon has been an extremely divisive issue in many denominations and still is in quite a few faith communities. Some denominations have sounded a clear no, and others an unmitigated yes. Some have at last introduced female ordination but still suffer from considerable internal dissent. In some quarters the discussion continues, with a gradually growing support for the option of female pastors and female elders and deacons. In other denominations the introduction of an ordained female clergy remains unlikely for the foreseeable future. The debate on ordination of women in the Adventist Church has now been going on for a number of decades.[18] In part the issue is, of course, theological. But in part it is also cultural and sociological. And it would be fair to say, at least in retrospect, that the various intermediate positions that the church has taken have not been totally consistent and have shown a rather confusing mix of theological arguments and administrative compromise.

In 1974 the General Conference Committee, when meeting in its Annual Council, took a first step to open the way for women to be ordained as local elders. It was decided to study the matter, but in the meantime the world divisions of the church were given a measure of freedom to proceed. A number of divisions began cautiously to allow women to be ordained as local elders. A definitive position was voted at the Annual Council of 1984. It was decided "to advise each division that it is free to make provisions as it may deem necessary for the election and ordination of women as local church elders."[19]

This, however, did not settle the issue of ordaining women for pastoral ministry. In 1990 the delegates at the General Conference session rejected a proposal to allow for the ordination of women to the gospel ministry but at the same time went on record that women were and remained welcome to serve in pastoral capacities. In 1995 the subject was back on the agenda of the General Conference session. This time it was proposed that each world region should be allowed to decide whether or not to allow the ordination of female pastors in the region of the world for which it is responsible. Again, the proposal to allow for the ordination of women, even if this change in policy was not forced on parts of the world where they felt they were not ready for such a step, was voted down.

All of this raises some important questions. Is ordination intrinsically different when it concerns an elder rather than a pastor? This seems to be implied in the decision to allow for the ordination of female elders, but not approve the ordination of female pastors. Also, the very proposal that was brought to the General Conference session in Utrecht in 1995 (that is, to leave the decision as to whether ordination of women was to be permitted to the various division committees) strongly suggests that the ordination of female pastors is not primarily a theological issue, for surely theological decisions are a matter of the entire denomination. The matter is further complicated by the fact that there is a clear standpoint regarding the ordination of female elders, whereas the position regarding the ordination of female deacons or deaconesses is rather ambiguous. The *Church*

Manual stipulates that elders (no differentiation is made between male and female elders) are to be ordained, but the word "ordination" is studiously avoided when it concerns the installation of deaconesses: "The church may arrange for a suitable *service of induction* for the deaconess by an ordained minister holding current credentials."[20] How does a "service of induction" differ from an ordination service if it requires the services of an ordained minister? It is no wonder that, as these words are written, the issue of the ordination of female deacons is back on the agenda of the General Conference.

A few world divisions of the Adventist Church were utterly disappointed by the decision of the General Conference session in Utrecht in 1995. A compromise has subsequently been sought in the use of a special credential for female pastors, the commissioned minister credential.[21] This credential is available for a number of categories of senior church employees, but also for "associates in pastoral care" (male and female). The main distinction with the regular *ministerial* credential is that the *commissioned* minister's credential is not valid outside of the administrative unit (conference or union) where it is issued, whereas the ministerial credential has worldwide validity. Also, a (female) commissioned minister does not have the authority to organize and disband local churches, as her (male) ministerial counterpart has. Performing marriage ceremonies is subject to some special conditions. A commissioned minister, however, can perform all the other functions of the ordained minister, including conducting baptisms and officiating at the Lord's Supper.

Some regard this compromise as a reasonable solution; others find it quite inadequate. Most agree that there is little or no theological rationale for this solution. In several areas of the world the distinction between "ordination" and "commissioning" is further obscured by the difficulty of finding adequate words for these two concepts in the local language.

There is at present no unanimity on the way forward. Many leaders in Western countries believe that those areas in the world that want to ordain women to the ministry ought to be allowed to do so. They feel that no time is to be lost, and usually point to the fact that the Adventist Church has over time moved backward on the issue of female participation in the ministries of the church rather than forward. Not only were there many female preachers of distinction in the Millerite movement,[22] but early Adventism also left a heritage of broad female participation in all vital ministries of the church.[23] They contend that it is difficult to understand why a church that has a woman (Ellen G. White) as one of its main founders finds it so difficult to move forward on the issue of female ordination to the pastoral ministry. But others believe that to give permission for ordaining women to the gospel ministry is to go against the clear injunctions of Scripture and is therefore totally unacceptable.

Theological Considerations

Although the debate about the ordination of women is not *only* of a theological nature, it most definitely has an important theological component. Those who are in favor of allowing, or are even promoting, the ordination of women will argue that it is their sacred conviction that this is what the Bible tells us to do, whereas those who oppose it will argue just as intensely that allowing for female ordination is to go against a clear biblical injunction that places restrictions on the role of women in the church. It should be noted that those who oppose the ordination of female pastors usually also believe that the church has erred in allowing for the ordination of female local elders and will also oppose the ordination of deaconesses.

The opposition against the ordination of women rests to a large extent on one basic argument and a few New Testament passages.[24] The fundamental argument runs as follows: Leadership in the family or household was placed on the husband (1 Cor. 11:3; Col. 3:18; Eph. 5:21-33). The church is described in the New Testament as the family or household of God (1 Tim. 3:15). Therefore, leadership in the church, as the family of God, is reserved for those who are heads of households. Some would argue that even as Adam and Eve were created, Adam was in some sense already "superior" to Eve, but that, in any case, after the Fall the "headship" of man was a divinely ordained fact. The priesthood in Israel was therefore a male prerogative, and in line with this, Christ chose only men to lead the early church.

A key passage in the argumentation against the ordination of women is 1 Corinthians 14:33-35: "As in all congregations of the saints, women should remain silent in the churches. They are not allowed to speak, but must be in submission, as the Law says. If they want to inquire about something, they should ask their own husbands at home; for it is disgraceful for a woman to speak in the church."

And another important passage is found in 1 Timothy 2:8, 11, 12: "I want men everywhere to lift up holy hands in prayer, without anger or disputing. . . . A woman should learn in quietness and full submission. I do not permit a woman to teach or to have authority over a man; she must be silent."

It would, at first sight, seem as if these biblical data present formidable problems for the supporters of the ordination of women. However, many scholars feel that these arguments are not as strong as they appear and that there are, in fact, stronger arguments to support the case *for* women's ordination. In his recent voluminous study on gender-related issues in the Old Testament, Andrews University professor Richard M. Davidson provides a convincing reply to those who feel that before and after the Fall men and women differed in status. He makes a solid case for the contention that the Old Testament teaches full equality of the sexes, without any hierarchy.[25]

He recognizes that the "curses" subsequent to the Fall (Gen. 3:15-19) implied a certain distinction in gender roles within the family. But the "ruling" of Adam over his wife, Davidson argues on linguistic grounds, lacks the connotation of the exercise of power and is predominantly a positive concept, not a negative one.[26] It expresses the idea of "a servant leadership of protection, care, and love." In the modern idiom, the husband is to "lovingly take care of his wife."[27] Furthermore, the way in which the context is structured, Davidson says, "reveals that it is not inappropriate for humankind to seek to roll back the curses/judgment and get back as much as possible to God's original plan . . . of total egalitarianism." In fact, this is what humanity has done with regard to several other components of the post-Fall curses.[28]

After having stated that throughout the Old Testament period the "divine pattern for husband-wife relationships established in Eden" remains the assumed paradigm, he reminds us that women could rise "to positions of influence, leadership and authority in the covenant community." He then approvingly quotes another author, Carol Meyers, who states that many people have misused the term *patriarchy* as a synonym for male dominance.[29]

Jacques Doukhan, another Andrews University Old Testament expert, has provided a number of convincing reasons the priesthood in Israel was reserved for men and why this fact should not lead us to the conclusion that today, therefore, female ordination should be out of the question.[30]

Many commentators feel that the passages in 1 Corinthians 14 and 1 Timothy 2 are *descriptive*, reflecting the culture of the time, rather than a *prescriptive* norm that would remain forever valid. It is difficult to see how Paul's statement that women ought to remain silent in the congregation (that is, ought not to address the congregation formally) can be taken in any absolute sense. Elsewhere in the same epistle it appears that women are allowed to pray or "prophesy" in public (1 Cor. 11:5) as long as they are modest in appearance, presumably by the cultural standards of that time.

It appears that in 1 Corinthians Paul is addressing some special situation that concerns the way some women in Corinth behaved in church and that must be seen in the context of the confusion around speaking in tongues that had led to disruptions in the church's worship.[31] *The Seventh-day Adventist Bible Commentary* does not go into any great detail when dealing with the passage in 1 Corinthians 14 and suggests that it must be understood against the cultural background of the first century.[32]

With regard to the aspect of female submission that is reflected in this passage, many commentators suggest that this likewise reflects a degree of tolerance for contemporary cultural circumstances, just as in other New Testament passages practices such as polygamy and slavery are not condemned outright. Most of those who argue against female ordination and cite New Testament texts that refer to the submission of women to men in support of their view would not read texts about polygamy or slavery in the same literal manner.

There are several good reasons such injunctions about women maintaining an attitude of silent submissions (as, for example, in 1 Timothy 2) should *not* be codified into church law. Rather, the church must do what it can to leave behind such undesirable accommodations to temporal circumstances, as were part of church life in the days of Paul and Timothy, and be determined to practice the spirit of the gospel, which points to full equality of all people—male and female—in Christ. Galatians 3:26-28 lays down a fundamental principle that should help decide all who are in doubt about the lawfulness of ordaining women: "You [brothers and sisters!] are all sons of God through faith in Christ Jesus, for all of you who were baptized into Christ have clothed yourselves with Christ. There is neither Jew nor Greek, slave nor free, male nor female, for you all are one in Christ."

Why does the issue of the ordination of women cause such heated debate? It is because the implications of the discussion go far beyond this topic. That is why Raymond Holmes, a retired Andrews University professor, gave his book the title *The Tip of the Iceberg* when he wrote his passionate plea to reject the ordination of women. He was correct in his opinion that one cannot detach one's view regarding female ordination from one's view of biblical inspiration in general.

On the one hand, some feel an honest reading of the Bible leaves them no other choice than to conclude that the Bible wants women to be silent in the church. On the other hand, others have a different view of inspiration, which does not lead them to that conclusion. They argue that the

Bible was written within a particular cultural context and that this explains the reluctance of the Bible writers, such as the apostle Paul, to preach a full functional equality between men and women. They believe that the fundamental truth that must be discovered underneath temporal cultural accommodations is that "in Christ" every inequality in status between male and female has been removed. For some, acceptance of women's ordination would be an extension of the women's liberation movement and feminism—a contention that does not make it any easier to look at the matter objectively. In many non-Western cultures, but also in quite a few subcultures in the West, male dominance is still the norm. In other cultures full equality between the genders is a value with high priority. Regrettably, however, in the minds of many, any defense of the ordination of women is simply part of a broader liberal agenda. All these factors, and still others, play a role.

But whatever the various factors are, the fact remains that to many the ordination of women remains rather ambiguous from a biblical point of view. Those who are opposed to it tend to lay emphasis on a particular set of texts, whereas those who are eager to allow for ordaining women tend to put stress on a different set of texts.[33] A final decision in the Adventist Church will, however, not result just from a theological discussion of this topic, in isolation from a broader debate on how Adventists read the Bible. This is even more so since the issue has become a symbol in the ongoing skirmishes between those who demand room for greater doctrinal diversity and those who are afraid of the "slippery slope" on which the church will glide from one compromise to the next.

---

[1] V. Norskov Olsen, *Myth and Truth, Church, Priesthood and Ordination* (Riverside, Calif.: Loma Linda University Press, 1990), pp. 128-130.

[2] Keith Mattingly, "Laying On of Hands in Ordination: A Biblical Study," in N. Vyhmeister, ed., *Women in Ministry*, p. 61.

[3] *Ibid.*, p. 62.

[4] B. Maarsingh, *Numbers: A Practical Commentary* (Grand Rapids: William B. Eerdmans Pub. Co., 1987), p. 98.

[5] E. G. White, *The Desire of Ages*, p. 296.

[6] Mattingly, p. 67.

[7] F. F. Bruce, *The Book of Acts*, in *The New London Commentary on the New Testament* (Grand Rapids: William B. Eerdmans Pub. Co., 1954), p. 130. For more insights regarding rabbinical ordination, see Olsen, pp. 130-138.

[8] *The SDA Bible Commentary*, vol. 7, p. 307.

[9] *Seventh-day Adventist Encyclopedia* (1996), vol. II, pp. 254, 255.

[10] E. G. White, *The Acts of the Apostles*, pp. 161, 162.

[11] Russel L. Staples, "A Theological Understanding of Ordination," in Vyhmeister, p. 141.

[12] Raoul Dederen, "A Theology of Ordination," *Ministry*, February 1978, p. 24L.

[13] Staples, p. 146.

[14] He was the author of the section on the church in the *Handbook of Seventh-day Adventist Theology* (pp. 538-581), which appeared in 2000 as volume 12 of the Commentary Reference Series.

[15] Dederen, "A Theology of Ordination," p. 24M.

[16] *Ibid.*, p. 24N.

[17] L. Staples, pp. 144-146, 153.

[18] The most comprehensive study on the issue of women's ordination was produced by a special committee of theologians connected with the Theological Seminary at Andrews University: Nancy Vyhmeister, ed., *Women in Ministry—Biblical and Historical Perspectives* (Berrien Springs, Mich.: Andrews University Press, 1998). Predictably, a response to this collection of studies soon came, written by another group of Andrews University professors and alumni: Mercedes H. Dyer, *Prove All Things—A Response to Women in Ministry* (Berrien Springs, Mich.: Adventists Affirm, 2000). These important books were preceded by other substantial publications, written from a pro or contra point of view. Charles E. Bradford, past North American Division president, by writing a foreword lent his weight to Patricia A. Habada and Rebecca Frost Brillhart, *The Welcome Table: Setting a Place for Ordained Women* (Langley Park, Md.: Team Press, 1995). Among those who strongly argued against female ordination were Samuel Bacchiocchi, *Women in the Church* (Berrien Springs, Mich.: Biblical Perspectives, 1987) and C. Raymond Holmes, *The Tip of the Iceberg* (Wakefield, Mich.: Pointer Publications, 1994).

[19] *Seventh-day Adventist Encyclopedia* (1996), vol. II, p. 255.

[20] *Seventh-day Adventist Church Manual* (2005) pp. 50, 51, 59. (Italics supplied.)

[21] See the policies under E5 in the *General Conference Working Policy*.

[22] Catherine A. Brekus, *Strangers and Pilgrims: Female Preaching in America, 1740-1845* (Chapel Hill and London: University of North Carolina Press, 1998), pp. 307-335. See also Susan Hill Lindley, *You Have Stept Out of Your Place: A History of Women and Religion in America* (Louisville, Ky.: Westminster John Knox Press, 1996).

[23] Bert Haloviak, "A Place at the Table: Women and the Early Years," in Habada and Brillhart, pp. 27-44.

[24] Everett Ferguson, *The Church of Christ—A Biblical Ecclesiology for Today* (Grand Rapids: William B. Eerdmans Pub. Co., 1996), pp. 341-344.

[25] Richard M. Davidson, *Flame of Yahweh: Sexuality in the Old Testament* (Peabody, MA: Hendrickson Publishers, Inc., 2007), pp. 22-35, and pp. 58-80.

[26] *Ibid.*, p. 72.

[27] *Ibid.*, p. 75.

[28] *Ibid.*

[29] *Ibid.*, p. 213-222. See Carol Meyers, *Discovering Eve: Ancient Israelite Women in Context* (New York: Oxford University Press, 1988.)

[30] "Women Priests in Israel: A Case for Their Absence," in Vyhmeister, pp. 29-43.

[31] W. Larry Richards, *1 Corinthians*, pp. 242-244.

[32] *SDA Bible Commentary*, vol. 6, p. 793.

[33] Mark Chaves, *Ordaining Women: Culture and Conflict in Religious Organizations* (Cambridge, Mass.: Harvard University Press, 1997), pp. 91-101.

Chapter 9

The Doctrine of the Church in History

We will now focus our attention on the development of the doctrine of the church in the course of church history. Some will ask: Why should this receive so much attention? Is it not sufficient simply to investigate what we can learn from the Bible and then do our utmost to apply this as best as we can to the praxis of church life? The answer is that this approach is rather shortsighted. Of course, we first need to understand what Scripture says. But by now we have discovered that the Bible does not address with concrete theological instructions all practical issues the church has had to face and that much was left to the creative thinking of God's people, who, led by His Spirit, were challenged to meet ever-changing circumstances on the basis of the broad *principles* the Bible offered them. This challenge remains with us as Christians who live in the twenty-first century—also with Seventh-day Adventist Christians. The dictum that we cannot understand the present without a thorough knowledge of the past also applies to our present domain of study.

It cannot be denied that church doctrine often developed in response to certain crises. This was very much the case with regard to the doctrine of the Trinity, as the church had to deal on the one hand with those who failed to see the threeness in the Godhead and, on the other hand, with those who overemphasized the threeness to the extent that they lost sight of the oneness. Intense debate preceded the wording of a doctrine that attempted to do justice to both aspects. A similar process occurred when the church of the early centuries needed to define the nature of Jesus Christ. Some denied His full humanity, whereas some denied His full divinity. How could the church best defend the view that Jesus Christ is fully God and fully human? And what words could be found to express adequately the relationship of the human and the divine natures of our Lord? Other doctrines and doctrinal formulas likewise owed their origin and development to continuing dialogue and study but usually in the context of debate and controversy—or even heresy.

This same process can clearly be noted with regard to the doctrine of the church, even though this area of Christian dogma was slower to develop. But from early on, important developments took place, and these have continued to take place as time progressed. As we look at church history in general and also at the history of the various traditions within Christianity, we will notice time and again that problems faced by the universal church in some form or another tend to resurface in particular denominations, not excepting the Seventh-day Adventist Church. Our survey in this chapter will have to remain far from complete, but we will attempt to cover the main ecclesiastical players and the main events that had a major influence on the way the thinking of the church about itself developed.

Apostolic Fathers and Apologists

We have looked at the biblical data about the church, its essence, its origin, and earliest development as reported in the writings of the New Testament. Just outside the canon of the New Testament is a group of documents that is usually referred to as the writings of the Apostolic Fathers. These writings, which in their literary form often resemble the writings of the New Testament, date from the early decades of the second century A.D. By that time Christianity had spread to Asia Minor, Syria, Macedonia, Greece, Rome, and even some areas farther away. The name *Apostolic Fathers* was given to these writings (usually eight documents are placed in this category) because of the claim that the authors had known the apostles. This is certainly not true in all cases, but the name suggested a special degree of authority.[1]

Clement of Rome (a presbyter who wrote from Rome to Corinth, c. A.D. 95) was one of these "apostolic fathers." He allegedly was the author of two letters to his home church in Greece, although there is great doubt that he actually authored the so-called Second Letter of Clement. He had an intense regard for the unity of the visible church and emphasized the need of obedience to the leaders. His letter shows awareness of a gradually developing threefold organizational structure: bishop, elder, and deacon. It appears that this Clement (many popes were to adopt his name) was the first to put forward the idea of some form of apostolic succession.[2]

The *Didache,* or *Teaching of the Twelve Apostles,* is a kind of manual on moral and Christian praxis that was discovered in Istanbul in 1873 and is usually also listed among the Apostolic Fathers. The precise date of origin is uncertain. It may come from a community in Palestine or Syria. It reflects a structure of elders/bishops and deacons, but prophets still appear to be of significance. The emphasis is placed on the need to distinguish between true and false prophets.[3]

The third author among the Apostolic Fathers, who shows an ecclesiological interest, is *Ignatius of Antioch,* who may have been a disciple of John. He wrote letters to seven churches while on his way as a prisoner from Antioch to Rome, looking forward to the martyrdom he was facing and hoping that he would be strong enough.[4] He worried about false doctrines and believed that the bishop serves as the guarantor of orthodox beliefs. Unity was the all-important concern for Ignatius.[5] Interestingly, he was the first to use the word "catholic."[6] In Ignatius' letters we see the emerging idea of one local *episkopos* presiding over a college of elders and deacons. The role of bishop was becoming increasingly significant in Ignatius' writings but was not yet fully defined.

The *Apologists* were a group of authors who wrote slightly later than the Apostolic Fathers (around the middle of second century—c. A.D. 130 to 180).[7] As the word indicates, they were challenged to defend the church against mainly false charges. While the Apostolic Fathers targeted the church members and the church leaders, the Apologists mainly addressed the surrounding world and its culture. Often they wrote for the benefit of the emperors, but a wider readership was also intended. Some of the more mundane accusations from the outside world were that Christians committed incest (as a community of "brothers" and "sisters"), ate children, and were involved in all sorts of orgies. Other accusations were of a more intellectual nature. The Gospels were supposedly full of internal contradictions, and Christians were accused of being utterly unpatriotic because they were opposed to emperor worship. Despite such challenges and periods of (local or more widespread) persecution, the church grew and spread. Gradually "rules of faith," simple creedal formulas, were formulated. By the time of the Apologists, there was also a large degree of consensus about the extent of the canon of Scripture.

The Apologists are important in this context because of the information they provide about church life and the further development of liturgical practices. They show that the episcopal system with one single leader (*episkopos*—bishop) became universally accepted, while bishops of prominent churches (in provincial centers) were acquiring a special status. The growing prestige of the Roman bishop is one aspect to be noted. This was, in particular, evidenced in the controversy about the day on which Easter ought to be kept. Polycarp, the bishop of Smyrna (c. A.D. 69 to c. 155), was involved in this debate, and so were Melito, the bishop of Sardis (d. c. A.D. 180), who reportedly was a prolific writer,[8] and later Church Father Irenaeus (c. A.D. 130 to 200).

In this so-called Quartodeciman Controversy, those who always wanted to celebrate Easter on the fourteenth of the Jewish month of Nisan (the day of the Jewish Passover) were vigorously opposed by those who wanted this Christian feast to be on the Sunday following Nisan 14. The bishop of Rome had clear views on the matter, and eventually "pope" Victor got himself involved and tried to settle the matter by excommunicating Polycrates, the bishop of Ephesus (c. A.D. 190). Nothing further is known of this Polycrates, but the conflict with Victor is an important signal of the growing importance of the role of the bishop of Rome.[9]

Irenaeus is a key theologian of the late second century. He was probably born in Smyrna in Asia Minor and later settled in Rome and from about A.D. 178 was bishop of Lugdunum in the Roman province of Gaul (today: Lyon in France). He remains best known for his defense of the Christian faith against the Gnostic heresies that were a major threat to the church of that period. His book *Adversus Omnes Haereses* (*Against All Heresies*) not only enlightens us about these Gnostic teachings but also informs us about Irenaeus' views on Scripture, tradition, and the church. He stated that it is impossible to understand the Christian truth without having access to the tradition that is handed down by the apostles rather than by means of the secret traditions of the Gnostics.[10] It is at that point that he introduced in his book against the Gnostic heretics the outline of the concept of apostolic succession.[11] It is because of the unbroken apostolic chain that the church is the sole repository of the truth.[12]

Developments in the Third and Fourth Centuries

Montanism was an important movement in the second part of the second century that illustrates another significant facet of the church's development. Montanism "represented the perennial protest that occurs in the church when there is an overelaboration of machinery and lack of dependence on the Spirit of God."[13] This statement may betray some bias, but students of church history will indeed discover a recurring tension between the ecclesiastical bureaucracy and the more prophetic or charismatic elements in the church. Glimpses of this phenomenon can also easily be detected in Adventist history and contemporary Adventist church life. The attraction that Montanism held for many illustrates a regularly recurring trend. When hierarchical bureaucracy becomes predominant, almost invariably there is on the part of many believers a deep desire for charismatic leadership and for a greater emphasis on the role of the Holy Spirit.

Montanism started around A.D. 156 in Phrygia, Asia Minor, was propounded by Montanus, an ex-priest of the goddess Cybele (a pagan goddess who was widely worshipped in the ancient world). Montanus believed that he was the mouthpiece of the Holy Spirit. He was soon joined by prophetesses Maximilla and Priscilla. The movement placed strong emphasis on the power of the Holy Spirit and was extremely critical of the development of an ecclesiastical hierarchy. This was accompanied by a fervent expectation of the Second Coming. The explanation of the rapid rise of Montanism is, at least in part, to be found in the steady decline of charismatic leadership in the church, as bishops and teachers replaced prophets.

The movement spread rapidly but became less "wild" as it came westward. It reached North Africa around A.D. 200. The fact that Church Father Tertullian joined the movement gave added prestige to it. Montanism survived until the sixth century, when it was crushed by Emperor Justinian (A.D. 527-565).[14]

A final conclusive evaluation remains difficult. The negative comments on the errors of Montanism originated with its opponents and were loaded with prejudice. The fact that a man like Tertullian became a Montanist gives, however, food for some thought and may indicate that Montanism may well have had some attractive features that are no longer highlighted.

Cyprian, the bishop of Carthage in North Africa (A.D. 248 to 258), was the first Church Father to formulate a somewhat detailed doctrine of the church. Many of the later Roman Catholic emphases are discernible in his main work *De Catholicae Ecclesiae Unitate* (*Unity of the Catholic Church*) (A.D. 251). His most famous dictum was: "*Extra ecclesiam nulus salus*" ("Outside the church there is no salvation"). Another well-known statement of Cyprian was: "You cannot have God as your Father if you do not have the church as your mother!" Cyprian consistently stressed the role of the bishop. Episcopal authority was directly linked, he argued, to apostolic authority, and since Peter was the "prince" of the apostles and the bishop of Rome, Peter's successor would naturally have first place among the bishops. Cyprian thus was the first to make the primacy of Peter an integral part of the theory of church governance.[15] From a Protestant perspective Cyprian is therefore, in particular, remembered for his "grand contribution to the progress of error and corruption in the church."[16]

Cyprian had to deal with the fallout of a movement that came to be referred to as Novatianism, a byproduct of the empire-wide persecution that was instigated by Emperor Decius (A.D. 249 to 251). The church members who had been directly subjected to these persecutions fell into four classes: (1) *martyrs,* who had sacrificed their lives; (2) *confessors*, that is, those who were put in prison and were later released, but did not deny their faith (they enjoyed a high prestige); (3) *sacrificati*, that is, those who had agreed to offer sacrifices in order to save their skin, and the *thurificati*, who had done likewise but had offered only incense; and (4) the *libellatici*, those who accepted a certificate, without actually bringing the sacrifice. When the persecutions relented, the issue was this: should the people in categories (3) and (4) get a second chance? Some argued they should not be allowed to retain or regain their church membership. Others wanted to be more lenient and to allow them to come back with or without conditions. Novatian, a Roman presbyter, became a leader among those who wanted to be very strict. Before too long the issue led to a major schism. Cyprian agreed to a large extent with Novatian's views, which led to very tense relationships between him and the bishop of Rome, who promoted a less strict attitude. Clearly Cyprian's respect for the bishop of Rome did not yet, at this stage, imply a blind subjection to the opinion of the Roman bishop.[17]

The Novatian controversy represents a very practical problem that is as relevant today as it was in the third century. It forced the church and its leaders to rethink the "borders" of the church. At what point can a person no longer be regarded as a member of the body of Christ? What are the conditions that may legitimately be imposed on people, who have openly apostatized, before they can be readmitted into church membership? The Novatian controversy led to still another hotly debated question. If people had been baptized by schismatics, was this baptism valid, or should such people be rebaptized when joining the regular church? Yes, Cyprian said, supported by many other bishops. No, said Stephen, the bishop of Rome. He maintained that baptisms performed by schismatics and heretics were not invalidated by their adherence to wrong doctrine, as long as those baptized had been baptized in the name of the Trinity. This particular point of disagreement has resurfaced time and again in different denominational settings.[18]

Subsequent Developments

The issue that caused the protest of Novatianism returned in an even more urgent form in the *Donatist movement* about a century later, during the fierce Diocletian persecution that lasted for about a decade (A.D. 303 to 313). (Donatus, who gave his name to the movement, was one of the leaders of the schism that resulted.) This time there was a group of *traditores*, who had not stood firm in the face of persecution but had been willing to surrender the copies of the Scriptures that they possessed when the Roman authorities had declared such possession illegal. What to do with them? Should they be rebaptized if they wanted to be readmitted to the church? The related question that we already noted above and that would keep coming back throughout history is this: Is the validity of the sacraments of the church (baptism and the Lord's Supper) affected by the spiritual state of the one who administers them?

The famous Church Father Augustine (A.D. 354 to 430), the bishop of Hippo in North Africa, was the main person to respond to this and a number of other doctrinal challenges (such as the controversy about faith and works, original sin, predestination, and the role of the human will). His autobiography still makes fascinating reading.[19] Augustine's most famous book probably remains his *De Civitate Dei* (*On the City of God*),[20] in which he explains how he views the relationship between the Christian faith and other religions and the relationship of the church to the Roman government. This "tale of two cities" (the city of God versus the pagans) provides a unique Christian philosophy of history that would remain extremely influential.

Of special importance for our present study are Augustine's views of the church. Augustine emphasized that in this life it will always be impossible to fully separate the wheat from the tares. The church is holy not because all its members are perfect but because it will be made perfect in holiness in the end of time. The visible church was important for Augustine. The apostolicity of the church was rooted in the apostolic succession, with the bishop of Rome in first place, but the visible church did not fully coincide with the invisible body of the elect. The church is always a mixed community, with sinners in various stages of spiritual growth. This conflicted with the Donatist view, which urged that the church be "pure."[21] Again we see an issue that has returned time and again throughout the church's history, in particular during the time of the Reformation and one that is not unfamiliar to Seventh-day Adventism. Many Adventists continue to struggle with the question whether the church is a community of saints or a school for sinners and continue to find it difficult to accept that somehow the church is both.

One aspect should be added that also had its echo throughout history. The Donatists, who insisted that their church was the real church because it was a fellowship of saints only, has often been regarded as a kind of prototype of the "free" churches that would later be established in protest against the "state" churches that had developed in post-Reformation times in several European countries. The Donatists refused to allow any interference of the Roman state, whereas Augustine did not fully separate the church from the state and at a given time was even willing to accept assistance from the state in dealing with what he considered a dangerous heresy.[22]

One of the most important processes in the period between the early centuries and the end of the Middle Ages and the onset of the Reformation was, of course, the further development of the power of the Roman pontiff and of the system of church governance that went with it. As the church expanded, several prominent centers gained in special esteem: Alexandria, Antioch, Constantinople, Jerusalem, and Rome. History testifies of intense rivalry between the leaders of these churches, but in particular between those of Constantinople and Rome. By the end of the fifth century A.D., the bishop of Rome, who since the third century was referred to as *papa* (pope), had clearly acquired a position of special prominence.

Pope Damasus of Rome (A.D. 366-384) refused to recognize an important council that was held in Constantinople (A.D. 381) because it had no participation from Rome. Innocent I (A.D. 402-417) played a major role in attempts to impose disciplinary and liturgical uniformity in the church in the West. His successor, Pope Zosimus (A.D. 417-418), claimed that Rome's authority was such that no one should dare to dispute a decision made by its bishop. Pope Leo "the Great" (A.D. 440-461) argued that his position exceeded that of other bishops and that his authority, as the heir and vicar of Peter, extended over the entire church. These claims were certainly not accepted by all other bishops, but they indicated the growing prestige of the bishop of Rome, which culminated with Pope Gelasius I (A.D. 492-496), who convened in synod in Rome (A.D. 495) which declared Rome's "principality" over the whole church.[23]

As the church developed, the role of the sacraments was increasingly emphasized, and the structure of the church was more and more characterized by a hierarchical system. The laity became fully subjected to those who had been ordained as professional clergy. The people's involvement in the selection of church leaders steadily diminished until it virtually disappeared. Celibacy had existed in the church since apostolic days, as a free option, but from the fourth century onward began to be imposed by disciplinary laws. While the difference grew between the nonordained and the ordained, another chasm deepened steadily between those who lived "normal" Christian lives and those who dedicated themselves to a monastic life of greater perfection.

Christian monasticism dates from the early centuries. It originated in Egypt and spread from there increasingly also to the West. As the Middle Ages progressed, monastic orders, each with their own rules, multiplied.[24] And although many positive things can undoubtedly be said about various aspects of monastic life and even though many men and women in the cloisters lived a life of great piety and were utterly dedicated to their God and to helping their fellow human beings or to pursuing all kinds of worthy academic goals, from a Protestant perspective both the separation between laity and clergy and the creation of a spiritual elite in the monastic orders were regrettable demonstrations of an almost total disregard for the biblical principle of the priesthood of all believers.

As the Middle Ages wore on, the balance of power in the church continued to shift toward Rome. Increasingly that power was not just spiritual but also very earthly. The popes believed they had the right to crown emperors and kings, and on several occasions popes felt that they could excommunicate or even depose rulers they felt dissatisfied with. The famous Bernard of Clairvaux (A.D. 1090-1153) applied the title "Vicar of Christ" to Pope Eugenius III. Pope Innocent III (A.D. 1160-1216) further expanded its application and interpretation. As in Christ priesthood and kingdom were combined, he argued, so the pope is both priest and king, and he therefore has greater authority than any earthly ruler.[25] The medieval growth of papal power, which climaxed with Pope Boniface VIII (A.D. 1294-1303) and his papal bull *Unam Sanctam*, in which he defended his jurisdiction over all creatures on earth, was not uncontested and there were those (the "conciliarists") who contended that general church councils should have the final say in ecclesiastical decisions rather than one man in Rome. Eventually, the "forerunners" of the Reformation, such as Wycliff and Huss, minced no words in rejecting the papal claims and the system the Papacy represented as contrary to Bible principles.

However, before a full-fledged Reformation took place in the sixteenth century, a major split in Christianity occurred when the schism between Western Christianity and Orthodox Christianity in the East came about. After a long process of increasing estrangement, the final separation came in 1054. A disagreement between the church of the West and the churches in the East about the word *Filioque* (which concerned the relationship between the Holy Spirit and Father and Son, respectively) figured prominently in the theological debates that took place just prior to the schism. But it is abundantly clear that questions of authority and power, in particular of the bishop of Rome, were at the real heart of the controversy. Other factors certainly also played a role (such as the role of Latin and Greek, respectively; the divergent views on the value of images; and the question of celibacy), and in the centuries to come the two ecclesiastic blocks would drift further and further apart. We easily recognize this deplorable phenomenon again and again, in the history of the church and in the history of individual denominations, that beneath the debate on theological subtleties, another issue—that of power—usually is at stake. Today the churches of the East are grouped in a number of independent national churches (the "autocephalous" churches), each governed by its own patriarch.

The Time of the Reformation

The sixteenth century reformation of the church, with Ulrich Zwingli, Martin Luther, and John Calvin as the main players, changed the ecclesiastical scene more drastically than any other event in church history. At first reluctant to separate from the mother church, the fierce resistance they encountered from the established church left the Reformers with no other option. Having broken away from the mainstream of the Catholic Church over the doctrine of grace, the Reformers came under increasing pressure to develop a coherent theory of the nature of the church, which would justify this break and provide a theological basis for the new evangelical churches springing up in the cities of Western Europe. "Where Luther is especially linked with the doctrine of grace, Martin Bucer and John Calvin are the ones who made the decisive contributions to the development of the Protestant understandings of the church. Those views have become increasingly significant in global Christianity." Thus Alistair E. McGrath succinctly summarizes the new chapter in the history of ecclesiology.[26]

Any reader who is not conversant with the main characters and events of the Reformation period would be well advised to take some time to brush up on the Reformation period. There were others Reformers before and besides Luther, Zwingli, and Calvin, but here we will briefly focus on just those three key leaders. We will have to limit ourselves to the main points that these men championed and to the movements of which they became the spiritual fathers, but we will also have a few words to add about the "radical" Reformers. It becomes quickly apparent that Adventism has been influenced by practically all of these persons and movements of the past, and those who are familiar with recent Adventist history will know that there also are some Adventist voices that prefer a more "congregationalist" model—as was advocated by several Reformers.

Martin Luther (1483-1546)

Since Luther rebelled against the established church and because of his insistence that individual Christians are quite capable of finding access to God when they read the Bible, Luther has often been depicted as someone who held a "low" view of the church. This is far from the truth. He even repeated the words of Cyprian that there is no salvation outside the church.[27] But in his understanding of the church, he moved far away from what he found in the established church of his days. One of the main points of Martin Luther's theology of the church is that church exists where the Word of God is purely preached and heard and where the sacraments are administered according to Christ's instructions.

The rediscovery of the miracle of divine grace leaves no role for a sacerdotal priesthood as special dispensers of grace. The only true priesthood is the priesthood of all believers. The public service in the church is entrusted to the ordained clergy, but the supreme authority in the church is found not in the clergy or the hierarchy but in the Word of God, which must be faithfully preached. Historical community with the early church, in his view, was not sufficient to establish its credential as the true church. A church and its office bearers are legitimized only by theological community with apostolic times.[28] Like Augustine, Luther insisted that the church consists of people who are sinners but that these sinners have been justified (*simul justus et peccator*). A communion of saints is always simultaneously a communion of sinners. In a sense, the church is a "hospital" for the sick. Significantly, Luther prefers the German word *Gemeinde* (community) over the word *Kirche* (church).

Luther further developed Augustine's doctrine of the two kingdoms or the two realms—both of which God created but with different roles. Though church and state each have their own spheres, Luther did not want total separation. He called upon the Christian princes in Germany to provide protection for the believers who faced persecution from the

133

Roman Church, and also allowed civil rulers a degree of control over some ecclesiastical matters. Defenders of the free-church principle have, with some fairness, concluded that eventually this doctrine of the two realms created a persecuting Lutheran state church.[29]

Of further interest to those who study these matters from an Adventist perspective is the fact that although Luther linked baptism with faith, he did not believe that faith has to *precede* baptism. Luther, unfortunately, defended infant baptism and rejected believers' baptism. His view of the Lord's Supper was likewise a compromise between the Roman Catholic doctrine of the Mass and the more biblical view of other Reformers, such as Ulrich Zwingli, who supported a symbolic meaning of the emblems of bread and wine.

Ulrich Zwingli (1484-1531)

The roots of Ulrich Zwingli, an important Swiss Reformer, were in Christian humanism. The Dutch scholar Desiderius Erasmus greatly influenced him. Zwingli's theology was in many aspects similar to that of the other key Reformers, such as Luther, but he also deviated in several ways from them. Zwingli exerted a strong influence on the Radical Reformation.

He was more radical than Luther in rejecting the traditions of the medieval church. Like Luther, Zwingli believed that there is an invisible as well as a visible church. The visible church must be kept as pure as possible, and the local church must play an important role in ensuring the necessary discipline.

Zwingli defended even a much closer connection between church and state than Luther did. (His actual practice came close to a form of theocracy.) Significantly, Zwingli died on the battlefield. Like Luther, he defended infant baptism, but he differed significantly from Luther in his views on the Lord's Supper. He rejected the "bodily presence" in the emblems of bread and wine and defended, as we noted above, a fully symbolical view.

John Calvin (1509-1564)

Of the Reformers, the Genevan pastor-theologian John Calvin made the greatest contribution to the Protestant doctrine of the church. He devoted a major section of his most famous work, *Institutes of the Christian Religion,* to his views on the church. His ideas continue to influence much of Protestantism, in particular the churches of the Reformed tradition.

Luther accepted the things that were not expressly forbidden by Scripture; Calvin accepted only what was clearly taught by Scripture.

Calvin proposed, similar to Luther, what one might call a minimalist definition of the church: the church is where the Word of God is purely preached and heard and where the sacraments are administered according to Christ's instructions. Calvin also differentiated between the perfect invisible church of all the elect and the visible church, in which both elect and reprobate are members. It is not the condition of the members but the presence of the authorized means of grace that determines whether it is the true church. The visible church is a sign of the invisible.

Calvin, in particular, emphasized the need for discipline, which is to be administered by the pastor. He did what he could to implement this in the church in Geneva, which he wanted to turn into a model community. His severe disciplinary actions were vehemently opposed by many, even to the extent that he was forced to leave Geneva temporarily. It led to situations of great intolerance and even to persecution of theological opponents. The best known victim was Michael Servetus (1511-1553), who denied some fundamental Christian doctrines. When arrested upon orders of John Calvin, he refused to recant and was subsequently burned as a heretic.

Calvin maintained that the Bible teaches a fourfold church order: pastor, teacher, elder, and deacon. He insisted that the church must return to the organizational model of early Christianity. Calvin also defended infant baptism. If faith must precede baptism, he reasoned, it becomes a kind of work and no longer symbolizes true grace. Calvin's view of the Lord's Supper is somewhere between that of Luther and Zwingli. He did not believe in the "real presence," but he also believed that Zwingli's view of "mere" symbolism is too meager. He held the opinion that the bread and wine are "signs," which in a very pregnant way show us how the blood and body of Christ are available to us.

In Calvin's thinking, church and state are closely connected. The state is subjected to the church and Christian statesmen are to defend true doctrine. Calvinism soon developed a theory of just war and of resistance against tyranny (on the condition that some clear conditions are met) and defended the use of the death penalty.

The Radical Reformation

Some Reformers were more "radical" than Zwingli, Luther, Calvin, and their associates. They rejected the close link between church and state that would lead to the establishment of "state churches" or "established churches." These "radical" Reformers also wanted to go further than the "mainline" Reformers in several other areas of reform. This at times led to unusual situations, to say the least. The best known episode of extremism was the founding of a theocratic regime in Münster, Germany (1534), by a group of Anabaptists (literally, rebaptizers).

Because of some early excesses, Anabaptism has often received a more negative press than it actually deserves. This is not so unexpected if we recognize that much of church history has been written from the perspective of the major, established churches. Some recent studies have, however, proved to be less biased.[30] The Radical Reformation has provided the roots for such movements as the Mennonites, the Quakers, the Baptists, and the "free" churches in general. Modern evangelicalism can trace some of its major ideas to the Radical Reformation.

One of the main emphases of the Radical Reformation was the outright rejection of infant baptism and the insistence on believers' baptism and a believers' church. Their work led to the formation of several movements and sects, that, because of their insistence that only people who can make a conscious choice to be baptized can belong to the church, were often rather restrictive with regard to church membership and at times extremely strict in the exercise of church discipline. Although some Anabaptist leaders did at times refer to the invisible church, "the main thrust of Anabaptist ecclesiology was toward the implementation in history of the visible church."[31] They wanted a restoration of the New Testament church and clear policies to maintain the purity of the local church. Anabaptists, like so many who were later inspired by their ideas, clearly opted for a congregational approach to church governance.

In contrast with the mainline Reformers, the Anabaptists vigorously defended the principle of total separation between church and state. In consequence of their conviction that faith cannot be coerced, the Anabaptists and their spiritual heirs became staunch defenders of religious freedom.

Methodism

Two Protestant denominations merit special mention. One is still a major world body; the other was small and quickly disappeared from the religious scene, but had a significant impact on the thinking of the Adventist pioneers. Some (for example, James White and Joseph Bates) had belonged to the *Christian Connexion*, an early nineteenth century reform movement in America and is usually labeled "restorationist," that is, desiring to return to simple, pure New Testament Christianity. The early developments of several Adventist doctrines owed much to this influence.[32] In its ecclesiology the "Christians," as they usually called themselves, at first maintained a strong antiorganizational stance, although before too long they formed some "conferences." On the whole, they tended toward a mainly congregational church structure and despised formal creeds.[33]

Other pioneers (as for example, Ellen G. White) came from a *Methodist* background. Methodist influences on Adventism are, in particular, noticeable in the area of church organization. Andrew Mustard notes the pragmatic approach to church organization that characterizes both Methodism and Adventism and refers to the role of camp meetings that were so characteristic of U.S. frontier Methodism and that soon also became a common practice in the Adventist world. Adventism also copied from Methodism the basic structure of local conferences and a General Conference—once they had conquered their earlier reluctance toward all forms of organization.[34]

Roman Catholic Ecclesiology

Adventist teachings regarding the church and its organization have to a large degree been built on the ideas of the Reformers rather than on those of the medieval church and post-Tridentine ideas (that is, after the Council of Trent [1545-1563], which formulated the Roman Catholic reaction to the Reformation) Roman Catholic thinking. From a Protestant perspective, the dominance in the late Middle Ages of scholastic thinking, heavily influenced by the heritage of Greek philosophy and epitomized in the work of Thomas Aquinas (1225-1274), is one of the main points to note. Aquinas' notions about the church were based on his teachings about grace.[35] It is the grace of the Spirit that brings the people to faith and unites them as believers in the mystical body of Christ, the church. The church continues to be seen mostly in its visible and institutional aspects, with the Eucharist as the most important sacrament by which the visible body of Christ grows and thrives.[36]

The other point Protestants regarded with great misgivings is the further development of papal power during the medieval period. The theological position that the kingdom of God virtually coincided with the Catholic Church fed the ambition of "great" popes, such as Gregory VII, Innocent III, and Boniface VIII, and gave the legitimacy to the Roman pontiff to demand that worldly rulers would defer to his authority. The

Roman Catholic ecclesiology was further shaped by the challenge to react to the views of the Reformers. The Council of Trent, which was called to deal with the crisis caused by the Reformation, did not yet venture to draw the ultimate conclusion about the position of the pope, because too many of the bishops were still claiming that their authority was derived from Christ and not from Rome.

In the post–Tridentine period such voices would continue to be heard, but other voices would eventually win the day. Cardinal Robert Bellarmine (1542-1621) defined the church as "the company of all who are bound together by the profession of the same Christian faith and by the use of the same sacraments and under the rule of legitimate pastors and principally Christ's vicar on earth, the Roman pontiff."[37] The development that, as we saw, began in the early centuries eventually culminated in the decisions during the *First Vatican Council* (1869-1870), when the papal power was defined as full and supreme in matters of faith and morals.

Vatican II: Lumen Gentium

Roman Catholic teachings regarding the church have basically remained as they were defined during Vatican I. Yet the Second Vatican Council did place some new accents. One of the key documents to come from the council was the Dogmatic Constitution on the Church, *Lumen Gentium* ("Light of the People"). The name reflects the first words of the document: "Christ is the Light of humanity." It was officially promulgated by Pope Paul VI on November 21, 1964.[38] The document is quite spiritual in tone and refers to the church primarily as "the people of God" rather than defining the church primarily as a juridical, hierarchical, clerical organization. Yet it is clear that these "people of God" belong mainly in the institutional Catholic Church.

The part about the relationship to other Christians evoked much criticism on the part of Protestants. Though the pope, in his opening address to the third session of the council, mentioned "the other Christians," he also insisted that these are "outside of the sheepfold."[39] Protestants found many positive elements in the "schema" on the church, but also discovered that there was no retreat on any of the important Catholic doctrines that relate to the church toward a more biblical position.[40] Several other documents voted by the Vatican II relate to the church, of which the "Declaration on Religious Liberty" was of special importance[41] and undoubtedly represented a change, or at least a revision, from the old doctrine of no religious liberty for non-Catholics.[42]

Since Vatican II, various documents have demonstrated a continuing Catholic interest in dialogue with other Christians and a desire to foster unity, as, for instance, John Paul II's encyclical *Ut Unum Sint* ("that they may be one") of 1995 indicates. This papal document deals with unity with the Orthodox churches as well as with Protestants. But there have since been other signals that have been less encouraging for Protestants and that question anew whether Protestant denominations could actually be called "churches" in the full sense of the word. The document *Dominus Iesus* ("The Lord Jesus"), which was issued by the Congregation for the Doctrine of the Faith and bears the signature of Cardinal Joseph Ratzinger, now Pope Benedict XVI, stated that other Christian denominations were seriously "defective" when compared to the Catholic Church.[43]

Some Contemporary Ecclesiologies

Two Protestant authors in the nineteenth century were very influential in the domain of ecclesiology: Friedrich Schleiermacher (1768-1834) and Albrecht Ritschl (1822-1889).[44] Schleiermacher's view that religion is mainly a matter of feeling influenced his ecclesiology, whereas Ritschl's emphasis on the moral aspect of religion also penetrates his ideas about the church, which he regarded primarily as a community that is faithful to Jesus' moral teachings. These ideas remained influential with liberal theologians at the end of the nineteenth and the beginning of the twentieth century.

A few words should also be devoted to two significant but more recent German theologians—Karl Barth and Hans Küng, an important Protestant and Roman Catholic voice respectively. Karl Barth (1886-1968) was the foremost architect of twentieth century Reformed thinking. But, though rooted in the Reformed tradition, Barth did, in fact, come close to the ecclesiological views of the "free" churches. He placed strong emphasis on the role of the local church and on the giftedness of all members. Barth adamantly opposed infant baptism and any kind of union between the church and the state.[45]

Hans Küng (1928-   ) is a very controversial Catholic thinker who eventually, in 1979, lost his official teaching position because of his alleged departures from official Catholic theology. His two main books on the church, *Structures of the Church*[46] and *The Church,*[47] were, however, written when he was still recognized by the church as an official teacher. His criticism of the concept of papal infallibility, in particular, was not welcomed by Catholic Church leadership.

Evangelical Protestantism

As noted earlier, evangelical Christianity owes much to the ideas of the "radical" Reformers of the sixteenth century. The concept of the church as a voluntary fellowship of believers who join the church of their own initiative through "believers' baptism" has had powerful worldwide appeal. Key emphases are: (1) separation from the world, (2) the importance of church discipline, and (3) the calling of all members to witness about their faith. This latter aspect has played a vital role in the strong growth of evangelicalism. Mission is for most evangelicals—as for Adventists—the raison d'être for the church.[48]

Pentecostalism has become the fastest growing segment of evangelicalism (an estimated worldwide total of 400 million members with an annual growth of some 19 million members). There is considerable theological diversity within the Pentecostal movement. Generally speaking, one notices a lack of carefully crafted theology—certainly in the area of ecclesiology—and a "low" view of history and tradition. Generally speaking, Pentecostals tend to be "restorationist," that is, focusing on returning to what they see as original New Testament religion. They manifest, in the view of most other Christians, a rather one-sided emphasis on the role of the Holy Spirit and on (some of) the gifts bestowed on the believers. A greater charismatic interest is, however, one of the general trends of our times, which can be noticed in many Christian denominations.

Our brief review of the main persons and currents in the history of the doctrine of the church would not be complete without a short reference to the postmodern perspective on the church.

Postmodernity is a reality to reckon with, in particular in the Western world. It has influenced people in their relationship to Christianity and to the church. It has also influenced many church members in more ways than the leadership often recognizes.

Postmodernists are often very open to religiosity of many different sorts, but are extremely suspicious with regard to anything bureaucratic and hierarchical. As a result, they distrust institutional structures and have little use for supralocal structures. If they are interested in the church, it is in the local congregation and not in national or global organizations. For postmodern Christians the local community is of prime importance. It tends to be more important than the actual propositional content of their faith (doctrine). For many, belonging comes before believing.

The content of faith, many postmodern theologians argue, is not based on absolute truth that can be objectively defined. All individuals have their own truth. There are many different interpretations of the Scriptures, one not being more legitimate than the other. It is within the context of a given community that faith receives its formulation in the language that this community happens to use and that is meaningful to that community (without necessarily being meaningful to those outside of that given community). It follows that in this sphere of relativity the urge to disseminate one's convictions is greatly diminished, and "mission" in the traditional sense disappears. It also follows that authority and church discipline will function very differently, if at all. Although postmodern thinking offers some fresh opportunities for the Christian church, it poses very major challenges that one needs to be aware of, especially if one lives and/or works in a largely postmodern environment.

---

[1] For the text of these writings, see, e.g., Edgar J. Goodspeed, *The Apostolic Fathers: An American Translation* (London: Independent Press, Ltd., 1950). The book also offers short notes concerning the authors, the genres they represent, and the most likely dates and areas of provenance.

[2] Justo L. Gonzalez, *A History of Christian Thought* (Nashville: Abingdon Press, 1970), vol. 1, pp. 63-67.

[3] *Ibid.*, pp. 67-71.

[4] *Ibid.*, pp. 71-80.

[5] Jaroslav Pelikan, *The Emergence of the Catholic Tradition,* vol. 1, *The Christian Tradition: A History of the Development of Doctrine* (Chicago/London: University of Chicago Press, 1971), pp. 159, 160.

[6] Letter to Smyrna 8:2.

[7] Louis Berkhof, *The History of Christian Doctrines* (Edinburgh: Banner of Truth Trust, 1937), pp. 56-61.

[8] Joseph B. Tyson, *A Study of the Early Church* (New York: Macmillan Co., 1973), pp. 249, 250.

[9] F. F. Bruce, *The Spreading Flame* (Grand Rapids: William B. Eerdmans Pub. Co., 1958), pp. 211, 276.

[10] Alister McGrath, *Historical Theology: An Introduction to the History of Christian Thought* (Malden, Mass./ Oxford, UK: Blackwell Pub., 1998), pp. 25, 40-42.

[11] Gonzalez, p. 169.

[12] J.N.D. Kelly, *Early Christian Doctrine* (London: A&C Black. 1968), p. 192.

[13] A statement made by Earl E. Cairns, *Christianity Through the Centuries*, p. 111, cited in Carl D. Radmacher, *What the Church Is All About: A Biblical and Historical Study* (Chicago: Moody Press, 1978), p. 53.

[14] For a concise description of Montanism, see W.H.C. Frend, *The Early Church* (London: Hodder and Stoughton, 1965), pp. 80-83.

[15] Bruce, p. 212.

[16] Quoted from William Cunningham, *Historical Theology*, Vol. I, p. 169, in Berkhof, p. 229.

[17] Gonzalez, pp. 242-244.

[18] For a good overview of the Novatian schism and the role of Cyprian, see Frend, pp. 111-115.

[19] A popular edition is Augustine, *Confessions* (London: Penguin Books, 1961).

[20] A good translation is provided by Henry Bettenson and was published in 1984 in the Penguin Classics Series, under the title *City of God*.

[21] Gozalez, vol. 2, p. 50.

[22] Radmacher, p. 54.

[23] For a good review, see Bernard P. Prusak, *The Church Unfinished: Ecclesiology Through the Centuries* (New York/Mahwah, N.J.: Paulist Press, 2004), pp. 120-148.

[24] See, for a good overview: C. H. Lawrence, *Medieval Monasticism: Forms of Religious Life in Western Europe in the Middle Ages* (London and New York: Longman, 1989).

[25] *Ibid.*, pp. 214, 215.

[26] McGrath, *Historical Theology,* pp. 168.

[27] Gonzalez, vol. 3, p. 61.

[28] McGrath, *Historical Theology,* p. 202.

[29] Radmacher, p. 62.

[30] William R. Estep, *The Anabaptist Story: An Introduction to Sixteenth Century Anabaptism* (Grand Rapids: William B. Eerdmans Pub. Co., 1975), pp. xi, xii.

[31] *Ibid.*, pp. 239, 240.

[32] See George R. Knight, *A Search for Identity* (Hagerstown, Md.: Review and Herald Pub. Assn., 2000), pp. 31, 32, 73, 74, 110; *Organizing to Beat the Devil*, pp. 15-18. Also, "Christian Connection," in D. G. Reid et al., eds., *Dictionary of Christianity in America,* p. 255.

[33] Andrew G. Mustard, *James White and SDA Organization: Historical Development, 1844-1881* (Berrien Springs, Mich.: Andrews University Press, 1987), pp. 29-33.

[34] For details about the early moves toward church organization among Methodists, see Richard P. Heitzenrater, *Wesley and the People Called Methodists* (Nashville: Abingdon Press, 1995), pp. 233-260.

[35] For the scholastic view of grace, see Berkhof, pp. 211, 212.

[36] C. Phan, *The Gift of the Church,* p. 30.

[37] Berkhof, p. 234.

[38] The document is found in Austin Flannery, ed., *Vatican Council II: The Conciliar and Post-Conciliar Documents,* study ed. (Northport, N.Y.: Costello Pub. Co., 1987), pp. 350-426.

[39] See, for a discussion from a conservative Protestant perspective, G. C. Berkouwer, *The Second Vatican Council and the New Catholicism* (Grand Rapids: William B. Eerdmans Pub. Co., 1965).

[40] For a discussion of the discussion on the church during Vatican II from an Adventist perspective, see B. B. Beach, *Vatican II: Bridging the Abyss* (Washington, D.C.: Review and Herald Pub. Assn., 1968), pp. 66-171.

[41] For the text, see Flannery, pp. 799-812.

[42] B. B. Beach, *Vatican II*, p. 216.

[43] The text is readily accessible on the Internet: http://www.vatican.va/roman_curia/congregations/cfaith/documents/rc_con_cfaith_doc_20000806_dominus-iesus_en.html

[44] R. Dederen, "The Church," *in SDA Handbook of Theology*, pp. 571-573.

[45] Barth's theology of the church is found, in particular, in the fourth volume of his monumental work *Church Dogmatics* (Edinburgh: T&T Clark, 1975).

[46] New York: T. Nelson, 1963.

[47] New York: Sheed and Ward, 1967.

[48] For a survey of the development in Evangelical theologies of the church, see Mark Husbands and Daniel J. Treier, *The Community of the Word: Toward an Evangelical Theology* (Downers Grove, Ill. InterVarsity Press, 2005).

Chapter 10

One Church for All?

It has often been said that the enormous fragmentation of Christianity is a scandal. Others say it is a sin because it contravenes Christ's direct command that His followers should be one. There is no doubt that, indeed, the degree of division in the Christian church is a scandal, in the original meaning of the word. In classical Greek the word *skandalon* referred to a piece of wood that kept open a trap for animals. In the New Testament the word has the root meaning of a bait or trap, an obstacle on the road that may cause us to fall, or more generally an offense or something that may cause us to stumble in our faith.[1] Unfortunately, many people have lost their confidence in the institutional church because of the endless quarrels and bitter controversies among Christian theologians and clergy as well as between denominations.

But is the fragmentation of Christianity also to be regarded as a sin? It is if sin is understood in the sense of having "missed the mark,"[2] for there is no doubt that the disunity of Christians falls far short of Christ's ideal for the church. If sin is defined as the breaking of a divine commandment and if that unity is defined as organizational unity, Christians are surely in blatant transgression of the divine instruction. Christ commanded in no uncertain terms that His followers should all be one (John 17:21-23). Champions of ecumenism therefore often speak of the "sin of division" in these terms.

However, if the lack of unity among Christians were only an organizational matter or a lack of uniformity in church governance, one could question whether one should speak of "sin" without careful qualification. The fact that church organizations have split has at times been positive. Separations can be fruitful and have "not infrequently provided spiritual and ecclesiastical stimulation."[3] If lack of uniformity in ecclesiastical policy, in worship styles, or evangelistic methods, etc., is viewed as "sin," as it is by some who regard their own method of doing things as the only bibli-

143

cally defensible way, one is clearly on the wrong track. For diversity in such matters is not a sin but rather a testimony to the richness of God's people, who have gathered from among all nations, languages, and cultural and ethnic backgrounds.

The unity that the New Testament looks for among Christ's followers is of a different kind. It is the unity of spirit that exists between kindred souls who share the same ideals and aspirations in their service of Christ. The unity that should exist among the disciples of Christ (John 17:11) must find its inspiration in the unity that exists between Christ and His Father. The twelve, to whom the command to be one was originally addressed, had recently been engaged in a controversy as to who would have the first places among them in the kingdom of Christ (Luke 22:24-30). The "complete unity" that Christ demanded from them would also be a key characteristic of all "those who will believe" in Christ as the result of their preaching of the gospel and would be an unmistakable testimony of the authenticity of their faith (John 17:20-23). "The unity springing from the blended lives of the Christians would impress the world of the divine origin of the Christian church."[4] There would be a diversity of spiritual gifts (1 Cor. 12), but the believers would all form parts of one "body," that is, share in the spiritual unity that is available in Christ. In 1 Corinthians 1:10 the apostle Paul exhorts the believers to avoid internal divisions. He then explains what he means: "That you may be perfectly united in mind and thought."

Does this perfect unity "in mind and thought" imply full theological agreement? Is that what we should also conclude from such statements as Ephesians 4:4, where we are reminded that Christians share "one Lord, one faith, one baptism"? Is that what Ellen White also presupposes in her comments on this subject? "God is leading a people out from the world upon the exalted platform of eternal truth, the commandments of God and the faith of Jesus. He will discipline and fit up His people. They will not be at variance, one believing one thing, and another having faith and views entirely opposite, each moving independently of the body. Through the diversity of the gifts and governments that He has placed in the church, they will all come to the unity of the faith."[5] The context makes clear, however, that she is referring to key points of the church's teachings and not to doctrinal minutiae, and in her works statements that underline her view that not all church members have to think alike in all points of scriptural interpretation abound.

Ellen White leaves no doubt that she views the unity Christ called for in spiritual rather than doctrinal or organizational terms. "The golden chain of love, binding the hearts of the believers in unity, in bonds of fellowship and love, and in oneness with Christ and the Father, makes the connection perfect, and bears to the world a testimony of the power of Christianity that cannot be controverted."[6] If we follow along this path, we can only conclude that a lack of spiritual unity among Christians is indeed sin. But in addressing this issue, we will begin not by looking at ways to remedy the organizational fragmentation of Christianity but by focusing on the sin in our own hearts that prevents us from living in unity with fellow believers in our own environment. And when we draw the circle wider, we will want to focus first on the lack of unity in our own church community before we say something meaningful about the wider disunity in Christianity. In essence, the goal of Christian unity is never primarily a program or a strategic plan. When we repeat the words of the credo of the early church about the "*one* holy, catholic and apostolic church" we confess that Christian unity is not mainly a human effort but is "a matter of the Christian faith, and not something subject to our disposition or a matter of considerations of mere utility."[7]

A Call for Restoration of Organic Unity

Through the centuries, persons and movements have tried to reverse the trend toward ever greater fragmentation of the church and have worked for a restoration of organizational unity. But the ecumenical movement as we know it today dates only from about a century ago. In the late nineteenth and early twentieth centuries a number of significant ecumenical congresses were held in which students and other young people took the lead. The Edinburgh Missionary Conference of 1910 is often seen as the formal beginning of the modern ecumenical movement. American church historian Mark Knoll lists it as one of the "turning points in the history of Christianity."[8] The congress was the result of an increasing awareness of the need for greater unity among Christians if its worldwide mission was going to be accomplished any time soon. After World War I further developments were the Faith and Order and the Life and Work movements. Eventually formal organizations were founded, including the World Council of Churches, which was born in 1948 in Amsterdam.

Soon many regional and national ecumenical organizations were established. The aim of these organizations is to work toward greater organizational unity. Some significant successes have been achieved. A fairly large number of denominations have, often after long and difficult negotiations, decided to mutually recognize the validity of the sacraments as administered in their traditions, and some denominations have actually fully merged and some important denominational alliances have been formed. In the United States between 1900 and 1970 some 30 mergers were realized, among them the United Methodists and the United Presbyterians. The united Church of South India is another significant merger.[9] A remarkable example is also the creation of the new 2-million-member Protestant Church in the Netherlands, in which two major denominations of Calvinist origin and a much smaller Lutheran Church fully merged.

It would seem, however, that in the past few decades the ecumenical movement has begun to run out of steam. Many conservative Protestant denominations have found the World Council of Churches and various other national ecumenical councils too liberal or too political and have either simply decided to stay outside or have formed their own organizations. The Orthodox churches of Eastern Europe have been remarkably open toward dialogue with other Christians, yet have tended to regard other churches as heterodox communities that must eventually accept their Orthodox teachings. The Roman Catholic Church has not joined the World Council of Churches, and Catholic ecumenical initiatives and involvements seem to have slowed down in recent years. By and large, the contemporary ecumenical movement tends to emphasize dialogue and the need for a better mutual understanding and cooperation in areas in which doctrinal diversity is no immediate problem, rather than striving mainly for "organic" unity. In addition, it should be noted that in our changing world, the spotlight is also increasingly on the non-Christian religions—Islam in particular. This development puts the relationship between Christianity and other world religions high on the agenda.

Adventists and Ecumenism

The Seventh-day Adventist Church continues to face a major dilemma. On the one hand, it is interested in positive relationships with other Christian bodies. Church leadership, therefore, seeks dialog with other Christians and will eagerly cooperate in any number of areas. On the other hand, a strong suspicion lingers with regard to the motives of many other Christian bodies, which is fueled by the Adventist views regarding the end of time and traditional Adventist self-understanding.[10] A clear concept of what the Adventist identity is and a sound ecclesiology are needed if the church wants to move from a mostly pragmatic and at times somewhat opportunistic approach toward ecumenism to a strategy that is, first of all, based on a theological understanding of the doctrine of the church.

From quite early on in its history, the Adventist Church has been willing—and sometimes eager—to dialogue with other Christians. When the World Missionary Conference in Edinburgh, to which we referred above, took place in 1910, three Adventist delegates were among the participants. It has been the consistent policy of the Adventist Church ever since to send observers to important ecumenical gatherings—for instance, to the four sessions of the Second Vatican Council (1962-1965)[11] as well as to major meetings of the World Council of Churches and other international ecumenical congresses.

Three ecumenical encounters between Adventists and others should perhaps receive special mention. During 1955 and 1956 a series of six conferences were held between Walter Martin and a few other Evangelicals and a small group of Adventists leaders.[12] Walter Martin, a member of the editorial staff of *Eternity* magazine, wanted to write a critical book about Adventism and had sought more information before starting his writing. The ensuing consultations led not only to a series of rather positive articles about Adventism in *Eternity* and to Martin's book *The Truth About Seventh-day Adventism* (which Adventists considered as quite fair), but also to an important Adventist publication: *Seventh-day Adventists Answer Questions on Doctrine.*[13] This book has remained rather controversial, but has undoubtedly played an important role in positioning Adventism as a truly "Christian" church.

Between 1965 and 1971 annual consultations were held between representatives of the World Council of Churches and the Seventh-day Adventist Church. The initial purpose of the talks was "to acquaint each side with the structure, functioning and thinking of the other side."[14] Subsequent consultations, however, moved from the level of a mere sharing of information to serious theological discussions on such issues as law and grace, Sabbath and Sunday, and eschatology. Although it became clear that these consultations would not lead to an application for membership of the Adventist Church in the World Council of Churches, they clearly resulted in a better mutual understanding and created channels for ongoing communication.

It should also be noted that the Seventh-day Adventist Church has for several decades fully participated in the meetings of the Christian World Communions, an interchurch forum that provides a regular opportunity for dialogue between leaders of "world confessional families," such as

Baptists, Adventists, Anglicans, Lutherans, etc. Since 1968, the Roman Catholic Church has also been represented at these meetings.[15]

Recent ecumenical encounters of Adventists with other Christians included serious bilateral conversations with the Lutheran World Federation[16] and extended dialogue with the World Alliance of Reformed Churches, the Salvation Army, the Presbyterian Church (U.S.A.), and the World Evangelical Alliance.

Adventists and Roman Catholics

Adventist leaders have untiringly emphasized that they are not anti-Catholic bigots. But they continue to maintain absolute disagreement with a number of Catholic doctrines and with what they consider unacceptable ambitions of the Roman Catholic Church. William G. Johnsson, former editor in chief of the *Adventist Review*, once admonished his readers that "there are devout men and women among Roman Catholics whose spirituality and ethical concerns put many Adventists to shame." He hastened to add, however, that Roman Catholic theology centers in the human priesthood and the Mass, whereas Protestantism centers in the salvation provided by Christ; Roman Catholicism builds its beliefs on the Scriptures *and* on tradition, whereas Protestantism rests on the Bible alone. Yet Johnsson was adamant that any Catholic-bashing ought to be a thing of the past.[17]

On April 15, 1997, the General Conference of Seventh-day Adventists released, through the office of its world president, a statement entitled "How Seventh-day Adventists View Roman Catholicism." The statement was triggered by a number of unfortunate incidents in which Adventists had attacked the Catholic Church. The statement underscores the validity of the traditional prophetic views of Adventism. It states that Adventists are convinced that eventually "world religions—including the major Christian bodies as key players—will align themselves with the forces in opposition to God and to the Sabbath." Nevertheless, the first paragraph of the statement is equally important: "Seventh-day Adventists regard all men and women as equal in the sight of God. . . . We gladly acknowledge that sincere Christians may be found in other denominations, including Roman Catholicism, and we work in concert with all agencies and bodies that seek to relieve human suffering and to uplift Christ before the world." The last paragraph is also worth quoting: "Adventists seek to be fair in dealing with others. Thus, while we remain aware of the historical record and continue to hold our views regarding end-time events, *we recognize some positive changes in recent Catholicism,* and stress the conviction that many Roman Catholics are brothers and sisters in Christ.[18]

Recently Adventist attention with regard to Catholicism has been focused on Pope John Paul II's pastoral letter *Dies Domini* of May 31, 1998, which urged Catholics to be more faithful in attendance at Mass and pleaded for a new respect for Sunday as the day of rest and worship. Naturally, Seventh-day Adventists read this publication with great interest. Not only did they disagree with some of its theology, but many felt alarmed at the pope's suggestions that there might be a role for the state in the protection of Sunday rest.[19]

The traditional Adventist interpretation of Daniel and the Revelation and the views of the end-time scenario that have resulted continue, to a very large extent, to set the parameters for the manner in which Adventists regard Catholics and other Christians. Seventh-day Adventists emphatically distance themselves from Roman Catholics and claim to be Protestant Christians. They also do not want to be classified as Fundamentalists, but many increasingly see themselves, and are seen by others, as part of Evangelicalism. It is not without significance that, when Donald W. Dayton and Robert K. Johnston planned their book *The Variety of American Evangelicalism,* they wanted to include a chapter on Adventism.[20]

Although Adventist anti-Catholic rhetoric has throughout recent decades been considerably softened, there is no consensus with regard to the question whether, and if so, how much current Roman Catholicism has changed in comparison to the past. Some argue that in all fairness we must admit that there have been changes—and some very positive ones—during and since Vatican II.[21] Many would contend that any changes that may have occurred are cosmetic rather than genuine. Others take a somewhere middle stance, asserting that there have been important changes but that the theological basics of the Roman Catholic Church remain untouched. A recent example of that approach was found in an article by Woodrow W. Whidden, in which he affirmed "that many positive things have taken place in Roman Catholicism" but then argues that it continues to preach a very distorted gospel.[22]

How to Relate to Other Christians?

When the World Council of Churches was established, the Adventist Church decided not to become a member and has consistently maintained that stance. As a rule, it has also declined to accept full membership in other important ecumenical regional and national councils. Adventists belong to those Christians who "out of concern for truth and the prophetic mission, kept their distance, not sailing on the ecumenical boat, but acknowledging some of the positive achievements, such as religious liberty, less hostile interchurch relations and greater justice in human relations."[23]

Not all objections to membership in ecumenical organizations have been a matter of principle. They are, at times, also pragmatic. One of the reasons that were a factor to keep both the Roman Catholic Church and the Adventist Church outside of the World Council was the fact that as a rule the member churches are national churches rather than worldwide movements.[24] The Adventist Church has consistently advised its organizational units in countries around the world not to accept full membership in ecumenical councils but to participate, where feasible, in an observer's role. This advice is followed in most cases, except where practical circumstances dictate otherwise. (For instance, in some instances observer status is not available.) Around the world many Adventist pastors have found it a positive experience to participate in local interchurch ministerial councils.

It is interesting to note that Ellen White, one of the founders of the Adventist Church, tended to be quite open toward interchurch contacts, in particular on the personal and local level. This is remarkable, considering her rather strong language about other Christian churches and in particular the Roman Catholic Church, in her book *The Great Controversy* and some of her other writings. Yet it is significant to see how she repeatedly appealed to "the brethren" to be careful not to create or cultivate the image of an enemy. Toward the end of her life she wrote: "We should not go out of our way to make hard thrusts at the Catholics. Among the Catholics there are many who are most conscientious Christians and who walk in all the light that shines upon them, and God will work in their behalf."[25] A similar statement is found in *Counsels to Writers and Editors*: "Let not those who write for our papers make unkind thrusts and allusions that will certainly do harm, and that will hedge up the way and hinder us from doing the work that we should do in order to reach all classes, the Catholics included."[26]

In a similar vein Ellen White commented on Adventist relationships with Protestant denominations: "The Lord has not given His people a work of making a tirade against those who are transgressing His law. In no case are we to make a raid on the other churches."[27] She advised Adventist pastors to associate with colleagues of other faith communities and not with the primary aim of convincing them of the correctness of Adventist doctrine. There is, she wrote, "common ground, upon which we can meet people of other denominations; and in becoming acquainted with them we should dwell mostly upon topics in which all feel an interest, and which will not lead directly and pointedly to the subjects of disagreement."[28] She advised Adventist pastors to pray for and with their non-Adventist colleagues. Note that she referred to these pastors of other churches as "shepherds" when she said: "Come near to the ministers of other denominations. Pray for and with these men, for whom Christ is interceding. . . . As Christ's messengers we should manifest a deep, earnest interest in these shepherds of the flock."[29] Ellen White practiced what she preached. During her travels she would at times gladly accept invitations to preach in churches of other denominations.[30] And it has become well known that she in her writings often quoted profusely from authors who belonged to various other Protestant churches.[31]

Principles for a Balanced View on Ecumenical Involvement

Any involvement in ecumenical activities should not be based primarily on pragmatic considerations, such as will it benefit the Adventist Church and/or its ministries and institutions insofar as it creates a useful network? Nor should a decision to refrain from membership in ecumenical councils or from participation in other ecumenical forums depend primarily on fear that a vocal minority of church members may react negatively. These and other pragmatic elements are not totally unimportant aspects, and, as we have seen, the way in which the church organizes itself and operates in the world will always necessitate a degree of creative interaction with circumstances—local, regional, and global. However, pragmatic decisions that may have to be made should be embedded in sound theology. Determining our attitude toward ecumenism and all that it involves requires sound ecclesiological principles. In the final part of this chapter we will attempt to bring some of the basic principles that we have outlined in earlier chapters together and to formulate six principles that may guide the corporate church, pastors, local churches, and individual members in their approach to ecumenical questions.

1. The focus should be on the biblical view of unity. The New Testament originated at a time that predates our present situation with its myriad of religious traditions, denominations, and sects. When the topic of unity is addressed by Christ or the apostolic authors, it concerns not ecumenism as we know it today but rather the spiritual unity among the brothers and sisters of the apostolic church. The church members had a Jewish or a Gentile background and from the beginning manifested a very considerable ethnic and cultural diversity, but there were as yet no formal organizational splits and therefore no questions as to how to work for organizational reunification.

The unity spoken of in the New Testament is a unity in Christ (Eph. 4:1-6), a unity that should not be threatened by a desire for power or an unhealthy attachment to particular leaders (1 Cor. 1:1-13). Any dividing wall between different factions caused by religious, cultural, linguistic, or ethnic traditions (Eph. 2:14-16) had been radically removed in Christ. Christian unity was a spiritual union in which all believers, through the Spirit, would dedicate themselves to the common good of the church (Eph. 4:13). The unity advocated in the New Testament is not unity of an organizational nature (however important that may seem to us), but a unity in the acceptance of Christ as the Lord of our lives and in the desire to be His disciples. This is the kind of unity we should experience in our own faith community—in our local church as well as denomination-wide—and it is the kind of unity we can also experience with many believers who do not belong to the Seventh-day Adventist Church but join us in their determination to follow the Lord Jesus Christ.

In this phase of history secularism is rampant in large parts of the world. Christians must be seen as one in the Spirit of Christ and not as feuding groups that spend most of their time competing against one another and forcefully denouncing one another. And in a time when several dubious postmodern tendencies also threaten the Seventh-day Adventist Church, it is important that Adventism remain united around a common core of beliefs, a common set of values, and a common missionary goal. This kind of "unity in the church reveals Christ's manner and grace more than sermons and arguments."[32]

2.   **Growing unity in doctrine should be the outcome of, rather than a precondition for, fellowship with brothers and sisters in Christ.** The Christ followers in New Testament times were far from united on every point of theology. In fact, during the first century much of the doctrinal fine print as we know it today had not yet been worked out. Views could seriously differ. Paul urged great tolerance with respect to fellow church members who had divergent views with regard to certain practices (Rom. 14). When we look at the history of our own denomination, there was certainly a spirit of unity among the early Adventist believers and their leaders, but nonetheless it took decades to arrive at a general consensus about some of the issues that are now considered fundamental Adventist teaching.

This is not to say that an ongoing search for a better understanding of the theological implications of the biblical writings is of little value. A desire to arrive at sound doctrinal conclusions, and not to be confused by unscriptural ideas, is important, and, as we noted earlier, a conscious denial of the basics of the Christian faith will place us outside of the family of God. In any discussion, whether with members of the religious community to which we ourselves belong or with adherents of other faiths, the goal should always be to advance prayerfully in our understanding of truth.

Several dangers should, however, be recognized and avoided. 1. Doctrinal debates can easily become acrimonious and may at times generate more heat than light. Church history abounds with examples in which small doctrinal differences led to outright war between various parties and at times led to denominational splits about issues that today even the people who belong to the new churches that were formed cannot explain. Any theological discussion that does not manifest Christian courtesy and love cannot be labeled a quest for truth. For, after all, Christ is the truth, and if He cannot be recognized in what happens, it brings a curse rather than a blessing. 2. The opposite point of view, which regards doctrine as totally irrelevant and suggests that all believers are entitled to their own brand of theology, is as popular as it is wrong. It can never be a matter of no consequence what God has revealed in His Word and, guided by the Spirit, we must do all we can to better understand its implications. 3. The third danger is never far when interfaith dialogue between Christians and non-Christians takes place, whether on the personal or the corporate level. It creates bridges when similarities are explored. But there can also be the temptation to deemphasize crucial differences and to overemphasize similarities in viewpoints. One can easily run the risk "of misrepresenting differences in order to make them more palatable to the partner in conversation."[33]

Full doctrinal unity will probably never be achieved, even if these dangers are avoided—not in internal discussions within a particular faith community, or in wider ecumenical consultations. Attempts toward better mutual understanding and finding common ground should, however, never be characterized by church political strategies or compromise, as if truth can be negotiated or can be arrived at by majority vote. It should also always be remembered that full unanimity in doctrinal understanding is not simply synonymous with perfect unity in Christ. But if there is unity in Christ, an important precondition is met to develop a greater degree of doctrinal unity.

3. God's church does not coincide with one particular denomination or religious tradition. This position is based on arguments that we discussed in chapter 5. God has His people in many places, and we should not try to determine whom God regards as His. Seventh-day Adventists believe that the distinction as to who belong to the (remnant) people of God and who have given their ultimate allegiance to Babylon will become clearer as the history of Planet Earth draws to a close.

This end-time scenario naturally tends to color our thinking about our present attitude toward other churches. Often the argument runs somewhat like this: *There may still be many true believers in other denominations, but these churches are on the wrong track, and one day soon they will show their true colors and turn against the remnant Seventh-day-Adventist Church. This,* the argument continues, *should make us careful in entering into any ecumenical dealings with them, even now.* This way of thinking has some serious flaws. First, it assumes that we know in detail what the time of the end will bring. That developments in the world of politics as well as in the realm of religion will escalate is clear from even a cursory reading or Bible prophecy. But God has not considered it necessary or wise to fill the enormous gaps that remain in our knowledge of the final phase of Christianity and with regard to the possible future role of other world religions. We have no idea whether or not the present religious structures (including our own) will even exist when things reach their final crescendo. Second (and this follows from the point just made), it is wrong to judge people and organizations that exist today in the light of what we surmise they might one day become.

From our Adventist perspective, many teachings and practices in other churches do not conform to the Bible. We should not deny or downplay this under the pressure of those who accuse us of being unchristian because they feel we show a lack of ecumenical enthusiasm. But we should gladly recognize the many good things that happen in other Christian communities and should give full credit where credit is due. We should also gladly recognize the intense missionary drive that characterizes some of these other churches. A fear of possible future developments in these denominations is no valid reason in the present not to maintain cordial relationships and not to work together in areas of common interest—even if at times we may be doctrinally at quite a distance from each other. When we consider our attitude toward these other denominations, we should ever be mindful of an incident recorded in the Gospel of Mark. It had come to the knowledge of the disciples that someone had been driving out demons in the name of Jesus. Contrary to what the disciples expected, Jesus did not want them to stop this person, even though the disciples felt that he "was not one of us." Jesus said: "Whoever is not against us is for us" (Mark 9:38–41). Jesus wanted His disciples, at the very least, to give others who might not be doctrinally sound the benefit of the doubt and to recognize the fact that someone who genuinely follows Jesus cannot simultaneously be against Him.

4. The previous three principles lead us to the next one, which has to do with our mission. What we just said under dangers 2 and 3 suggests that Adventists should cooperate with other Christians where and when they can and should happily assist in ecumenical organizations, and that Adventist end-time expectations should not keep us from doing so. There is, however, an important other consideration. If we accept the Adventist self-understanding that we discussed earlier and insist on mission as the raison d'être of the remnant, our priorities become clear. Communicating Christ to those who do not yet know Him and sharing those aspects of Bible truth that many other Christians are not yet familiar with will be the main focus of all that the Adventist Church does—in word and very much also in deed. This may well cause us to decide that our focus on gospel outreach takes preeminence over spending a lot of energy on ecumenical activities, especially since studies show that often strong ecumenical involvement may hamper rather than stimulate mission.[34]

5. Respect for other Christians linked with the conviction that the "remnant" church has a special task will ensure that Adventists communicate their message in full transparency and honesty. Adventists want to go into "all the world," but they gladly recognize that other missionary agencies are "also part of the divine plan for the evangelization of the world."[35] They recognize the full right of church members to change their religious conviction and to leave the Adventist Church, but also insist that all other persons, whatever their religious affiliation (or without such affiliation), should have that same right. Adventist evangelism knows of no human-made boundaries, but should always be conducted according to the highest standards of Christian courtesy and honesty.[36]

6. Relationships with other Christians, whether on the corporate level or between individual Christian believers, ought to be marked by a truly Christlike spirit of humility. In the famous chapter about Christ's unparalleled humility (Phil. 2), God's people are told to be "like-minded" (verse 2) and to do nothing "out of selfish ambition or

155

vain conceit, but in humility [to] consider others better than yourselves" (verse 3). Christians cannot look down on other Christians, because they supposedly are less committed or less sound theologically or in other aspects do not quite reach the norm that they believe their own church has reached or even surpassed. It is unfair to compare the best in one's own church with the worst in someone else's church. It is also unfair to be willfully selective in quoting from various and often outdated sources when criticizing viewpoints that are held by other churches or that their representatives may have held in the distant past.

God's church has no room for triumphalism. We are all sinners, whatever denomination we belong to (Rom. 3:23). And those who feel that they have been blessed with a special divine assignment do well to ever keep in mind the words of Jesus: "From the one who has been entrusted with much, much more will be asked" (Luke 12:48).

[1] Colin Brown, ed., *The New International Dictionary of the New Testament,* (Exeter, U.K.: Paternoster Press, 1976), vol. 2 , pp. 707, 708.

[2] Reinder Bruinsma, *Key Words of the Christian Faith* (Hagerstown, Md.: Review and Herald Pub. Assn., 2008), pp. 66-69.

[3] B. B. Beach, *Ecumenism: Boon or Bane?* (Washington, D.C.: Review and Herald Pub. Assn., 1974), p. 114.

[4] *The Seventh-day Adventist Bible Commentary,* vol. 5, p. 1053.

[5] Ellen G. White, *Testimonies for the Church* (Mountain View, Calif.: Pacific Press Pub. Assn., 1948), vol. 3, p. 446.

[6] Ellen G. White, *God's Amazing Grace* (Washington, D.C.: Review and Herald Pub. Assn., 1973), p. 237.

[7] V.-M. Kärkkäinen, *An Introduction to Ecclesiology,* pp. 79, 80.

[8] Mark A. Knoll, *Turning Points: Decisive Moments in the History of Christianity* (Grand Rapids: Baker Academics, 2000), pp. 268-294.

[9] Bruce L. Shelley, *Church History in Plain Language* (Nashville: Thomas Nelson Pub., 1995). pp. 446-448.

[10] A number of aspects that pertain to this topic are dealt with in B. B. Beach and John Graz, *101 Questions Adventists Ask* (Nampa, Idaho: Pacific Press Pub. Assn., 2000).

[11] B. B. Beach was one of the observers, and attended all four sessions. He regularly reported for the *Adventist Review* on these meetings, and also wrote a book, *Vatican II: Bridging the Abyss* (Washington, D.C.: Review and Herald Pub. Assn., 1968).

[12] R. W. Schwarz, *Light Bearers to the Remnant* (Pacific Press Pub. Assn., 1979), pp. 542f. See also T. E. Unruh, "The Seventh-day Adventist Evangelical Conferences of 1955-1956," *Adventist Heritage* 4 (winter 1977): 35-46.

[13] Washington, D.C.: Review and Herald Publishing Association, 1957. A new, annotated edition was more recently published: George R. Knight, ed., *Seventh-day Adventists Answer Questions on Doctrine* (Berrien Springs, Mich.: Andrews University Press, 2003).

[14] *So Much in Common: Documents of Interest in the Conversations Between the World Council of Churches and the Seventh-day Adventist Church* (Geneva: World Council of Churches, 1973). p. 98.

[15] Ans J. van der Bent, "Christian World Communions," in Nicholas Lossky et al., *Dictionary of the Ecumenical Movement* (Grand Rapids: William B. Eerdmans Pub. Co., 1991), pp. 156-159.

[16] These encounters resulted in a substantial publication titled *Lutherans and Adventists in Conversation* (Silver Spring, Md.: General Conference of Seventh-day Adventists, 2000).

[17] William G. Johnsson, "Adventists and Roman Catholics," *Adventist Review,* June 26, 1997, p. 5.

[18] "How Seventh-day Adventists View Roman Catholicism," *Adventist Review,* May 22, 1997, pp. 21, 22. (Italics supplied.) The statement is also found in *Statements, Guidelines and Other Documents,* pp. 90, 91.

[19] *Dies Domini,* par. 67. See Samuele Bacchiocchi, *The Sabbath Under Crossfire* (Berrien Springs, Mich.: Biblical Perspectives, 1998), pp. 17-58.

[20] Russell L. Staples, "Adventism," in Donald W. Dayton and Robert K. Johnston, *The Variety of American Evangelicalism* (Downers Grove, Ill. InterVarsity Press, 1991), pp. 57-71.

[21] Reinder Bruinsma, "Adventists and Catholics: Prophetic Preview or Prejudice," in *Spectrum,* vol.27, no. 3 (summer 1999): 45-52.

[22] Woodrow W. Whidden, "The Antichrist: Is the Adventist Interpretation Still Viable?" *Adventist Review,* May 25, 2000, pp. 8-13.

[23] Beach and Graz, p. 92.

[24] Beach, *Ecumenism—Boon or Bane?* pp. 286, 287.

[25] White, *Testimonies,* vol. 9, p. 243.

[26] Ellen G. White, *Counsels to Writers and Editors* (Nashville: Southern Pub. Assn., 1946), p. 60.

[27] White, *Testimonies,* vol. 9, p. 236.

[28] White, *Evangelism,* p. 144.

[29] White, *Testimonies,* vol. 6, p. 78; *Evangelism,* pp. 143, 144, 562.

[30] Herbert E. Douglass, *Messenger of the Lord: The Prophetic Ministry of Ellen G. White* (Nampa, Idaho: Pacific Press Pub. Assn., 1998), pp. 128, 129.

[31] *Ibid.,* pp. 456-465.

[32] White, *Evangelism,* p. 342.

[33] Angel Manuel Rodríguez, "Adventists and Ecumenical Conversation," *Ministry,* December 2003, p. 8.

[34] Beach, *Ecumenism—Boon or Bane?* pp. 177-188.

[35] *Working Policy of the Seventh-day Adventist Church,* Policy O 10.

[36] See "Relationships With Other Christian Churches and Religious Organizations" in *Statements, Guidelines and Other Documents* (Silver Spring. Md.: Communication Department, General Conference of Seventh-day Adventists, 2005), pp. 219, 220.

Chapter 11

The Church and Social Justice

In its proclamation, to what extent should the church focus on social issues? Should the church take the lead in campaigns against injustice, discrimination, and poverty? Should the church use some, or a great deal, of its resources in the war against hunger, the battle against HIV/AIDS, and earmark money and human resources for the realization of humanitarian projects in the developing nations? Should the church raise its prophetic voice against events and developments in the political arena and against specific legislation in particular countries, or should it hesitate to voice a political opinion? Should the church perhaps leave initiatives in all such areas to other organizations and focus the limited resources of its own labor supply, institutions, and finances uniquely on the preaching of the gospel in the special context of the times we live in?

Different answers have been given. In times long past most charitable activities, such as almshouses, care for widows and orphans, and even hospitals were in the domain of the medieval church. Later both Catholic and Protestant missions in foreign lands were usually accompanied by strong initiatives in the realm of healing and teaching.[1] Even the world-renowned Red Cross has Protestant roots in Geneva.

When the modern nation-state developed and carved out an increasingly large societal role for itself, the church and church-related organizations such as certain monastic orders and charitable foundations largely abandoned this field of action. But there were also a few other developments that should be mentioned, which had a major impact on the way in which the church—and in particular the Evangelical movement—related to social challenges in the world.

One of these developments was the prominent role of the so-called Social Gospel movement during the late nineteenth and early twentieth centuries. It was a (mainly Protestant) response to the widespread social abuses that accompanied the rapid industrial development in the Western

158

world, and it prided itself on being "Christian." It wanted to Christianize the social, economic, and political institutions in society, as well as family and individual life, since the kingdom of God was to embrace the entire human life. The church has the task, it was argued, to be the conscience and guide for the transformation of social order.[2]

Walter Rauschenbusch (1861–1918), a Baptist minister in New York City, in his famous book *A Theology for the Social Gospel*[3] provided the movement with what came closest to a systemic theological foundation. Rauschenbusch's book was widely praised by many but was also heavily criticized because of its alleged liberal approach to the gospel. The present realization of the kingdom of God receives primary emphasis. "The saving power of the church," Rauschenbusch wrote, "does not rest on its institutional character, or its continuity, its ordination, its ministry, or its doctrine. It rests on the presence of the kingdom of God within her."[4] The Social Gospel movement placed strong emphasis on (1) the immanence of God and the realization of the kingdom of God in society, (2) justice rather than mere charity, and (3) the connectedness of personal salvation and the salvation of society at large.[5]

The ideas espoused in the Social Gospel movement remained influential. Martin Luther King, Jr., is but one important leader who acknowledged his intellectual debt to Rauschenbusch. But it also aroused strong opposition from the Roman Catholic Church, as well as from orthodox Protestants and from early-twentieth-century revivalist preachers.[6] The growing evangelical segments of Christianity vehemently rejected the Social Gospel and its kingdom theology.[7]

The Roman Catholic Church, for a long time, had to use much of its energies in its struggle with the political forces in Europe, and it was not until the papacy of Leo XIII (1878–1903) that the church began to pay real attention to social issues in the world. The famous 1891 encyclical *Rerum Novarum* gave a clear sign that at last the church was ready to address matters of grave social concern. The pope urged the creation of a network of clerically led Catholic associations for social, benevolent, and economic purposes.[8] This emphasis on "Catholic Action" and the call for the membership to refrain from any political and social organizations that were not Catholic has long characterized the approach of the Roman Catholic Church to activities in the social sphere. Since *Rerum Novarum* several other important documents have been published by the Catholic hierarchy.

As the Catholic social tradition developed, a number of elements emerged. The most prominent among them are (1) the emphasis on the dignity of the human person, as, in particular emphasized in the 1968 encyclical *Humanae Vitae* ("Of Human Life"), by Pope Paul VI;[9] (2) the emphasis on the family as a basic societal unit; (3) the dignity of work and of the worker, and (4) the preferential option for poor individuals.

The social activities of the Catholic Church, especially through the many religious orders that were dedicated to helping humanity, should not be underestimated. Yet in many places in the world the Catholic Church was not, even by a majority of its own members, perceived as having truly opted for those who were poor and those disenfranchised. This fact was one of the main conditions for preparing the way for another prominent current in Christian thought, so-called liberation theology.

The expression "liberation theology" in itself is rather vague, and one might well ask how many different such theologies exist. Several local theologies around the world have strong resemblances to the main features of liberation theology, and feminist theology as well as Black theology are closely related to it. The most prominent theologians of the movement are individuals such as Gustavo Gutierrez, José Miguez-Bonino, and Leonardo Boff.

Liberation theology is rooted in Latin America, where its origin must be understood against the background of colonial oppression and, subsequently, the enormous inequality between those rich and poor people. The institutional church was usually seen as protecting rich persons rather than defending poor people. Although liberation theology looks to the Bible for inspiration in its fight against injustice, it is heavily impacted by the social sciences for its methodologies, and its leaders were convinced that political involvement was essential if any concrete success in fighting poverty was to be obtained.[10] In North America and Europe this type of theology got a very mixed reception. In many liberal and ecumenical circles it was quite favorably received, while, in particular, most Evangelicals (even in Latin America) believed that liberation theology caricaturized the gospel. One Evangelical author summarized it as follows—and no doubt expressed a sentiment that was (and is) quite common in Evangelicalism: "True Liberation Theology is not merely ardent social concern wedded to orthodox Christian Beliefs: it is a theological and doctrinal revolution that stands in opposition to the very foundations of traditional Christian doctrine."[11] Evangelicals feared that salvation would no longer be expected from Christ's heavenly intervention but rather from human social and humanitarian effort.

The great hesitancy on the part of Evangelicals to place major emphasis on social issues and to make the caring for physical and social needs a vital part of their mission outreach was certainly also reinforced by the Modernist-Fundamentalist controversy in the early and mid-twentieth century, in which the sympathy of most Evangelicals lay with the Fundamentalists to a large extent. The heavy emphasis on biblical truth and correct doctrine tended to eclipse all other concerns. In addition, the fact that much of the earlier optimism that fueled the Social Gospel movement had evaporated—a process that was further strengthened by the depression of the 1920s and 1930s and World War II—did not help to put social concern on the ecclesiastical agendas of orthodox Protestants and Evangelicals.

There was, however, a remarkable change in Evangelical thinking in the 1950s, which has at times been referred to as "the great reversal."[12] Since that time many Evangelical agencies for national and international aid have been founded, and increasingly Evangelicals have come to believe that the mandate given to the Christian church is not limited to preaching but must include healing, teaching, and advocacy for justice.

The Adventist Church and Social Concerns—in the Past

The history of Adventist activities in the realm of healing, teaching, and development work has some similarity with what we can see in the Evangelical world at large, even though there are also major differences. For one thing, Adventism from its very inception, not in the least through the influence of James and Ellen White, not only concentrated on discovering and disseminating "present truth," but soon recognized health and education as part and parcel of the Adventist contribution to Christianity. From the opening of the first Adventist health institution, the Western Health Reform Institute, in Battle Creek in 1866 and the founding of the first school, a small primary school in Battle Creek in 1853, Adventists have incessantly built, enlarged, and improved their educational networks and health systems. Though there have been several crises and many strong disagreements about strategies and methods, and though many difficulties had to be overcome—whether or not these activities were intimately connected with the gospel preaching was never in doubt.[13] The emphasis on eating healthful food was and remained an important stewardship aspect.

Less institutional and gradually diminishing in scope were reform activities in a number of other areas. One of these was the concern for the basic human right of religious liberty. The interest in this domain reached its climax in the late nineteenth century when Adventists felt that some of

161

their basic rights, such as worshipping on the day of their choice, were in serious jeopardy.[14] The immense interest in "temperance" goes back as far as Joseph Bates, one of the first pioneers and founders of the Adventist Church. Abstinence from alcohol, tobacco, and other harmful drugs became one of the hallmarks of the Adventist identity. But there is little doubt that the temperance concern played a more dominant role and had a more pronounced activist form in the late nineteenth century than ever since.

Although never strictly pacifistic, Adventists from the Civil War period onward opposed active participation in the killing or wounding of fellow human beings and promoted alternative forms of serving one's country.[15] To some extent, noncombatancy has continued to be the preferred option in the Adventist Church, though not in the same measure everywhere around the world. Finally, there was yet another area of social engagement in early Adventism. Surprising to many, certainly in the light of some later developments in the area of race relationships, there was an active involvement of several early Adventist leaders in the campaign against slavery, and some early Adventists actively assisted fugitive slaves.[16]

In some of these areas Adventists long had the edge over many other Christian communities. However, developments within the Adventist Church in a number of ways also reflected, as time went by, what happened within conservative Christianity and more specifically within Evangelicalism. Adventists by and large reacted negatively toward such currents as the Social Gospel movement and later liberation theology.[17] Although many of the goals of these movements were sympathetic to Adventists with their wholistic philosophy of life, the liberal context and its ecumenical associations made Adventists, together with other conservative Christian bodies, suspicious and reticent to place too much emphasis on social involvement.

Just as in the wider Evangelical world, there was a "reversal" during the post-World War II period. Institutional health work continued as before, but community work became a much more important aspect from the 1950s and 1960s onward.[18] SAWS (Seventh-day Adventist Welfare Service) was established in 1956. The name of the organization was changed into Seventh-day Adventist World Service in 1973, and the organization was reorganized as ADRA (Adventist Development and Relief Agency) in 1983.[19] Today ADRA operates in about 100 countries and is one of the larger Christian aid organizations in the world.

Even though currently the Adventist Church is probably active on more social fronts than most other Christians denominations, not much systematic theological thought has been given to the underlying rationale, the methodology, and the challenges that yet might need to be addressed as well as the possible limitations. And there is a noticeable lack of emphasis on the connection between biblical stewardship and care for Planet Earth. Before we continue to chart the way in which the Adventist Church has responded and should further respond to social, political, and environmental issues, we need to look at the available biblical data. How do they inform us not only about the responsibilities of each individual Christian but also about the responsibilities of the church?

Poverty and Injustice—the Biblical Data

Let us look at how the Bible deals with issues of poverty, human rights, hospitality, and justice.[20] Are these among the key values that belong to the identifying marks of the kingdom of God? Do these and related issues give substance to what it means to be a steward and a disciple in the twenty-first century? Does a church that claims to have special attention for the gift of prophecy also recognize that it has a responsibility in speaking prophetically about events and trends in the world? And does all this also impact on what the church must consider as its mission in the world?

First of all, it needs to be emphasized that in the Bible injustice and poverty and their opposite poles—justice and solidarity—are not mere abstract legal or economic terms. They have, of course, legal and economic connotations, but justice and injustice are primarily to be understood as *relational* concepts. Neither is poverty something abstract but concerns "a group of human beings who have names, who are made in the image of God, whose hairs are numbered and for whom Jesus died."[21] Likewise, justice has a human face. God's justice is not just about judgment and punishment but also about healing, forgiveness, and restoration. With that in mind, let us zoom in a little further on poverty and injustice and the way in which the Bible wants us to deal with them.

Liberation theologians are correct when they affirm that God shows a preferential attitude toward those who are poor and oppressed. Yet wealth as such is not condemned. The patriarchs were rich people. "Abraham had become very wealthy" (Gen. 13:2). Likewise, Isaac "became rich, and his wealth continued to grow" (Gen. 26:13). Job was on the list of the richest men in the Middle East before he fell victim to a series of misfortunes (Job 1:3, 8; 2:3), and he became even richer when his ordeals ended (Job 42:12-15). Boaz was "a man of standing," which also meant that he was quite well-to-do in material respects (Ruth 2:1). Among the early kings Solomon in particular was noted for his wealth (1 Kings 4:22, 23; 9:28: 2 Chron. 8:17, 18). Even the prophet Daniel prospered at the Babylonian court (Dan. 2:48). Among New Testament examples of well-to-do followers of Jesus was Joseph, "a rich man from Arimathea" (Matt. 27:57), and among the early Jerusalem believers we find people with substantial means (Acts 4:34). Many other biblical examples of rich people could be cited.

At the same time, although wealthy people were not criticized for the mere possession of earthly goods, it is also clear that the Scriptures repeatedly warn us about the seductive power wealth has. We are reminded that "the love of money is a root of all kinds of evil" (1 Tim. 6:10). And once you get really hooked on money, your spiritual life, we are told, is in trouble: "You cannot serve both God and Money" (Matt. 6:24; Luke 16:13). Money can become an obstacle between us and salvation, as the story of Jesus' encounter with the rich young man (Matt. 19:16-30) illustrates. The story of King Hezekiah affords a well-known case of someone who became obsessed by his wealth rather than being overcome by gratitude because of his miraculous recovery from his nearly fatal illness (2 Kings 20:12-20; Isa. 39). It proves the point made in Deuteronomy 8:14, where we are reminded of what we have seen happen all too often: When you begin to amass wealth, "your heart will become proud and you will forget the Lord your God." The sad truth is that "whoever loves money never has money enough" (Eccl. 5:10).

There is no indication in Scripture that God demands a form of total communism, in which all wealth is equally distributed. Apart from the fact that schemes to produce such a situation have always miserably failed, there is no divine directive that all should have the exact same amount. Even the spiritual talents are not spread equally among the believers! But this does not mean that God has no deep compassion with the plight of poor people and has no interest in how His people relate to poverty. At this point the ideas of poverty and injustice are connected. Poverty is often the result of the grave injustices that people have to suffer.

Poverty can be the result of misfortune, beyond anyone's control, as in the case of Job. Sometimes it results from one's own mistakes or sheer laziness, as the book of Proverbs repeatedly indicates. Often people find themselves trapped in a cycle of poverty, as is abundantly visible in our inner cities. But, tragically, a lot of poverty comes from human (or should we say inhuman?) injustice. God, however, is not indifferent when injustice occurs. "He who oppresses the poor shows contempt for their Maker" (Prov. 14:31). He condemns the tricks of rich persons to take advantage of those who are poor. "Shall I acquit," He asks through His prophet Micah, "a man with dishonest scales, with a bag of false weights?" (Micah 6:11). His anger is kindled when laborers do not receive a fair wage. "Woe to him who builds his palace by unrighteousness . . . making his countrymen work for nothing, not paying them for their labor" (Jer. 22:13). When He sees injustice, "the Lord enters into judgment against the elders and leaders of his people," who have "the plunder from the poor in [their] houses" (Isa. 3:14). Isaiah 10:1-4 sums it up how God regards injustice and abuse of the poor, and what He will do about it:

Woe to those who make unjust laws,
to those who issue oppressive decrees,
to deprive the poor of their rights,
and without justice from the oppressed of my people,
making widows their prey and robbing the fatherless.
What will you do on the day of reckoning . . . ?
To whom will you run for help?
Where will you leave your riches?
Nothing will remain but to cringe among the captives
or fall among the slain.

We find in the Old Testament a number of divine directives aimed at alleviating, at least to some extent, the plight of poor people. When reaping their crops or picking their grapes, farmers were not supposed to be too thorough. They were told to leave something for "the poor and the alien" (Lev. 19:10). "When you are harvesting in your field and you overlook a sheaf, do not go back to get it" (Deut. 24:19). It was likewise not allowed to take essential items as a security for a debt (Deut. 24:6, 13; Ex. 22:26), nor was charging interest to "a brother" permitted (Deut. 23:19, 20; Ex. 22:25). The Israelite institution of "redemption" enabled people to regain a property that had been lost. The best-known example of the action of a *go'el* (redeemer) was Boaz (Ruth 4:1-10), who qualified as such and regained the family possessions of Elimelech on behalf of his daughter-in-law Ruth. A rather detailed account of a similar transaction is found in Jeremiah 32.

The sabbatical year and the jubilee offered further evidences of God's concern for those who were poor. Although there is little information about the actual application of these provisions in Israelite society, the divine instructions show that God was painfully aware of the circumstances of poor people and of those who (even among His own people) had lost their freedom and had become someone else's property. The sabbatical year (once every seventh year) and the jubilee (every fiftieth year) were intended as opportunities for some of the misery of poverty to be redressed and for slaves to regain their freedom (Ex. 21:2; Deut. 15:1-18; Neh. 10:31; Lev. 25:8-17, 23, 55).

The biblical antidote against an unhealthy love for money is clearly the faithful giving of tithes and offerings. Not the *amount* given is of paramount importance but the *attitude* of the giver. Jesus Himself knew what it meant to be poor. Though He was rich, the apostle Paul reminds us, He became poor for our sake (2 Cor. 8:9). Jesus stated a fact that was obvious to His audience when He said, "Foxes have holes and birds of the air have nests, but the Son of man has no place to lay his head" (Matt. 8:20). So He could utterly identify with those who were poor. He knew the true value of the two small copper coins that the poor widow brought to the treasury of the Temple (Mark 12:41-44). God "loves a cheerful giver" (2 Cor. 9:7). The early Christians learned to practice solidarity. "Proper recognition" was to be given to "widows who are really in need" (1 Tim. 5:3). Timothy was to give the people in his charge the following instruction: "If anyone does not provide for his relatives, and especially for his immediate family, he has denied the faith and is worse than an unbeliever" (verse 8). In several places in the New Testament we are told of Paul's efforts to model the virtue of solidarity by collecting money for the mother church in Jerusalem (Rom. 15:25-29; 1 Cor. 16:1-4; 2 Cor. 9:5).

What Does God Want From Us?

The prophet Micah sums matters up as succinctly as we find anywhere else in the Scriptures: "What does the Lord require of you? *To act justly and to love mercy and to walk humbly with your God*" (Micah 6:8). Reading the short book of the prophet Micah, we find a threefold cycle of criticism and accusations on the one hand, and of promises, hope and healing on the other. The prophet is crystal clear: God hates sin, and pious behavior cannot make up for that. He hates the rich whose only purpose in life is to get more. He hates dishonesty and violence. And He hates leaders who do their work just for the sake of money and status. The prophet singles out one particular issue—those in poverty are deprived of their land and livelihood. Thus, there are many who are left behind, and many—women and orphans in particular—are mistreated.

This is, the prophet says, what the situation requires: The people must "act justly," or "do justice." The Hebrew text uses the term do *misphat*, which means practice the requirements of the law that relate to other people. It requires "a relationship that gives back what is due and even goes on to deliver the oppressed and the downtrodden. The requirement is relational, ethical, and concerned for others' welfare."[22] Mere obedience to cultic laws and sacred traditions will not suffice. God's covenant with His people requires that people relate in justice to Him and to one another.

In addition, God wants His people to love mercy, not from a sense of duty, but because that has become second nature to them. This term assumes a covenant relationship and "connotes the fact of deliverance or protection of another as a way of being faithful to their mutual covenant."[23] Of course, we do not have to look far to find the One who gave us a perfect example of the challenge Micah holds before his contemporaries as well as before those who later read his words, including us in the twenty-first century.

Jesus Christ acted justly and loved mercy! That was His calling. Quoting from Isaiah 58:6 and 61:1, 2, Christ proclaimed that He had come to set captives free, release the oppressed, and heal the brokenhearted. In this direct reference to the jubilee ("the year of the Lord's favor" [Isa. 61:2]) we hear Christ's mission statement. No doubt, His mission is spiritual, but His specific reference to the jubilee most certainly implies also a social and humanitarian dimension. And the way in which He spent His three years among humanity leaves us in no doubt that His ministry was perfectly wholistic, combining spiritual, social, and humanitarian dimensions while manifesting an unparalleled concern for justice. Whoever doubts this last aspect should spend some time in meditating upon one of the great stories of the Gospels—the woman caught in adultery and the manner in which Christ defused the situation that ensued (John 7:53-8:11)!

Following the example of our Lord in taking the words of Micah as our guiding principle is, of course, an individual challenge. It concerns each one of us. To act justly has very concrete implications for the Christian, who takes discipleship and stewardship seriously. As an individual—in my family, toward my partner, my children, my friends—do I act justly? Can they rely on me? Do I always do what is right and fair?

Acting justly means that we understand that some things are totally unfair and absolutely wrong, some things that are totally nonnegotiable. It also means that we understand that the life we have is a gift from God and that we must be good stewards of that precious gift, understanding that the resources of this earth must be shared in a fair and equitable way. To act justly means that we do the little bit we can to ensure that the farmers in Africa and South America get a fair price for their produce. It demands that we are consistent—that we not just sign letters for Amnesty International but also determine to refrain from putting our savings in funds that are invested in companies that oppress people or fabricate weapons. And, of course, it pre-supposes that we support agencies that help people in need. Remember, this is not just *advisable*. This is what God *requires* of you and of me.

What About the Church?

So far we have focused on the individual Christian, but what about the church? The answer to that question can be rather short. The church is a community of people who want to follow Christ in theory and practice. The corporate church in its various facets cannot ignore the issues of poverty and injustice and related matters. If Christ was in the healing business and made sure that the hungry were fed, so must the community that represents Him in this world. If Christ combined the preaching of the Word with acts of kindness and justice and was willing to be poor among those who were poor, so must the church that professes to follow Him as its Lord. The church cannot turn a blind eye to poverty, because God does not do this. God hears the cry of the children in this world who go to bed on empty stomachs and of the millions of human beings who must find shelter under a few rusty sheets of metal or less, and the institutional church cannot pretend not to notice this.

If the church professes to take the Bible as its source of inspiration, it cer-tainly cannot overlook the fact that there are more than 2,000 references to poverty in the Scriptures. Bono, the lead singer of the band U2, is not my favorite artist, but the words that he spoke at the forty-fifth National Prayer Breakfast in the Washington Hilton in 2006 keep ringing in my ears: "God is in the slums, in the cardboard boxes where the poor play house. God is in the silence of a mother who has infected her child with a virus that will end both their lives. God is in the cries heard under the rubble of war. God is in the debris of wasted opportunity and lives. . . ."[24]

If the church is truly God's church, it must "act justly." It must be-come actively involved in development work. Combating illiteracy, work-ing for better health care, clean water, and nutritious food, are domains that must not be left to government agencies and humanistic NGOs—the church as well must show its concern for justice and mercy. Activities such as ADRA, Community Services, orphanages, language schools, medical mission work, etc., must not be motivated by a need for good public relations, but must be seen as an integral part of the mission that Christ has given His church. And although these activities must of necessity target people in need, regardless of creed and color, ethnicity or culture, and although they must never become disguised ways of improper proselytizing, they are more than mere acts of Christian kindness. There is a theological rationale for involvement in development work and social projects. As one definition aptly points out: *"Development is a movement toward that freedom and wholeness in a just community which persons will enjoy when our risen Lord Jesus returns at His second coming to bring the kingdom in its fullness."*[25]

A concern for mercy and justice on the part of the church reaches further than encouraging individual members to get involved in social activities for the benefit of their fellow citizens nearby and the disenfranchised in faraway lands. And it goes beyond facilitating the establishment and the governance—and even subsidizing—of church-sponsored humanitarian agencies. It impacts on every level of the church's organization. Do the church's administrators "act justly" in the way they "run" the church? Do they know what it means to truly share their resources? Or do they tend to look primarily after the needs of their own "field" or their own congregation? Does the local congregation look after the weak and the vulnerable in its midst? Can pastors and denominational employees be sure that they are always treated fairly? Do board members consistently vote for what is right, or do they at times compromise or choose what is cheapest, or easiest, or least controversial?

This becomes a very personal question. As a pastor, am I sure that acting justly has always been and always will be my main concern? Or am I sometimes tempted to support the people with means and status, rather than simply doing what is right? Was I, as a now-retired administrator, known as someone who acted fairly and straightforwardly? who kept his promises? Did the church workers in my care always get what they were entitled to?

A Prophetic Voice

Micah spoke as God's prophet. Does the church, through its individual members and by means of its corporate voice, continue to speak and act prophetically and to declare publicly what it believes God expects from people today? Many denominations have over time spoken out on key issues. But sometimes churches and church leaders have remained tragically silent when they should have raised their voices but deemed it not opportune to do so.

169

The Seventh-day Adventist Church has spoken clearly in an official and public way about many ethical and social issues. Some of the resulting statements may not have received as wide a circulation as church leaders may have wished. In some cases it would seem that more could have been said on a particular topic or that a different emphasis might have been given. But the very fact that the statements and guidelines that have been issued in the past decade or so fill a 250-page book signals that the Adventist Church has been serious in raising its prophetic voice and has addressed issues such as AIDS, assault weapons, climate change, human rights, racism, environment, gambling, and many more.[26] But this does not mean that the prophetic voice could not, at times, have been clearer and louder.

Just as quite a few Evangelical Christians maintain, so some Adventists will argue that the church should simply focus on preaching "the truth" because "time is short." There is, however, a fairly wide consensus in the Adventist Church that the church's mission has a twofold dimension (apostolate and diaconate), even though as yet, as indicated above, there has hardly been a serious attempt to define the various aspects of the mission outreach, in particular its social dimension, in theological terms. We will return to this in the next chapter.

The Role of the Church at Present

Missiologist George W. Peters provides an apt summary of what the church's responsibilities in the world must include if its witness is to be wholistic and true to the example of the One who founded the church. Note the following five points.

1. "The church must be specific, emphatic and directive in its teachings relative to culture and development." This is clearly part of the mandate that humans should subjugate, cultivate, and advance the earth that we received at Creation (Gen. 1:28).

2. "The church must teach its constituency the responsibility of nation and culture building, and prepare and motivate its members to occupy and/or even strive for relevant positions and administration, as well as general service, in order to be the salt of the earth and the light of the world" (see Matt. 5:13-16). There are numerous biblical examples of believers who took this calling seriously, either by choice or as a result of choices others made for them.

3. "The church must be the prophetic voice in the world and function as the conscience of society. All issues that affect the woe or welfare of

mankind must also become the concern of the church." The church has the prophetic calling to point out biblical and divine principles and to warn the leaders in society that violation of such principles and ideals will sooner or later carry far reaching consequences. One has, at the beginning of the twenty-first century, plenty of reason to wonder whether the Adventist community, considering its tradition, should not raise its prophetic voice more forcefully in the areas in which it once seemed to be much more outspoken and proactive, such as health reform, substance abuse, religious liberty, and related human rights.

4. "The church must itself demonstrate the operation of divine principles and ideals: love, justice, equality, compassion, service, sacrifice, suffering, etc." and join, where conscientiously possible, those forces that also seek to promote those same ideals.

5. "The church must be prepared to take the initiative, if need be, to demonstrate the possibility of higher and noble principles and active participation in the service of mankind. . . . The church must be God's showcase and living example of what God is, and what His kingdom implies."[27]

I believe it is important to add one further element. The Adventist community has a rich tradition of emphasizing stewardship. In a time when the global ecosystem is under threat, when the rich part of the world irresponsibly and egotistically utilizes an inequitable portion of mineral and other natural resources, when climate change has turned into a real threat for millions who live in low coastal areas, when consumption of luxury goods and unnecessary gadgets has become a key aspect of the postmodern lifestyle, when hunger and lack of sanitation and basic health care and the absence of safe water still threaten the present—let alone the future—of hundreds of millions of men, women, and children—in such a time a community of disciples of Christ carries stewardship responsibilities, individually and collectively, as never before!

Seán McDonagh, author and professor of anthropology, wrote these significant words: "It is beginning to dawn on many people that alleviating poverty, healing nature and preserving the stability of the biosphere is the central task for those who wish to follow in the footsteps of Jesus in today's world. Human creativity, inventiveness and technology will have a very important role to play in this healing, *but religious energies flowing from the life, death, and resurrection of Jesus are also crucial.*"[28]

The Need for Balance

Christians, on both the individual and the corporate level, have often failed to maintain a healthy balance. Often they have opted for preaching rather than helping, but the reverse has also been true. Seventh-day Adventism has not been exempt from these temptations. There have been times when social involvement and care for poor and disenfranchised persons have been sadly neglected. But Adventist history also has examples in which some tried to build a benevolent empire that almost eclipsed all other branches of church work. George Knight coins this "the Kelloggian vision," referring to the clash between the visionary but dominant doctor who worked incessantly to bring his dream of a nondenominational international chain of charity organizations to reality.[29] This was opposed by other leaders, Ellen White foremost among them, who were determined to focus on the preaching of the "messages of the three angels."[30]

In our attempts to determine how Christians who expect the soon coming of Jesus Christ must live while they wait for the climax of history—how they "must occupy till He comes" (see Luke 19:13)—we must always look at the example of the ministry of Jesus while He lived on earth. In contrast to those who want to put all their resources in the temporary betterment of this world, Jesus did not intend to set up an earthly kingdom. Yes, healing had an important part of His ministry, but talking with His disciples and other people and preaching to those who came to listen to Him always remained preeminent. He healed many, but not all. He raised a few persons from death, but allowed most people to die and await the resurrection.

It is clear that Christians have a mandate to care for this earth; that they must be responsible stewards of the resources of this planet; that they must feed the hungry, provide clean drinking water, houses, education, and health care. It is all part of the command to love our neighbors as ourselves. But while we "occupy till He comes" in activities that will alleviate suffering, we must be aware of two things. First, our endeavors will not bring a final and complete solution for the problems of the world. It is the divine intervention in Christ's parousia that will usher in a new world in which righteousness rules (2 Peter 3:13). Second, we have received a broader mandate—to preach the gospel in all the world (Matt. 28:19, 20 and parallels). There is an "eternal gospel" to be preached "to every nation, tribe, language and people," with a number of important end-time emphases (Rev. 14:6-12).

The apostles were not insensitive to the needs around them, but the biblical record leaves us in no doubt that spreading the "eternal gospel" was their highest priority. That should be a model for us to follow. On a practical level, the church is continuously faced with the problem of how to distribute its limited resources wisely when different branches of the church compete for them. This fact does not mean that the church has no responsibilities apart from direct preaching, but it does mean that the main priority of the church—to proclaim its message—must never suffer and that all denominational activities must be driven by that overall purpose.

Institutions have a natural desire to grow and branch out into even more lines of activities. However useful and good these may be, choices will have to be made and a healthy balance has to be maintained. As Ellen White warned: "In the institutions that have long been established there is sometimes a desire to grasp more and still more advantages. But the Lord declares that this should not be. The money in His treasury is to be used in building up the work all over the world."[31] One further quote from the same source emphasizes, possibly even more succinctly, the need for setting priorities and maintaining balance: "God's ministers must come into close companionship with Christ, and follow His example in all things— in purity of life, in self-denial, in benevolence, in diligence, in perseverance. To win souls for the kingdom of God must be their first consideration."[32]

Models of the Church

Earlier in our study of the nature of the church, we let ourselves be informed about essential aspects of the church by focusing on a number of biblical metaphors. In closing this chapter, I want to mention two models of the church that illuminate further what this chapter is about. When we speak of models of the church, we refer to numerous images that are not directly based on biblical terms but seem to do justice to our understanding of what the church is, based on the total biblical testimony. Avery Dulles says we may speak of a model "when an image is employed reflectively and critically to deepen one's theoretical understanding of a reality."[33]

Some of these models are very useful in any discussion about what the church should be in today's world. They relate to the question as to what is the church's divine calling par excellence.

The various models overlap and should not be seen as mutually exclusive. And not all aspects apply when a particular image or model is used. (The church may be compared to a flock. This is a powerful image that inspires us to follow obediently the master, but Cardinal Dulles reminds us that it does not follow that church members must begin to grow wool!)[34]

173

Biblical truth is always deeper and broader than one or two human terms can define. And there can be a certain trendiness in the application of particular models. It is important to remain critical and to ask ourselves which models come closest to what the Bible says about the essence of the church.

Two models, in particular, emphasize the comprehensive calling of the church: the model of (1) the church as a herald and that of (2) the church as a servant!

The church as herald. While Roman Catholics often prefer such models of the church as "the mystical body of Christ" or the church as a "sacrament," Protestants have tended to stress the element of proclamation. A herald has a message he or she is commissioned to deliver. This model is clearly present in the writings of Paul and was used extensively by Luther and, more recently, by Karl Barth. Hans Küng, though a Catholic, was also attracted to this model. Bultmann and the so-called post-Bultmannians added their own perspectives. Theologians such as Gerhard Ebeling and Ernst Fuchs stress the role of language in a rather postmodern manner. But though it has been stretched in many directions, this model helps believers to focus on the overarching mission of the church to proclaim God's message. Some have argued that this model stresses proclamation but neglects the element of action. Here we must remind ourselves that the models are complementary, and the model of the servant stresses precisely that aspect.

A model that has recently received much emphasis is that of the church as a *hostel*, a safe haven, a place where people are welcome at the table. The images of a meal, of being a guest at the table, of being invited to a feast, etc., are rather obvious building blocks for this model. It stresses the need for the church to be "open," not merely as a strategy for recruitment but as a way of being! The model of the church as *servant*, however, also receives a lot of attention—and rightly so. In combination with that of the *herald* model, it gives forceful expression to the biblical notion of the witness of the church as *diakonia*.

Diakoneo/diakonos and related terms are, as we noted earlier, frequently used in the New Testament to denote service of a general kind, such as serving at the table and other kinds of loving service, but also in a more specifically Christian sense, as "servant" of the new covenant. As such, it refers to the office of deacon in the church, but it has a much wider application. It is not by accident—and very appropriately—that many recent books about Christian leadership stress the idea of servant leadership.[35]

Christ came to proclaim the truth (John 14:6). And He came to serve

(Phil. 2:7). His church has no other option but to follow suit and to do all it can to maintain the same balance between the two aspects they find in Him whom it professes to follow.

---

[1] George W. Peters, "The Church and Development: A Historical View," in Robert L. Hancock, *The Ministry of Development in Ecumenical Perspective* (Pasadena, Calif.: William Carey Library, 1979), pp. 3-18.

[2] "Social Gospel Movement" in *Dictionary of the Ecumenical Movement* (Grand Rapids: William B. Eerdmans Pub. and Geneva: WCC Publications, 1991), pp. 928, 929.

[3] See, e.g., the edition published by Abingdon Press (New York: n.d).

[4] *Ibid.*, p. 129.

[5] "The Social Gospel," in William A. Dyrness and Veli-Matti Kärkkänen, eds., *Global Dictionary of Theology* (Downers Grove, Ill.: InterVarsity Press, 2008), p. 836.

[6] *Ibid.*, p. 838.

[7] C. Peter Wagner, "A Missiological View of Christian Relief and Development," in Edgar J. Elliston, ed., *Christian Relief and Development* (Dallas: Word Publishing, 1989), p. 117.

[8] Williston Walker, *A History of the Christian Church* (New York: Scribner, 1985), p. 672.

[9] For the text, see http://www.vatican.va/holy_father/paul_vi/encyclicals/documents/hf_p-vi_enc_25071968_humanae-vitae_en.html.

[10] David L. Smith, *A Handbook of Contemporary Theology* (Wheaton, Ill.: Victor Books, 1991), pp. 203-226.

[11] Raymond C. Hundley, *Radical Liberation Theology: An Evangelical Response* (Wilmore, Ky.: Bristol Books, 1987), p. 3.

[12] Elliston, pp. 25, 26.

[13] For a good overview of the history of Adventist interest in health "reform," see D. E. Robinson, *The Story of our Health Message* (Nashville: Southern Pub. Assn., 1943). See also George W. Reid, *A Sound of Trumpets* (Washington, D.C.: Review and Herald Pub. Assn., 1982) and Richard W. Schwarz, *John Harvey Kellogg: Pioneering Health Reformer* (Hagerstown, Md.: Review and Herald Pub. Assn., 2006).

[14] See the relevant chapters in Warren L. Johns, *Dateline Sunday, US* (Mountain View, Calif.: Pacific Press Pub. Assn., 1967).

[15] Douglas Morgan, *Adventism and the American Republic* (Knoxville: University of Tennessee Pres, 2001), pp. 31-34.

[16] *Ibid.*, pp. 26-29.

[17] See Atilio Dupertuis, *Liberation Theology—A Study in Its Soteriology* (Berrien Springs, Mich.: Andrews University Press, 1997).

[18] "Community Services," in *Seventh-day Adventist Encyclopedia* (1996), vol. 10, pp. 400-403.

[19] "Adventist Development and Relief Agency International," in *Seventh-day Adventist Encyclopedia* (1996), vol. 10, pp. 12-14.

[20] Reinder Bruinsma, *De Christen en zijn Geld: Rentmeesterschap Vandaag* (Kampen, Netherlands: Uitgeversmaatschappij J. H. Kok, 1990), pp. 12-50; 90-121.

[21] B. L. Myers, "Poverty," in Dyrness and Kärkkänen, p. 687.

[22] Jon L. Dybdahl, *The Abundant Bible Amplifier: Hosea-Micah* (Boise, Idaho: Pacific Press Pub. Assn., 1996), p. 215.

[23] *Ibid.*, p. 216.

[24] In Reinder Bruinsma, "To Act Justly," *Ministry,* March 2008, pp. 21-23.

[25] Ronald J. Sider, in "God and the Poor: Toward a Theology of Development," Hancock, p. 35.

[26] *Statements, Guidelines, and Other Documents.*

[27] Peters, in Hancock, p. 26.

[28] Seán McDonagh, *Greening the Christian Millennium* (Dublin, Ireland: Dominican Publications, 1999), p. 23.

[29] G. R. Knight, *If I Were the Devil,* p. 266; for a discussion of this issue, see pp. 251-269.

[30] For a summary of this episode in Adventist history, see Richard W. Schwarz and Floyd Greenleaf, *Light Bearers—A History of the Seventh-day Adventist Church* (Nampa, Idaho: Pacific Press Pub. Assn., 2000), pp. 264-272.

[31] Ellen G. White, *Gospel Workers* (Washington, D.C.: Review and Herald Pub. Assn., 1915), p. 455.

[32] *Ibid.,* p. 31.

[33] A. Dulles, *Models of the Church,* p. 15.

[34] *Ibid.*

[35] See Robert K. Greenleaf, *Servant Leadership* (New York: Paulist Press, 1977).

Chapter 12

The Mission of the Church

Missiology is the theological subdiscipline devoted to the study, the rationale, the biblical basis, and the history and practice of Christian missions. In a general book about the doctrine of the church we can devote only limited attention to some of the main aspects of missiology, but we cannot skip this topic, since mission has to do with the very heart of ecclesiology. The people of Israel in Old Testament times were called for a mission, and likewise, God's people now exist for the sake of their mission to the world.

In actual practice the church has not always placed a high emphasis on its missionary calling. During long periods of its existence, the Christian church did not give the highest priority to preaching the gospel in "all the world." That was true for the medieval church and, later, also for Protestantism. Although in all centuries there have been courageous and committed missionaries and amazing mission projects have been launched, the worldwide missionary enterprise as we know it today dates, to a large extent, from the nineteenth century.[1]

Seventh-day Adventists are very mission-minded, even though it took a few decades before the church had a clear vision of its missionary calling. In the aftermath of the 1844 disappointment, Adventist believers held the conviction that the "door" of grace was "shut" and that their mission work was to be confined to the "gathering" of those who had in the past few years listened to the "midnight cry" and had fervently expected the coming of the Lord. Gradually they came to the realization that there was a further task of preaching the specific "present truths" that they were discovering in ever-greater clarity and detail, but it was not until the 1870s that a clear understanding of a mission assignment beyond the immediate American scene began to emerge.[2]

The history of Adventist missions shows that the church had the greatest missionary drive in the 1920s.[3] The church is still growing—in some areas, even exponentially—but it no longer focuses on its mission in quite the same way as was happening about a century ago. Currently a much smaller percentage of the church's income and human resources is actually devoted to extending the presence of the church into "unentered" territories.

While this is true, initiatives such as Global Mission (started in 1990) have contributed significantly to a positive trend in the Adventist missionary enterprise. Furthermore, the Adventist missionary outreach has been miraculously successful, as a few statistics will confirm. While the baptized membership in the Adventist Church was only about 75,000 in 1900, it grew to 1 million by the middle of the twentieth century and presently (2009) stands at some 16 million. Outside Adventism during the past 100 years, the Christian mission has also seen considerable results. There were about 500 million Christians in the world in 1900, whereas in the year 2000 about 2 billion people identified themselves as Christian. The enormous population growth meant, however, that the percentage of Christians of the total world population stagnated at a little above 30 percent.[4] By comparison, Adventist growth has been remarkably stronger. Whereas some 50 years ago there was only one Adventist for every 2,500 people in the world, the ratio is now 1:425.[5]

Why Mission? The Biblical Perspective

The word "mission" is derived from the Latin *mittere,* "to send." Mission has to do with the one who sends, those who are being sent, and the purpose for which people are sent. To be sent implies a willingness to go, which often means the crossing of one or more borders. These borders can be not only physical but also ethnic, linguistic, or cultural.[6]

Mission is no divine afterthought, but is rooted in God's very nature. He is the Creator, who wants people to relate to Him. He is outgoing, He is the Light (1 John 1:5) and is not withdrawn or absent. He is love (1 John 4:8, 16) and therefore seeks relationships, restoration, and wholeness. The theology of mission, therefore, is not an appendix to doctrinal theology in general. "No doctrine of God, Christ or the Holy Spirit had been expounded completely according to the Bible until it has established the triune God as the outgoing God of mission, the God of saving purpose and relationship to mankind who undertakes a program for the progressive realization of his purpose."[7]

Mission is a dominant theme in the Old Testament. Genesis 1-11 tells us about God's missionary effort to deal with the human race as a whole.

Genesis 3:15 is the protoevangelium, which highlights that salvation will be available for all. Israel was called to be a missionary people. The blessings of the covenant would be universal (see for example, Gen. 12:1-3; Ex. 19:5, 6). Israel's history was to be more than national history: it would be *salvation* history!

The Old Testament stresses the universality of God's purposes. God leaves no room for other gods and for syncretism. The nations are included in His plan (2 Chron. 6:32, 33; Isa. 53; Ps. 86:9, 10; 67). The stories of Jonah, Esther, Ruth, Naaman, etc., strikingly illustrate God's deep interest in other peoples besides Israel. Israel was to care for strangers (Ex. 12:48; 22:21; Num. 9:14; 15:14; Deut. 1:16; 31:12)—a concept not readily found in other religions. Of particular importance is the concept of Israel as a priesthood (Ex. 19:5, 6). Israel was to mediate the only true God to the other nations that did not worship Him.

Mission is also a crucial theme in the New Testament. We note the particularistic aspect. In some parts of the New Testament the focus is on Israel (Matt. 15:24; 10:5, 6). But underlying this is always the universal aspect: God so loved the *world* (John 3:16). And beyond this, we even find a cosmic dimension, for sin has not only affected human beings but also the entire creation is "groaning as in the pains of childbirth" (Rom. 8:22) because of its alienation from God. This will, however, prove to be temporary because as the result of divine intervention, everything will soon be made new (Rev. 21:5) and then the sign "mission completed" can be given.

Christ was and is the supreme missionary. He was sent by the Father (John 17:18, 21), yet came voluntarily (Mark 10:45; Phil. 2:6-8). He recognized no social, cultural, or ethnic barriers. Examples in the Gospels of how He ministered to people of all kinds of backgrounds and all walks of life and of how His teachings emphasized the universal nature of God's boundless offer of grace abound. In His personal ministry Christ gave a powerful preview of how His followers, once the church had been established, would similarly disregard the nationalistic, cultural, and religious barriers that had often seemed so definitive and immutable to them (Acts 10; 11).

The Gospel story climaxes in the missionary mandate (Matt. 28:18-20; Mark 16:15, 16; Luke 24:46-49; John 20:21, 22; Acts 1:8; 26:13-18) just prior to Christ's ascension. A comparison of the ways in which this mission charter is worded in the four Gospels brings out various complementary aspects. Matthew stresses the authority behind it as well as its all-inclusive nature and duration. Mark lays special stress on the urgency and geographical scope, whereas the wording in Luke impresses through its Christocentric nature and universal tone. John points, in particular, to the spiritual nature of the mission mandate and the spiritual equipment needed.

The Gospels tell the disciples of Christ that they are to go! They are to cross boundaries, travel far and near, face untold adventure and numerous difficulties, reach into the unknown. They are to preach and teach, to baptize and make disciples with the intention that these new disciples will also go and repeat the cycle. The commission is given to the disciples as a group and through them to the community of disciples that would be formed—the church. Ellen White comments: "The Savior's commission to the disciples included all the believers. It includes all believers in Christ to the end of time. . . . All to whom the heavenly inspiration has come are put in trust with the gospel. All who receive the life of Christ are ordained to work for the salvation of their fellow men. For this work the church was established, and all who take upon themselves its sacred vows are thereby pledged to be co-workers with Christ."[8]

It is significant that the gospel is to be preached to all nations (Matt. 24:14; 28:19; Rev. 14:6). The biblical concept of a "nation" is not to be confused with that of the modern national state. It does not imply that the gospel commission will have been fulfilled as soon as a Christian presence has been established in each of the 230 states that are internationally recognized. The Greek word that is translated as "nation" is *ethnos*, which has a much wider connotation. Of course, in its immediate context, the emphasis is on the fact that the gospel must be preached to both Jews and Gentiles.[9] But it has correctly been observed that the word refers, in fact, to all "people groups"—all linguistic and social and cultural groups that can be identified. A good working definition runs as follows: "A people group is a significantly large . . . sociological grouping of individuals who perceive themselves to have a common affinity with one another."[10] There may be as many as 24,000 such "nations," that is, such people groups.

The challenge is enormous. But the risen Christ, to whom has been given "all authority in heaven and on earth" (Matt. 28:18), will be with His church "always, to the very end of the age" (verse 20). The Dutch missiologist Johannes Verkuyl points out that authority can often be used to wrong ends but that this does not apply to the authority of Christ. "A saving and liberating authority proceeds from Him, the victim who became a victor. He is the crucified Lord who now rules. His power is not that of a despot bent on destruction; instead He uses his power for our healing and liberation and accomplishes these goals by love, reconciliation, and patience."[11] He takes continuing responsibility for the success and progress of the mission.

The power and authority of the Lord were channeled to the church through the Holy Spirit, who came as promised (John 14:15, 18, 25-27; Acts 1:8), propelling the church to a magnificent start (Acts 2) and endowing the members and leaders of the church with diverse gifts for mission (Eph. 4:11-13; 1 Cor. 12). The book of Acts chronicles the fulfillment of Christ's promise and demonstrates that the assurance about His authority and power and of His presence through the Spirit were not empty words. The gospel message reached Jerusalem (Acts 1), and on the day of Pentecost the message was heard by all those who visited the city, "God-fearing Jews from every nation under heaven" (Acts 2:5). The gospel influence soon extended farther into Judea and into Samaria (Acts 8:1), while chapter 10 relates how it first reached the Gentiles. From the thirteenth chapter onward the circle widens further to include the entire region we now call the Middle East—with Paul as the greatest apostle to the Gentiles.

The mission theme is ever present in the New Testament Epistles, sometimes explicit, sometimes implicit. *Mission is the core business of the church.* "The church of Christ on earth was organized for missionary purposes, and the Lord desires to see the entire church devising ways and means whereby high and low, rich and poor, may hear the message of truth."[12] The church is to be God's missionary agency par excellence. It must not leave the mission task to the world to para-church organizations, which can only provide extra support. But a sound ecclesiology demands that mission remain the prime responsibility of the church. "However much the days and ages may change as the church carries out her mission on the six continents, one fact never changes: Jesus Christ is urging on His church to complete its missionary calling as He guides her to her final destination. And this missionary movement which emanates from Him will not cease until the end of the world. Thus, even though the methods of carrying it out must be changed continually, the task itself remains the same."[13]

The Uniqueness of Christianity and of Adventism

Getting involved in missions makes sense only if it makes a difference whether one does or not. The gospel is about God's grace. His greatest desire is to see people saved for eternity. The apparent delay in the Second Coming is because of this: God is patient with humanity, "not wanting anyone to perish" (2 Peter 3:9). When the moment of Christ's coming arrives, the remnant may, therefore, be surprisingly large! For the gospel is good news. "It is not an announcement of terror, but news of God's boundless generosity."[14] The song written more than 150 years ago by Frederick W. Faber states a truth never to be forgotten: "There's a wideness in God's mercy, like the wideness of the sea" and "The love of God is broader than the measure of man's mind."[15]

The biblical data do not, however, point toward universalism, that is, the view that ultimately all will be saved. Many will be saved, but regrettably many will also be tragically lost. All the straightforward texts about the judgment and about the rejection and punishment awaiting those who continue to rebel against God cannot be explained away by interpreting them as mere hyperbolic speech.

A related issue, about which there is an ongoing debate, is the salvific status of Christianity among other religions. Again, we can deal with this topic only briefly. Three main positions have emerged.[16]

1. Pluralism. According to this view, God reveals Himself in all religious traditions. Every religion is said to provide a road to the beyond. These roads are all historically and culturally conditioned. This sounds like an attractive idea, and it certainly appeals to postmodern minds. It has, however, serious consequences for the whole concept of missions. For if this view is correct, why "go" out into the world and try to persuade adherents of all religions to become Christians? They will be saved anyway!

2. Universalism. Those who defend this idea focus on a rather limited number of biblical passages that appear to stress the universal impact of divine grace. A favorite text of the universalists is 1 Corinthians 15:22-28. It refers to the sequence in which various groups will be saved, with the glorious end result that "God may be all in all" (verse 28). Other oft-quoted texts include 1 Timothy 2:3, 4; Romans 2:6-16; 1 John 2:2; Romans 5:12-19; and Philippians 2:9-11. The proponents of this view do not, however, take into account the clear passages that emphasize other aspects of God's interactions with humankind. Those texts that speak about eternal damnation are played down and explained as hyperbolic figures of speech. Some universalists believe that those who have not chosen rightly in this life will have a postmortem chance to remake their choices. The statements in 1 Peter 3:18-20 and 4:6 are cited in support. This is a striking example of how at times one or two problematic texts are used to give support to a certain theory, while a multitude of texts that affirm the opposite position are fully ignored!

3. Exclusivism or Restrictivism. This theory defends the view that salvation is only through Christ. People need to hear the gospel and must re-

spond. *There is no other name that brings salvation than the name of Christ*, the supporters of this view say. The most popular texts in support of this view include Acts 4:12; John 14:6; Mark 16:16; and 1 Timothy 2:5. If some "honest" people will be saved without having had the opportunity to hear the full gospel, their salvation will—whether they realize it or not—be through the merits of Jesus Christ. One cannot escape the conclusion, however, that ultimately some people will be lost and that somehow the church's missionary effort does make an eternal difference for humanity.

Adventists are among those who believe that when all the biblical data are fully considered and weighed, the only defensible view is the last one. They do not believe that non-Christians are beyond God's reach of grace, and they also believe that through Christ people may be saved, even though they never had the opportunity to hear about Him and to consciously decide to follow Him. Ellen White remarked in this connection: "Even among the heathen there were men through whom Christ was working to uplift the people from their sin and degradation."[17] And she adds that this continues to be the case in the present: "Among the heathen are those who worship God ignorantly, to whom the light is never brought by human instrumentality, yet they will not perish."[18]

Christians should not apologize for the uniqueness they claim for their faith. It makes a vital difference whether one is a Christian or not. If all religions were equally valid, a fully secular worldview would be just as acceptable. Together with many other Christians, Adventists defend the uniqueness of Christianity because of the uniqueness of its Founder, Jesus Christ. They recognize that there are similarities between most of the world religions, but they also are convinced that there are crucial differences between Jesus and the founders of other religions. No other religious founder ever claimed to be the eternal Creator-God, forgave sins, or rose from the dead. The main criterion is not whether a religion can satisfy the religious needs and sentiments of its adherents. The truth claim cannot be brushed aside. Since the various religions make mutually incompatible claims about reality, logic demands we recognize that they cannot all be equally true. This does not mean that all religions—except one—are totally bad and that we cannot learn anything from them. It does mean that a choice has to be made. For Christians that choice is and remains for or against Christ as the Savior of humanity!

The Adventist Self-understanding in Mission

Even when it is accepted that Christianity is unique among the world religions and that Christ is the only avenue toward salvation, the question will remain whether Adventism has a unique status within Christianity. The answer to this question has two aspects. On the one hand, Seventh-day Adventists do not believe that they are the only agents in God's plan for the salvation of humanity. On the other hand, Adventists see themselves as key players in the end-time missionary thrust. From early on in their history they have considered themselves "the remnant." There seems to be a certain shift, however, in the Adventist remnant theology, from stressing the fact that *they are the remnant* to an increasing emphasis on the fact that a special *message must be brought to the remnant* of this world.[19]

The message to be preached is the good news of the "eternal gospel" (Rev. 14:6). It is eternal, and in that sense it is not new. It is the biblical message of salvation in Christ, with the accompanying call to dedicated discipleship. It is the good news that Jesus is the Messiah of prophecy, and its proclamation pays attention to everything that leads up to His coming and results from it.[20]

But the proclamation of the gospel message in the end of time now focuses on a number of particular issues that are communicated in Revelation 14:6-12. The proclamation of the good news is based on the *eternal* gospel, but it also becomes, in a special sense, *present* truth. The three messages of the angels in Revelation 14 refer to issues and developments that the Adventist pioneers of the nineteenth century recognized as happening in their own time. The message of the first angel referred, in their view, to the forceful proclamation of the expected second coming of Christ during the 1830s and early 1840s, and the second message about the "fall" of Babylon was understood as the rejection by mainline Christianity of this Advent message. The message of the third angel was applied to the (partly still future) controversy between those who had discovered the truth of the seventh-day Sabbath and those who had or would reject this symbol of loyalty to God.[21]

As time progressed and Seventh-day Adventism defined its mission to the world more precisely, a further interpretation developed, and verse 12 of Revelation 14 began to be perceived as part of the third angel's message.[22] These three messages were to be the ongoing focus in the preaching of the eternal gospel and were of great significance for the Adventist identity. This was in particular true of the third message, which was understood not just as the climax of all three messages but also as including the first two. This "special message" of Revelation 14 was not to be disconnected from the gospel message as traditionally understood, as if other

Christians were preaching the gospel in general terms, while Adventists were concentrating only on their special message. When people asked Ellen White whether the "eternal" gospel message of justification by faith could be linked to the message of the third angel, she replied, "It is the third angel's message in verity."[23]

The messages of the three angels are, in the Adventist interpretation, not just related to the issue of Sabbath versus Sunday and the expected end-time consequences thereof, but also to other specific doctrinal insights, such as the beginning of the initial stage of the divine judgment, while the first message also lays great stress on the fact that God is the Creator-God—a very "present" truth in a time when God is no longer seen by the majority of the so-called intelligentsia as the ultimate explanation for the existence of our universe, the earth, and each one of us.

Ellen White summarized the importance and comprehensiveness of the three messages, which are at the core of how Adventists understand their mission, in these words: "The proclamation of the third angel's message calls for the presentation of the Sabbath truth. This truth, with others included in the message, is to be proclaimed; but the great center of attraction, Christ Jesus, must not be left out."[24]

Adventists can understand their movement basically in three different ways:

1. The Adventist Church is the "true" church, and other churches are "false." Adventists, therefore, are the only true witnesses and carry out the only true Christian missionary work. We have noted that this view misses a firm biblical foundation and does not reflect official Adventist thinking.

2. The Adventist Church is one among many different segments of current Christianity—it is just one option among many other valid options. It is not so important that people are "reached" by Adventists, as long as they are "reached" by the Christian message in some form or another. This view has the advantage that it emphasizes the fact that Adventists share many beliefs with other Christians and recognizes the brotherhood that exists, or should exist, between them and all others who are committed to following Christ.

3. Even though Adventists do not claim to be the only ones involved in Christian missions, they do claim to present a Christian option that offers a number of insights not readily available elsewhere (in particular the relevance of the passage in Revelation 14:6-12) and to correct certain opinions and traditions that are widely held among other Christians. They also place special emphasis on certain neglected but essential elements of

Scripture. In other words: Adventism makes a vital contribution to the richness of Christianity. The third view is the traditional view within Adventism.

Contextualization

As discussed in the previous chapter, the outreach of the Adventist Church must have two foci: (1) the preaching of the gospel as understood by Seventh-day Adventists and (2) a practical manifestation of the power of the gospel in humanitarian and social work. The content of what is preached and done in the context of fulfilling the gospel commission is of paramount importance, but the form in which what is preached and done is translated and packaged is also crucial. The content of what is said and done must of necessity be packaged into a particular form. In the Christian West there has long been a close alliance between the Christian faith and Enlightenment ideas. Many of us have become so used to the form in which the message comes to us that we hardly realize this package is shaped by modern Western culture and its underlying philosophies. What is needed, Leslie Newbigin affirms, is that this alliance be disentangled, "so that the word of the gospel can be heard distinctly in its own right and not as part of a world view into which it has so generally been domesticated."[25]

Every effort must be made to ensure that the Christian message, in word and deed, is not obscured or modified in the communication process. But it is just as true that this process does not take place in a void. The apostle Paul asks the pregnant question: "How, then, can they call on the one they have believed in? And how can they believe in the one of whom they have not heard? . . . Consequently, faith comes from hearing the message" (Rom. 10:14-17). People must hear the gospel before they can respond to it.[26] The hearing implies not just the reception of some audible or even audiovisual stimuli by the brain but presupposes that the message is delivered and received in such a way that the receiver perceives what it is about and can respond to it. Communication is never a simple process. But when the "sender" and the "receiver" belong to different cultures (which may well be the case even though they live in the same geographical location or have the same nationality), the communication process becomes infinitely more complicated. The Holy Spirit must be at work if the message, which is spiritual in nature, is to be understood by carnal people, who have often to a major extent lost the affinity with religious notions, feelings, and emotions. God facilitates the communication process through His Spirit, but He always uses human channels and expects them to "translate" what He wants to say in terms that the target audience will understand. That is to say, the message must always be thoroughly contextualized. The unchanging content of the good news must be presented in such a form that it can be understood by people who live in a particular historical, cultural, and social context and belong to a particular age bracket, speak a particular language, and are steeped in particular traditions. If the church wants to be serious about its mission, it has the God-given challenge to "translate" its message in ways that will ensure that what it proclaims remains "present truth" for all the "nations" to which it must be preached.

Although the term *contextualization* (or its equivalent, *enculturation*, which was often preferred by Roman Catholic theologians) may be of rather recent vintage, there is nothing new about the concept itself. In biblical times divine revelation always came within a given historical context. Students of the Old Testament have long been aware of parallels between the Old Testament and certain aspects of other ancient cultures. Israel was allowed to share in many of the forms that were current in its day. "The biblical evidence underlines the importance of careful attention to the cultural horizons of the audience," writes Jon Paulien in his challenging book *Everlasting Gospel, Ever-changing World*.[27] That was true in Old Testament days, as it has always been—as long as the meaning of rites, ceremonies, architectural designs, etc., were not compromised. Whatever criticism feminist theology may rightfully deserve, it has greatly, and justifiably, increased the awareness of theologians and nontheologians alike that the form in which the message of the Old Testament has been transmitted to us bears the stamp of the patriarchal culture of the times. (Traditionally, Christian theology has been the domain of Western men. It is not only legitimate but absolutely necessary that women and people from non-Western cultures contextualize the Christian message for the population segments they represent.)

Signs of contextualization also abound in the New Testament. The events that occurred in Palestine were soon reported to a non-Jewish audience, and the meaning of what had transpired was soon to be expressed in Greek terms. Paul deliberately attempted to contextualize his message. He did not expect his Gentile audience to adopt the Jewish culture in which he himself had grown up.[28] He said, "I have become all things to all men" (1 Cor. 9:22). He adapted what he said (and did) linguistically and culturally to the various publics he sought to reach.

The incarnation of Jesus Christ provides the indisputable argument

187

that contextualization is essential to God's method of communication and should therefore be the key to any mission strategy the church devises. "It is nothing short of amazing that the God of all the universe would choose our familiar turf, our way of life, our language, our total frame of reference rather than His own to be the context within which He interacts with us."[29]

The history of the Christian church and of Christian missions in particular provides us with many examples of where a neglect of contextualization led to missionary failure. One dramatic case is, for instance, the almost total demise of the Christian faith along the West African coast after Catholic missionaries had made promising inroads, especially during the sixteenth-century kingdom of Congo. The early successes were not sustained, mainly because Christianity was never truly indigenized. It remained a foreign element and almost totally disappeared until a new beginning was made in the nineteenth century.[30] Looking at the church in another part of Africa, we see that the church did not survive in North Africa and Nubia, whereas the church in Egypt and Ethiopia was able to withstand the threat of Islam, at least to some extent. How is this to be explained? The difference in the degree of contextualization was probably the most important factor. In North Africa the Christian faith was never sufficiently "owned" by the indigenous people and was ultimately abandoned in favor of Islam, which proved to be more affirming of the local cultures.

From about 1800 the strong belief of most missionaries in the superiority of Western culture led to a greatly diminished emphasis on the need for adaptation. The 1800 to 1950 period has been referred to as the era of noncontextualization.[31] Even today we find in many places of the world the tragic results of what happens when foreign forms are forced upon the people, and, as a result, the Christian faith, in many ways, remains a foreign religion. There is little doubt that the explosive growth of many independent churches in Africa must, at least in part, be understood as a rejection of noncontextualized forms of Christian religion and as a sincere attempt "to make Christianity relevant to the totality of the African experience of life."[32] Contextualization is not just an option to be considered. It is imperative because the church is called to follow in the footsteps of the Master, who was prepared to enter a totally foreign culture and who contextualized His truth in word and deed to fit within the context of early-first-century Jewish life in Palestine.

In Ellen White's day the issue of contextualization had not emerged in its more recent forms, and we can therefore hardly expect that she would have addressed the topic in current terms. Yet, although she did not know the term, she repeatedly stressed the need for the church, its workers, and its members to contextualize their missionary methods: "The servants of Christ should accommodate themselves to the varied conditions of the people. . . . Labor will have to be varied to meet the people where they are."[33] In another publication she stated that this process goes beyond the mere adaptation of methods: "The people of every country have their own peculiar, distinctive characteristics, and it is necessary that men should be wise in order that they may know how to adapt themselves to the peculiar ideas of the people, and so introduce the truth that they may do them good. They must be able to understand and meet their wants."[34] The following remark certainly has a broader application than originally intended: "We need to move with the greatest wisdom, that we shall not in anything create prejudice by giving the impression that Americans feel themselves superior to people of other nations."[35]

Contextualization has many different aspects. It impacts the way Bible translators struggle to find words and expressions that do not compromise the meaning of the Word but can be readily understood by the intended audience. It has to do with the words and metaphors that are chosen to express doctrinal truth and the choice of real-life illustrations that are used to explain what the doctrinal statements intend to convey. It impacts the way the church organizes itself, the way in which it worships, and the methods it uses in evangelization. It may well be that in today's world a critical contextualization of worship forms must have special priority, so that all age groups and ethnic groups may have as meaningful a worship experience as possible. Theology will, inevitably, always develop in a particular context, within a given faith community. Theology will, therefore, always, at least to some extent, be contextualized theology. It should be, if theology is to connect with real life.

Any kind of contextualization must, however, always be critical contextualization. That holds true for theology in general and also for all the other aspects we just mentioned. It cannot be emphasized enough that forms and methods may be borrowed and/or adapted, but the pure content of the message must never be compromised. Syncretism (an uncritical mixture of elements from different cultures and religions, such as in the New Age movement) is unacceptable. Jon Dybdahl, Old Testament scholar and missiologist, lists six key principles that may guide the church in its attempts to safeguard contextualization from syncretism: 1. Maintain

189

a close connection with the Scriptures. 2. Pray for and trust in God's leading. 3. Check our own motives and attitudes; are we truly trying to proclaim the gospel as clearly as possible, or are we mainly following some
popular missiological trends? 4. Consult the community of believers. There
is always wisdom in listening to what the Spirit says to the body of Christ.
Believers in the targeted culture should lead out in the process of contextualization. The danger of syncretism is greatly reduced if many
thinking and praying minds cooperate. 5. Realize that over time, truth
surfaces. Wrong decisions can be rectified if we allow the Spirit to work.
6. Maintain concern for "the weak." The principle outlined by Paul in
1 Corinthians 9:22, 23 still stands. The opinions and feelings of fellow
believers who express fears and doubts about the contextualizing process
must be considered.[36]

---

[1] One of the best surveys of mission history remains Stephen Neill, *A History of Christian Missions* (Penguin Books, 1964).

[2] For a concise survey of the development of Adventist missions, see George R. Knight, *A Brief History of Seventh-day Adventists* (Hagerstown, MD: Review and Herald Publishing Association, 1999), passim. See also Richard W. Schwartz and Floyd Greenleaf, *Light Bearers: A History of the Seventh-day Adventist Church,* in particular chapter 9, "Worldwide Outreach, 1868-1885" (pp. 130-145), and chapter 14, "Mission Advance, 1887-1900" (pp. 207-224). For the theological developments that stimulated and accompanied increased mission outreach, see P. G. Damsteegt, *Toward the Theology of Mission of the Seventh-day Adventist Church* (Grand Rapids: William B. Eerdmans Pub. Co., 1977).

[3] Schwartz and Greenleaf, pp. 273-292.

[4] A number of specialized agencies collect such statistics. A good, annually updated source is the *International Bulletin of Missionary Research.*

[5] *Statistical Report to the Annual Council of the General Conference Committee 2008* (Washington, D.C.: Office of Archives and Statistics, General Conference of Seventh-day Adventists, 2008). See http://www.adventistarchives.org/docs/Stats/ACRep2008.pdf.

[6] A basic but very informative guide to the theology and practical reality of missions (from an Adventist perspective) is Erich W. Baumgartner et al., eds., *Passport to Mission* (Berrien Springs, Mich.: Andrews University, Institute of World Mission, 1999).

[7] George W. Peters, *A Biblical Theology of Missions* (Chicago: Moody Press, 1984), p. 27.

[8] E. G. White, *The Desire of Ages*, p. 822.

[9] David J. Bosch, *Transforming Mission: Paradigm Shifts in Theology of Mission* (Maryknoll, N.Y.: Orbis Books, 1991), pp. 63-65.

[10] Patrick Johnstone, *Operation World* (Grand Rapids: Zondervan Pub. House, 1993), p. 654.

[11] Johannes Verkuyl, "The Biblical Foundation of the Worldwide Mission Mandate," in Ralph D. Winter and Steven C. Hawthorne, eds., *Perspectives on the World Christian Movement: a Reader* (Pasadena, Calif.: William Carey Library, 1992). p. A 62.

[12] E. G. White, *Testimonies*, vol. 6, p. 29.

[13] Verkuyl, in Water and Hawthorne, p. A 63.

[14] Clark H. Pinnock, *A Wideness in God's Mercy: The Finality of Jesus Christ in a World of Religions* (Grand Rapids: Zondervan Pub. House, 1992), p. 178.

[15] *The Seventh-day Adventist Hymnal,* no. 114.

[16] See Gabriel Fackre, Ronald H. Nash, and John Sanders, *What About Those Who Have Never Heard?* (Downers Grove, Ill.: InterVarsity Press, 1995). Also Leslie Newbigin, *The Gospel in a Pluralist Society* (Grand Rapids: William B. Eerdmans Pub. Co., 1989); Harold A. Netland, *Dissonant Voices: Religious Pluralism and the Question of Truth* (Grand Rapids: William B. Eerdmans Pub. Co., 1989); Paul F. Knitter, *No Other Name? A Critical Survey of Christian Attitudes Toward the World Religions* (Maryknoll, N.Y.: Orbis Books, 1990); John Sanders, *No Other Name: An Investigation Into the Destiny of the Unevangelized* (Grand Rapids: William B. Eerdmans Pub. Co., 1992).

[17] E. G. White, *The Desire of Ages,* p. 35.

[18] *Ibid.,* p. 638.

[19] George R. Knight, "Remnant Theology and World Mission," in Jon L. Dybdahl, ed., *Adventist Mission in the 21st Century* (Hagerstown, Md.: Review and Herald Pub. Assn., 1999), p. 94.

[20] Hans K. LaRondelle, *How to Understand the End-Time Prophecies of the Bible* (Sarasota, Fla.: First Impressions, 1997), p. 331.

[21] See "Three Angel's Messages" in the *Seventh-day Adventist Encyclopedia* (1996), vol. II, pp. 773, 774.

[22] See G. R. Knight, *A Search for Identity,* pp. 47-50, 75-81.

[23] Ellen G. White, in *Review and Herald,* Apr. 1, 1890.

[24] E. G. White, *Gospel Workers,* p. 156.

[25] Leslie Newbigin, "Preface," in James M. Phillips and Rover T. Coote, eds., *Toward the 21st Century in Christian Mission* (William B. Eerdmans Pub. Co., 1993), p. 5.

[26] The following paragraphs reflect my article "Contextualizing: Option or Imperative?" in *Ministry,* December 1997, pp. 14-16.

[27] Nampa: Pacific Press Pub. Assn., 2008, p. 14.

[28] Oscar I. Romo, *American Mosaic: Church Planting in Ethnic America* (Nashville: Broadman Press, 1993), p. 64.

[29] Charles H. Kraft, *Communication Theory for Christian Witness* (Maryknoll, N.Y.: Orbis Books, 1991), p. 14.

[30] J. Herbert Kane, *A Concise History of the Christian World Mission* (Grand Rapids: Baker Book House, 1991), pp. 69, 70.

[31] Paul G. Hiebert, "Critical Contextualization," *International Bulletin of Missionary Research,* July 1987, p. 104.

[32] Peter B. Clarke, *West Africa and Christianity* (London: Edward Arnold Publishers, 1986), p. 163.

[33] E. G. White, *Testimonies,* vol. 2, p. 673. See also E. G. White, *Gospel Workers,* pp. 117-119.

[34] Ellen G. White, *Testimonies to Ministers and Gospel Workers* (Mountain View, Calif.: Pacific Press Pub. Assn., 1923), p. 213.

[35] Ellen G. White, letter 24, 1884, in D. A. Delafield, *Ellen G. White in Europe* (Washington, D.C.: Review and Herald Pub. Assn., 1975), pp. 135, 136.

[36] Jon Dybdahl, "Cross-cultural Adaptation: How to Contextualize the Gospel," *Ministry,* November 1992, p. 16.

Chapter 13

The Future of the Church

W e began our study of the doctrine of the church with some observations about the many challenges that increasingly beleaguer the
Christian church—in particular in the Western world—at the beginning of
a new millennium. We noted that there is indeed a crisis of momentous
proportions in many sectors of Christianity and that the Christian message
appears to lose much of its power, first under the impact of the nineteenth-
and twentieth-century celebration of the sufficiency of human reason and
more recently because of the postmodern ways of thinking. But we also
suggested that in many areas of world the church is still very much alive
and even growing by leaps and bounds and that also developments in the
Western world suggest an often surprising vitality in old ecclesiastical structures as well as many refreshing grassroot initiatives. In the final chapter of
a book such as this, it is fitting to give further attention to the future of the
church.

Thousands of books have been published in recent years about the future of the church. Many of the voices that we hear are pessimistic, but
there are also sociologists of religion and other experts who increasingly
argue for an important place for the church in the years to come, even
though many doubt whether most of the current ecclesiastical structures
will survive and suggest that the baby boomers may well be the last generation that finds a spiritual home in the existing churches.[1] Even Evangelical
leaders admit that denominational loyalties are in serious decline.[2] Some
believe that as a result of less doctrinal emphasis, mergers between denominations will become easier. Many believe that we are moving to forms of
postdenominational Christianity, in which doctrine will no longer play a
significant role as an ever-greater variety of spiritual traditions are welcomed to cater for the smorgasbord of religious needs and tastes. Brian D.
McLaren, author and senior pastor of the Cedar Ridge Community
Church in the Washington, D.C.-Baltimore area, writes: "The spiritual

resurgence that I see brewing is unconventional and even irreverent at times, outside the boundary of our institutional religion."[3] Many church planters and others who experiment on the edge of today's denominations suggest that we simply do not know what kind of church will "emerge." "Emerging churches are communities," they say, "that practice the way of Jesus within postmodern cultures."[4] The "kingdom practices" of these communities will "deconstruct" the conventional church practices, and these communities will be "families" rather than institutions.[5]

Indeed, many questions may be asked about the ways in which future Christianity will manifest itself in our world. Some of the new forms that are developing may be quite legitimate, considering the challenge of con-textualization. But at the same time, questions will continuously need to be raised about the biblical and theological legitimacy of how the future of Christianity is shaping up.

The Future of Adventism

Many questions can likewise be raised about the future of Seventh-day Adventism. Adventism is not immune to most of the challenges that Christianity in general faces. Is the Adventist Church in crisis, as many crit-ical voices within the church maintain, and as both the title of a recent book by a sociologist at Georgia Southwestern State University and the title of a book by an Adventist theologian suggest?[6] The answer to that question probably depends mostly on how we define the word "crisis."

In his important book *The Church as a Social Institution: The Sociology of American Religion,* which has become a classic, David O. Moberg[7] argued that every denomination will, like any other organization, move through a life cycle in which five stages can be identified. In his terminology these are: (1) incipient organization; (2) formal organization; (3) maximum effi-ciency; (4) institutionalism; and (5) disintegration. Does this apply to the Adventist Church as well? George R. Knight suggested in 1995 that the Adventist Church in North America is "teetering on the divide between stages three and four."[8] That assessment may, I feel, be too positive, and it should also be added that it does not apply just to North America. On the other hand, Knight correctly emphasizes that according to Moberg, the process is not totally inevitable and may be reversed! This may not be easy, however, for it is also true that *"the history of the Adventist Church indicates that it never makes structural changes of a major sort until it is on the brink of or-ganizational and financial collapse."*[9] And "the only thing that can be said with certainty now is that Adventism will be swept down the river by the same sociological forces [that have swept many other denominations before it] unless it *deliberately chooses and courageously acts* to reverse the patterns of institutionalization and secularization."[10]

Other voices in contemporary Adventism strike similar warnings. William G. Johnsson, former general editor of the *Adventist Review*, lists 10 issues that are fragmenting the church today.[11] A. Leroy Moore, pastor and church administrator, wrote about "issues that divide us" in his book *Adventism in Conflict*.[12] And a regular perusal of independently published Adventist magazines such as *Spectrum* and *Adventist Today* (on the "left") and *Adventists Affirm* (on the "right"), as well as of denominationally sponsored journals, reveals how widespread the feeling that dangerous ideas and practices may destroy the church or, at least, seriously hamper its mission is.

To many, the wide theological diversity that can now be found in the church—in sermons from the pulpits, in Adventist university classrooms, in the denominational and independent print media, DVD productions, television programs, as well as in the theological thinking (or the lack thereof) by members in the pew—is greatly alarming, and many wonder how much theological diversity the church can tolerate without falling into apostasy.

The Future Is Secure

We must be realistic, but we need not be prophets of doom. For although Christianity is currently passing through heavy weather, the ship of the church will not go under and will, in the end, safely dock at its port of destination. When Christ departed, He promised to be with His followers "always, to the very end of the age" (Matt. 28:20). Twenty centuries of church history testify to the truth of these words. The church has survived the continuous onslaughts of its numerous enemies from without and within. This can also be said of the Adventist Church. More than a century and a half of Adventist history gives ample credence to the oft-quoted words of Ellen White: "In reviewing our past history, having traveled over every step of advance to our present standing, I can say, Praise God! As I see what God has wrought, I am filled with astonishment, and with confidence in Christ as leader. We have nothing to fear for the future except as we shall forget the way the Lord has led us."[13] This statement finds its echo in words written more recently: "The denomination has everything to hope for in terms of the future as long as it submits to the progressive leading of God."[14]

Interesting though a discussion based on sociological and historical developments may be, the question that concerns us above everything else is to what extent the Bible informs us about the future of the church. No doctrine of the church is balanced and complete without anchoring the church in its divine origin and solidly affirming its ultimate glorious future success.

There are some very good and very basic reasons to be optimistic about the future of the church. They all, in fact, are aspects of the one inestimable truth: The church is, in essence, not a human institution. *It is not our church. It is the church of Jesus Christ.* If it were our church, there would indeed be reason for despair. Since it is God's church, we can be sure that He will finish what He has begun (Phil. 1:6). Our certainty that all is going to be well stems from a number of foundational truths:

1. Christ founded the church. He said to Peter, and through him to all of us: *I* will build *my* church! (Matt. 16:18). The building comes with the best possible guarantee that it will endure.

2. The church is not based on some human ideal, philosophy, or program. It is built *on the Rock*, on the Truth, in which all other truths find their anchor: the confession that Jesus Christ is the Son of the living God (Matt. 16:16–18). This is the foundation for the salvation of humanity. It is not something that fills only a very temporary need and has only temporary appeal.

3. Christ is the head of the church. "He is the head of the body, the church . . . , so that in everything He might have the supremacy" (Col. 1:18).

4. Christ has given His Spirit to sustain His church and to give it the directions it needs. "The Holy Spirit, whom the Father will send in my name, will teach you all things, and will remind you of everything I have said to you" (John 14:26).

5. He has commissioned us with a charge that knows of no temporal or geographical limit (Matt. 28:19; Mark 16:15). The gospel message that is to be communicated is not a message that has a limited application, and there is no moment when the church can lean back and conclude that its assignment is completed.

6. The church will not be allowed to fizzle out but will be further empowered by **a final outpouring of the Spirit** (Joel 2:28–32).

7. Christ will not forsake His church, but **will always be with His people** (Matt. 28:20). And at last He will come for them to take them home (John 14:1–3).

In the first chapter of the book of Revelation we encounter a sublime picture of Christ's intimate connection with His church. (I referred to this earlier, but it is so beautiful and encouraging that I want to mention it again.) When John was "in the Spirit," he heard a voice, and when he turned to see whom the voice belonged to, he had a vision of Christ. Christ is described as "someone like a son of man." He is identified as "the First and the Last," "the Living One" (Rev. 1:9-18). John saw Christ and he saw "seven golden lamp stands," and Christ was walking in the midst of these candlesticks (as they are referred to in other Bible versions). The seven lampstands are identified in the final verse of the chapter as "the seven churches" (verse 20). What more encouraging picture could there be than that of the risen Christ walking in the midst of His church! This must have been an enormous boost for the morale of those seven small local first-century churches near the coast of ancient Asia Minor who were the first recipients of the book of Revelation. But since these seven churches clearly represent the church universal, it is likewise a tremendous encouragement for Christians today. This deep interest in His church and His continuing presence among the communities of His followers is further reflected in the seven letters that are recorded in chapters 2 and 3. Each of these letters shows that He is totally aware of what His people are going through. None of their worries and challenges escapes His loving notice, and for each church He has a promise that in the end all will be well.

What Will the Church of the Future Be Like?

There is no doubt that the Christian church will continue to change. As we noted earlier, in the past few decades the church is moving south. Pentecostals and some other segments of Christianity continue to experience enormous gains, while year after year many traditional churches see their membership erode. In many areas in the world relationships between Catholics and Protestants have dramatically improved, and many hope this development will continue—while this is one of the greatest fears of many others. In many Christian denominations, moral codes that once seemed to be absolute have lost their grip on the people. How one thinks about these and many other developments depends to a large extent on how one reads the Bible and to what extent the "thus says the Lord" is considered normative. At the same time it must, of course, be remembered that changes in external forms are to be expected as times and circumstances change and that it is not the change in forms but the change in content that we should worry about.

This also holds true for the Adventist Church. That the church would change in its forms, its organizational arrangements, its evangelistic methodologies, etc., was to be expected. Change in form—continuous critical contextualization—is needed if the church is to connect with the audience it faces in the twenty-first century and not to become like a museum. (Not even all *theological* development or refinement is by definition wrong and dangerous. It has been one of the fundamental characteristics of the Adventist Church to grow theologically as time goes by and to leave behind many concepts that once seemed quite valid.) Methods will (hopefully!) continue to change. It is impossible to predict how this will affect the way the church will go about its business a few decades from now.

The church may decide to drastically overhaul its administrative system and to adapt its organizational and leadership structures because of political circumstances or other external pressures, financial restraints, or for a multitude of other reasons. According to Barry Oliver, a prominent Australian church administrator, "flexibility of administrative structures is needed in the Seventh-day Adventist Church so that the continuing internationalization can be facilitated on a global scale. The flexibility is permitted by the ecclesiological functionalism of the church, the commitment of Ellen White to the need for change if necessary [as clearly demonstrated during the radical reorganizations in 1901-1903], and the priority of principle over form." The church must determine "whether its commitment to global mission is to be the organizing principle which is ultimately determinative of its structural form."[15]

Whether the church remains true to its calling does not depend on the way it is organized, as long as fundamental biblical principles about the nature of the church are not compromised. And it does not depend on worship styles, mission methods, or other forms in which the church manifests itself, as long as the core content of the gospel message is not diluted. The key question has always been and will continue to be in the future: Does the church maintain its loyalty to its Lord? Or, in biblical parlance: Does the church still consist of people who "obey God's commandments and hold to the testimony of Jesus" (Rev. 12:17)?

The End-time Church

As difficult as it is to extrapolate present trends in the world of world religions and in Christianity—including Adventism—this is even more the case when we look at developments from an eschatological perspective. On the basis of biblical apocalyptic prophecy it is safe to predict that the

197

final events in the religio-political history of this world will not be mere intensifications of present trends but may turn out quite differently from what we now might expect on the basis of trends we currently discern or expect. This is not to say that the end-time scenario is not linked to events, worldviews, institutions, and powers that have been and presently are part of human history. But the things that will take place as history reaches its climax will be of a magnitude and intensity that is as yet unheard-of and is quite unfathomable. And, therefore, it would appear to be wise, on the one hand, to underline that humankind is in for something that is extremely serious and that is as yet quite unimaginable. Whereas on the other hand, we should refrain from detailed predictions as to how these events will shape up and what powers will eventually play precisely what role.

The book of Revelation pictures a development that leads to a final and absolute polarization: Jerusalem against Babylon—those who reject the Creator-God with His offer of grace through His Son, Jesus Christ, and who refuse to live by His directives, over and against those who belong to a faithful "remnant" and have decided to be and remain on God's side regardless of whatever happens.

In this last Bible book we read about ("experience" might be an even better word when we immerse ourselves in the scenes that are presented to us and use all our senses to imagine what it will be like) a final battle between two confederacies—between the powers of evil and all those who are loyal toward the true God. A number of Adventist Bible scholars have in recent books given a fresh and very thoughtful interpretation of the events described in Revelation 12-22. Jon Paulien, dean of the faculty of theology at Loma Linda University, is foremost among them. He provides a clear and concise summary of the main elements.[16] The holy triune God—Father, Son, and Holy Spirit—are opposed in a life-and-death struggle by an unholy trinity—the "dragon" (Rev. 12), a "beast coming out of the sea" (Rev. 13:1-10), and "another beast, coming out of the earth" (Rev. 13:11-18), also referred to as the "false prophet" (Rev. 19:20).

Everything the triune God does will be counterfeited by His threefold adversary. A pure woman (a virgin bride) represents Jerusalem (Rev. 21:9, 10), the ultimate symbol for all those who have remained loyal to God, whereas a prostitute represents Babylon (Rev. 17:1-6), the ultimate symbol for the "end-time global confederacy of false religion."[17] God's people are commissioned to preach the everlasting gospel, as defined in a final appeal that is symbolized as a threefold angelic message (Rev. 14:6-12).

The global axis of evil tries to destroy God's people in every possible way. Its message is represented as a message of "three evil spirits that looked like frogs; they came out of the mouth of the dragon, out of the mouth of the beast and out of the mouth of the false prophet" (Rev. 16:13). God's enemies are collectively referred to as Babylon. God's people hear and heed the call to leave Babylon (Rev. 18:4). The final destiny of the worshippers of the beast (who bear the "mark of the beast" [see Rev. 14:11]) is reached when an angel with "a sharp sickle" cuts down all rebels so he can throw them "into the great winepress of God's wrath" (Rev. 14:17-20), whereas another angel, also equipped with a sickle, goes out to "reap" the harvest of grain at that final moment when "the time to reap has come, for the harvest of the earth is ripe" (verse 5) to gather those who have the seal of God. Those who are lost suffer the "second death," whereas this second death has no power over those who are eternally saved. All men and women who have deliberately chosen the side of the evil trio and have refused to listen to the final message of grace will eventually devour each other (Rev. 17:16). God's people, on the other hand, will be invitees at the "wedding supper of the Lamb" (Rev. 19:9).

Defining the "Remnant"

Is it possible to define those who will remain faithful in the face of this immense confederacy of evil and apostasy more precisely? Can we identify them with some organization or community that already exists today? It is tempting to do so. At the same time it is important not to move beyond the biblical data and to refrain from speculation. The history of prophetic interpretation should provide enough warning that it is easy to go astray and to point fingers in the wrong direction. Paulien believes that "the end-time religious opposition to God has a Christian face at an institutional level."[18] From our present perspective this seems quite likely, and recent and current developments in the religious world provide us with plenty of reasons to believe that several of the powers and trends that we have noticed in the past and continue to observe in the present will be part of the final axis of apostasy. But it is probably best not to proceed beyond that point.

Likewise, we must be careful not to move beyond the clear biblical data in defining the identity of the loyal believers. Is there an institutional continuity between those who today preach the gospel message with the specific end-time emphases of Revelation 14 and those who will remain loyal when the final crisis is there? The symbolism and vivid imagery of the

Revelation hardly allows for the continued existence of any kind of institutional life and organizational arrangements among God's people as we know them today when the great controversy reaches its crescendo. The persecution of the believers will almost certainly no longer leave any room for this.

There is lately a considerable discussion among Adventist theologians about the identity of the remnant.[19] Angel Rodríguez, a theologian at the church's headquarters office, lists six different views: (1) the traditional position that the Seventh-day Adventist Church is God's remnant community of the faithful; (2) the remnant concept that is broadened to include both Adventists and non-Adventists; (3) the remnant is to be found *within* the Adventist Church but may constitute only a small minority of Adventists; (4) the remnant is an invisible entity and includes all believers in any religious structure who are determined to remain faithful to God; (5) the remnant is still future, and it is impossible for any church to refer already to itself as the remnant; or finally, (6) the remnant is to be understood primarily in a sociological sense—those who belong to the remnant will work for justice and peace in this world. Rodríguez himself defends the traditional viewpoint, which identifies the Adventist Church as the remnant. But he accepts that there are believers outside the Adventist Church who should be included among the remnant.[20] He wrote: "The remnant is indeed larger than the historical manifestation in the Adventist Church as God's remnant. There is an invisible dimension to the remnant that transcends its historical and visible expression. But at the close of the history of sin, when the human race will be polarized, God's full and faithful remnant will be clearly distinguished from the rest of humanity. They will remain loyal to Christ as Savior and Lord, to the law of God and to the Scriptures. Adventists see themselves as instruments of God in gathering the faithful, eschatological remnant of God before the return of the Lord."[21]

Other Adventist scholars, however, increasingly suggest a wider application of the remnant concept, in particular in the future. Hans K. LaRondelle, a prominent systematic theologian who has written extensively on eschatology, points to the apostolic church, which saw thousands of new believers added to its number. He continues: "So shall the remnant church witness the predicted influx of 'believing remnants' of many peoples, who want to be instructed and saved on 'Mount Zion.' "[22] But he also maintains that in the present, as we live in the time leading up to the very end, the remnant is not merely an invisible remnant scattered through the Christian denominations but certainly also a visible faith community.[23]

The book *Seventh-day Adventists Answer Questions on Doctrine* continues to stir debate among Adventists. This is also true for what it states about the identity of the remnant: "Seventh-day Adventists firmly believe that God has a precious remnant, a multitude of earnest, sincere believers, in every church, not excepting the Roman Catholic communities, who are living up to all the light that God has given them."[24] And further: "We believe that finally the 'remnant' people will include every true and faithful follower of Christ."[25] Although *Questions on Doctrine*, as the book is popularly referred to, has been a highly influential book and was written by some of the foremost Adventist theologians of the church in the 1950s, there is no proof that it reflects in all aspects the majority thinking by church members.

Recently Jon Dybdahl has moved a little further than the authors of *Questions on Doctrine*. He maintains that neither in Scripture nor in the writings of Ellen G. White is the remnant directly equivalent to an institutional structure, church organization, or denominational entity. People inside the church can be lost, and since followers outside of it can be saved, he sees the "remnant people" as "those who are never satisfied with the status quo, but want to examine, learn, grow, and gather those 'scattered gems.' "[26] He wrote these words in 1996. A decade later he proposed that the Adventist Church is drawing a remnant not only from Christian backgrounds but from all religions. People from all kinds of religious backgrounds respond positively to the remnant message, even though they often do not at this point in time join the visible institutional form of the Adventist Church.[27]

Perhaps it would be best to focus on the clear characteristics that God's end-time people must exhibit: Obeying God and being firmly rooted in the faith of Christ—committed to a last-day mission to call the people all around the world to loyalty to their Creator. The most important question today, for me as an individual, is: Are these characteristics evident in my life, and am I totally serious about communicating a saving faith to others? This is what the Adventist community must constantly worry about: Does this church truly manifest these marks that underline its special role in the divine plan of redemption and is it faithful to its missionary calling? And is the Adventist Church today itself a "sign of the times," a clearly visible signal that the gospel is being preached to the world?[28]

Is there to be a direct link between the Adventist community and the people of God in the final crisis? It would be tragic if that were not the case. On the other hand, it is not very fruitful to try to predict how precisely the ranks on the two sides in the final battle for the mind of humankind will line up. Says Paulien: "The results of the final gospel proclamation is a worldwide confederacy of the saints, known as the remnant (Rev. 12:17); the 144.000 (Rev. 7:1-8 and 14:1-5); the great multitude (Rev. 7:9-17 and 19:1); the saints (Rev. 13:7; 14:12); the called, chosen, and faithful followers of the Lamb (Rev. 17:14); and the watchful ones who hang on to their garments (Rev. 16:15; 3:17, 18), which have been washed in the blood of the Lamb (Rev. 7:15-17; 19:7, 8). The multitude of images portray the one people of God at the end of time."[29]

Let's leave it at that, with the somewhat paradoxical assurance that although the Scriptures speak of a remnant (Rev. 12:17—the *hoi loipoi,* the remaining ones), the harvest will be astounding and result in "a great multitude that no one could count, from every nation, tribe, people and language" that will stand "before the throne and in front of the Lamb" (Rev. 7:9).

All Ends Well

This text in Revelation 7 that speaks of the multitude of the redeemed brings us to the end of our study. We have arrived at the point where we can speak of "the church triumphant." No longer are the saints a suffering remnant, their loyalty tested to the point of death, but in the graphic symbolism of the Revelation they wear white robes and they shout for joy: "Salvation belongs to our God, who sits on the throne, and to the Lamb" (verse 10).

As the apostle John was in the midst of this vision of the great multitude of those who had been saved, a heavenly being ("one of the elders") asked him, "These in white robes—who are they and where did they come from?" (verse 13). John answered with a short "Sir, you know" (verse 14). Then the heavenly speaker continued: "These are they who have come out of the great tribulation; they have washed their robes and made them white in the blood of the Lamb. Therefore, they are before the throne of God and serve him day and night in his temple; and he who sits on the throne will spread his tent over them. Never again will they hunger; never again will they thirst. The sun will not beat upon them, nor any scourging heat. For the Lamb at the center of the throne will be their shepherd; He will lead them to springs of living water. And God will wipe away every tear from their eyes" (verses 14-17). In other words, here are

God's people—at long last they have reached their destiny. They are with God and their future is forever secure.

It is no coincidence that the heavenly being in this vision refers to the Temple, the sublime symbol of God's atoning presence among His people. The symbol also occurs in the last two chapters of the Bible, where the eternal home of the church is depicted: a new earth with the New Jerusalem as its capital. Now there is no Babylon anymore anywhere to threaten God's people in Jerusalem. The city gates no longer need to be locked at night to protect the inhabitants from evildoers. God now "dwells" with His people, living in their midst. That is why this city is described as a cube—as wide as it is long and high! (Rev. 21:16). It has the shape of the Holy of Holies in the Old Testament sanctuary, which also was as wide as it was long and high (1 Kings 6:20). The Most Holy Place of the sanctuary was where God manifested His presence in a special way. Now, in all eternity, God is there with them. His people now have immediate access to Him. Our human minds do not grasp what eternal life in His presence will be like, but "life in the new Jerusalem is God's final word to futile hopes and utopian dreams of prosperity based on human strategy and effort. The New Jerusalem offers life without end and happiness without limit."[30]

The pilgrimage of the church has been long and difficult. There have been many detours, one-way streets, accidents, and obstacles along the road. But God did not leave His church without a Guide, and at last His people are home!

Let me end on a very personal note. As I write the final paragraphs of this book, we still live in the here and now. Planet Earth continues as the battleground between good and evil. The church is still imperfect and often fails to live up to its high calling. But the church is God's people, and the glorious truth is that we can be part of His people if we so choose. I embrace that privilege with all my heart. Many years ago I joined the Seventh-day Adventist Church, and I continue to cherish that choice. I know that God's people cannot simply be defined in terms of membership in a denomination, but I consider it a privilege to share in the insights in God's Word and the understanding of His dealings with humanity that Adventists have been entrusted with. I am proud to be a small cog in the mighty wheels that turn incessantly to reach the world with the Advent message of hope. And I sincerely hope that many of my brothers and sisters will, after reading this book, have a still better appreciation of what it means to be part of God's people.

[1] Eddie Gibbs and Ryan K. Bolger, *Emerging Churches* (London: SPCK, 2006), p. 21.

[2] Leith Anderson, *A Church for the 21st Century* (Minneapolis: Bethany House Pub., 1992), p. 28.

[3] Brian D. McLaren, *A New Kind of Christian,* (San Francisco: Jossey-Bass, 2001), p. 25.

[4] Gibbs and Bolger, p. 44.

[5] *Ibid.,* pp. 95ff.

[6] Laura L. Vance, *Seventh-day Adventism in Crisis: Gender and Sectarian Change in an Emerging Religion* (Chicago: University of Illinois Press, 1999); Jack W. Provonsha, *A Remnant in Crisis* (Hagerstown, Md.: Review and Herald Pub. Assn., 1993).

[7] Englewood Cliffs, N.J.: Prentice Hall, Inc., 1962, pp. 120, 121.

[8] George R. Knight, *The Fat Lady and the Kingdom* (Boise, Idaho: Pacific Press Pub. Assn., 1995), pp. 17, 18, 23-30; also G. R. Knight, *If I Were the Devil,* pp. 28, 29.

[9] Knight, *The Fat Lady and the Kingdom,* p. 18

[10] *Ibid.,* p. 35.

[11] William G. Johnsson, *The Fragmenting of Adventism* (Boise, Idaho: Pacific Press Pub. Assn., 1995).

[12] A. Leroy Moore, *Adventism in Conflict* (Hagerstown, Md.: Review and Herald Pub. Assn., 1995).

[13] E. G. White, *Testimonies to Ministers,* p. 31.

[14] Knight, *If I Were the Devil,* p. 38.

[15] Barry D. Oliver, *SDA Organizational Structure: Past, Present and Future* (Berrien Springs, Mich.: Andrews University Press, 1989), pp. 356, 357.

[16] See Jon Paulien, *Armageddon at the Door* (Hagerstown, Md.: Autumn House Pub., 2008), pp. 116-203.

[17] *Ibid.,* p. 125.

[18] *Ibid.*

[19] See Angel Manuel Rodriguez, "The Remnant and the Adventist Church," http://www.adventistbiblicalresearch.org/remnantSDAchurch.htm

[20] He recognizes that there is an article from Ellen G. White that points in that direction: "They Shall Be Mine, Saith the Lord of Hosts," *Signs of the Times,* Nov. 30, 1904, p. 1.

[21] Angel M. Rodríguez, "The SDA Church and the Christian World," in *Lutherans and Adventists in Conversation,* pp. 172, 173.

[22] H. K. LaRondelle, "The Remnant and the Three Angels' Messages," in R. Dederen, ed., *Handbook of Seventh-day Adventist Theology,* p. 870.

[23] Hans K. LaRondelle, *How to Understand the End-Time Prophecies of the Bible,* p. 280.

[24] *Seventh-day Adventists Answer Questions on Doctrines, Aanotated edition,* pp. 162, 163.

[25] *Ibid.,* p. 164.

[26] Jon L. Dybdahl, "It's God's Call: What It Means to Be the Remnant," *Adventist Review,* May 9, 1996, p. 14.

[27] Jon L. Dybdahl, "Doing Theology in Mission," *Ministry,* January 2006, p. 14. See also George R. Knight, "Remnant Theology and World Mission," in J. L. Dybdahl, ed., *Adventist Mission in the 21st Century,* p. 94.

[28] A point emphasized by Jan Paulsen, "The Adventist Church and the Signs of the Times," *Adventist Review,* Sept. 25, 2008, pp. 3-5.

[29] Paulien, *Armageddon,* p. 160.

[30] R. Stefanovic, *Revelation of Jesus Christ,* p. 599.

Index of Biblical References

Index of Names and Topics

Library of Adventist Theology, Book 1

At the very heart of Christianity is the issue of sin and atonement. George R. Knight addresses some of the crucial topics surrounding this issue, such as God's justice, the human response to salvation, and God's solution for reversing the consequences of sin. 978-0-8280-2067-1. Hardcover, 158 pages.

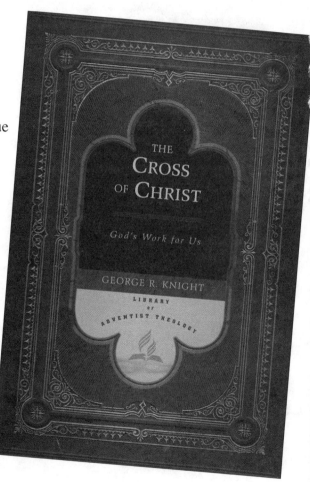

3 WAYS TO SHOP